1981

*On History*

# FERNAND BRAUDEL

## *On History*

Translated by Sarah Matthews

The University of Chicago Press

The University of Chicago Press,
Chicago 60637
Weidenfeld & Nicolson
London SW4 7TA

86  85  84  83  82  81  80      5  4  3  2  1

Library of Congress Cataloging in Publication Data

Braudel, Fernand.
  On history.

    Translation of Écrits sur l'histoire.
    Bibliography:  p.
    Includes index.
    1.  History—Collected works.  I.  Title.
D7.B7513        901        80-11201
ISBN  0-226-07150-2

FERNAND BRAUDEL is one of the world's
foremost historians. He became
president of the École Pratique des Hautes
Études in 1937, a professor at the Collège
de France in 1949, and president of the
Centre de Recherches Historiques in
1948. His books include *The Mediterranean
and the Mediterranean World in the Age of
Philip II* and *Capitalism and Material Life.*

# Contents 901
B827

Preface   vii

*Part 1*
*Time in History*

*The Mediterranean and the*
*Mediterranean World in the Age*
*of Philip II:* Extract from
the Preface   3

The Situation of History
in 1950   6

*Part 2*
*History and the Other*
*Human Sciences*

History and the Social Sciences:
The *Longue Durée*   25

Unity and Diversity in
the Human Sciences   55

History and Sociology   64

Toward a Historical
Economics   83

Toward a Serial History: Seville
and the Atlantic, 1504–1650   91

Is There a Geography of
Biological Man?   105

On a Concept of
Social History   120

Demography and the Scope of
the Human Sciences   132

*Part 3*
*History and the Present Age*

In Bahia, Brazil: The Present
Explains the Past   165

The History of Civilizations: The
Past Explains the Present   177

Index   219

96045

v

# Preface

This collection did not originate with me. Two or three years ago, my Polish and then my Spanish friends decided to collect and translate the few articles and essays which I had published in the past twenty years on the nature of history. This volume is the final result. If it had not happened this way, would I have thought of making such a collection myself? That is the question I ask myself as I finish reading the proofs.

Like everyone else, I cannot recognize my own voice when I hear it recorded. Nor am I sure whether I can immediately recognize, in any real sense of the word, my thoughts of yesterday on reading them. More than anything else, rereading these articles one after the other has reminded me of all sorts of past occasions. I see myself once more pacing around the camp in Lübeck with Henri Brunschwig during our interminable imprisonment; dining in the rue Vaneau with Georges Gurvitch; even more often, chatting with Lucien Febvre, or rather listening to him, as on that evening at Souget, his house in the Jura, when we sat beneath the cedars in the garden in the gathering gloom. Are such thoughts fed on so many echoes, so many memories, in which voices once heard come spontaneously to life again, really *my* thoughts? Yes and no. So many things have happened since then, so many new things beset me today! Since I am not a man for polemic, being concerned only with my own path, my own particular path, and since polemic and dialogue are a double and unavoidable necessity, here I am holding dialogues and engaging in polemic with myself, in a natural process of detachment from texts for which I obviously remain responsible. It was this sentiment which led me recently to rewrite *The Mediterranean*.

This time there is no question of rewriting anything. Apart from a few minimal factual corrections, these pages appear in their original form and with their original dates. So it is logical that I should view them from something of a distance and as a whole. Their coherence is a source of pleasure to me. I find throughout the book the same preoccupation which even today leads me to confront history—our profession—with the other human sciences, to try and see what light they can throw on our particular field, and on the other hand what we historians could have to offer our neighbors, reluctant as they are to seek or even listen to our advice.

A useful understanding has to be arrived at (as I have said before, and will say again) that the way to study history is to view it as a long duration, as what I have called the *longue durée*. It is not the only way, but it is one which by itself can pose all the great problems of social structures, past and present. It is the only language binding history to the present, creating one indivisible whole. Perhaps I still have time to explain my position with regard to this crucial preoccupation, with regard to the place of history in the contemporary society which is taking shape around us, with regard to the way in which history is rooted in the society in which the historian lives. For the one thing that fascinates me in our profession is the extent to which it can explain the life of men as it is being woven before our very eyes, with its acquiescences and reticences, its refusals, complicities, or surrenders when confronted with change or tradition.

The present collection does not cover all these problems. All it does is to map out their general area. I had no wish to slip into any of the empty spaces the pages of my recent lectures, given over the past few years, on the convergence of the human sciences, the place of statistics, the role of the computer, the possibility of coming to an understanding with social psychology and psychoanalysis, or with political science, slow as it is to become scientific.

The most difficult aspect of this restructuring of all the human sciences concerns, as always, the crucial relationship between history and sociology, that massive, rather confused science, crammed with all the riches of the past and of the future. Since the disappearance of Georges Gurvitch, it has become the rule, or the fashion, to break sociology up into many smaller sectors. This denies us outsiders any easy way of grasping it and of gaining access to it. Which sociologist today would again take charge of Georges Gurvitch's "global society"? But these are the tools and the concepts we need to integrate ourselves as much as possible with our neighbors' work. In a recent and once again disappointing discussion in which I sat facing several specialists in the social sciences, I. Chiva smilingly advised me, and all other historians, to construct our own sociology, since the sociologists did not have one ready-made for us. And then, I suppose, we should construct our own economics, our own psychology . . . Is it possible?

Having said this, if I may differ a moment with Emmanuel Le Roy Ladurie, I fear that there is an element of illusion or of alibi in asserting, when speaking of "statistical history," that the historian of the future "will be either a computer programer or nothing at all." What interests me is the programer's program. The historian for the moment should concern himself with gathering the human sciences together (could data processing help them to build up a common language?) rather than only with perfecting his own line. The historian of tomorrow will build up this language—or will be nothing at all.

*Paris, 16 May 1969*

*Part 1*                    *Time in History*

# The Mediterranean and the Mediterranean World in the Age of Philip II

## Extract from the Preface

This book is divided into three parts, with each part being an attempt to explain one aspect of the whole.

The first is an inquiry into a history that is almost changeless, the history of man in relation to his surroundings. It is a history which unfolds slowly and is slow to alter, often repeating itself and working itself out in cycles which are endlessly renewed. I did not wish to overlook this facet of history, which exists almost out of time and tells the story of man's contact with the inanimate, nor when dealing with it did I wish to make do with one of those traditional geographical introductions to history, which one finds placed to such little effect at the beginning of so many volumes, with their brief reviews of the mineral deposits, the types of agriculture, and the local flora, none of which is ever mentioned again, as if the flowers did not return each spring, as if the flocks were frozen in their migrations, and as if the ships did not have to sail on an actual sea, which changes as the seasons change.

Over and above this unaltering history, there is a history of gentle rhythms, of groups and groupings, which one might readily have called social history if the term had not been diverted from its full meaning. How did these deep-running currents affect the surface of Mediterranean life? That is the question I set myself in the second part of my book, looking successively at economies and states, societies and civilizations, and finally attempting to show, in an effort to clarify my own conceptions of history, how all these forces from the depths came into play in the complex arena of war. For war, as we know, is not an arena governed purely by the actions of individuals.

Lastly comes the third part, concerned with traditional history, history, so to speak, on the scale not so much of man in general as of men in particular. It is that history which François Simiand calls *"l'histoire événementielle,"* the history of events: a surface disturbance, the waves stirred up by the powerful movement of tides. A history of short, sharp, nervous vibrations. Ultrasensitive by definition, the slightest movement sets all its gauges quivering. But though by its nature the most exciting

From the Preface to *La Méditerranée et le monde méditerranéen à l'époque de Philippe II* (Paris: Armand Colin, 1949; 2d ed., 1966); *The Mediterranean and the Mediterranean World in the Age of Philip II*, trans. Sian Reynolds, 2 vols. (New York: Harper and Row, 1972–74).

and richest in human interest of histories, it is also the most perilous. We must beware of that history which still simmers with the passions of the contemporaries who felt it, described it, lived it, to the rhythm of their brief lives, lives as brief as are our own. It has the dimensions of their anger, their dreams, and their illusions. In the sixteenth century, after the true Renaissance, there came a Renaissance of the poor, the lowly, all avid to write, to speak of themselves and of others. All these precious records give a somewhat distorted view, invading that lost time and taking up an excessive amount of space in it. A historian, reading some papers of Philip II as if he were in his place and time, would find himself transported into a bizarre world, missing a dimension. A world of vivid passions, certainly, but a blind world, as any living world must be, as ours is, oblivious of the deep currents of history, of those living waters on which our frail barks are tossed like Rimbaud's drunken boat. A perilous world, granted, but one whose spells and dangerous enchantments we will have exorcised by having previously charted those great underlying currents which so often run silently, and whose true significance emerges only if one can observe their workings over great spans of time. Resounding events often take place in an instant, and are but manifestations of that larger destiny by which alone they can be explained.

Thus we have been brought to the breaking-down of history into successive levels. Or rather to the distinction, within historical time, of a geographical time, a social time, and an individual time. Or, again, to the breaking-down of man into a succession of characters. Perhaps it is that which will be found hardest to forgive in me, even though I maintain that the traditional divisions also split up the fundamental integrity of the living body of history, even though I maintain, despite Ranke or Karl Brandi, that narrative history is not an objective method, still less the supreme objective method, but is itself a philosophy of history; even though I maintain and then demonstrate that these levels are intended only as means of exposition, and that I have not refrained from passing from one to another as the need arose. But what is the use of pleading my case? Though I may be criticized for having put the elements of this book together badly, I hope that its parts will at least be found to have been satisfactorily constructed, according to the rules of our historical workshops.

I also hope that I will not be held to have been overambitious for having felt the need and the desire for taking a wide view. Surely history need not simply be condemned to the study of well-walled gardens? If it is, will it not fail in one of its present tasks, of responding to the agonizing problems of the hour and of keeping in touch with the human sciences, which are at once so young and so imperialistic? Can there be any humanism at the present time, in 1946, without an ambitious history, conscious of its duties and its great powers? "It is the fear of History, of history on the grand scale, which has killed History," wrote Edmond Faral in 1942. May it be reborn!

# The Situation of History
in 1950

History today finds itself faced with formidable but challenging responsibilities. This must be so, for history, in its essence and through all
its permutations, has always been dependent on concrete social conditions. "History is the child of its time." So its preoccupations are the
same as those which weigh on our own hearts and minds. And should its
methods, its projects, those answers which only yesterday seemed so
rigorous and dependable, should all its concepts suddenly collapse, it
would be from the weight of our own thinking, our own study, and, most
of all, the experiences we have undergone. Now, over the past forty
years those experiences have been particularly harsh for all of us; they
have thrown us violently back into our deepest selves, and thence into a
consideration of the whole destiny of mankind—that is to say, into the
crucial problems of history. It is a time to lament our state, to agonize, to
ponder, a time in which we must of necessity call everything into question. Besides, why should the fragile art of writing history escape from
the general crisis of our age? We are quitting a world of which we have
not always had the time to understand or appreciate the benefits, the
errors, the certainties, and the dreams—the world, shall we say, of the
early twentieth century? We are leaving it, or rather, it is slipping in-
exorably away from us.

## I

Great catastrophes may not necessarily give birth to genuine revolutions,
but they infallibly herald them and make it necessary to think, or rather
to think afresh, about the universe. Out of the agony of the great French
Revolution, which for years embodied the entire dramatic history of the
world, the meditations of the Comte de Saint-Simon were born, and then
those of his disciples and adversaries, Auguste Comte, Proudhon, Karl
Marx—meditations which still have not ceased to torment the minds and
reasoning of men. Or to take a small example from nearer our own time:
during the winter which followed the Franco-Prussian War of 1870–71,
what onlooker could have been more sheltered than Jacob Burckhardt
within the walls of his beloved Basel University? And yet he felt unquiet,

Inaugural lecture given to the Collège de France, 1 December 1950.

and was driven to formulate his grand vision of history. That term he taught a course on the French Revolution. In a prophecy which has since turned out to be only too true, he declared that it was merely the opening scene, the curtain-raiser, the initial moment in a cycle, in a century of revolutions which would go on and on. What an endless century it has been, indeed, leaving its bloody mark on Europe and on the whole world. But there was a long respite for the West between 1871 and 1914. And who can say how much those relatively peaceful, almost happy years diminished the scope of history? As if, to be on the alert, our profession has a constant need of suffering and of the manifest insecurity of men.

How can I convey how moved I was to read, in 1943, Gaston Roupnel's last work, *Histoire et destin*—that delirious, prophetic book, half lost in a world of dreams, but borne up by a wealth of compassion for the "sorrows of men"? Later he was to write to me: "I started [this book] at the very beginning of July 1940. In my little village of Gevrey-Chambertin, I had just seen the waves of refugees go past along the main road, the whole sorry exodus of unfortunates, in cars, in carts, on foot, a miserable muddle of people, all the wretchedness of the roads, and mixed up with all this there were the troops, soldiers without their weapons. . . . And this great panic, this was France! . . . Added to my declining years, to all my irremediable private misfortunes, there came this sense of a public, a national misfortune." But in Gaston Roupnel's last meditations it was just this wind of affliction which swelled the sails of history, and history, great, bold history, set off once again. Michelet became once more his God: "It seems to me," he wrote to me, "that Michelet's genius informs all history."

Our age is only too rich in catastrophes and revolutions, dramas and surprises. The social reality, the fundamental reality of man has been revealed to us in an entirely new light and, whether we would or not, our old profession of historian is endlessly burgeoning and blossoming in our hands. What changes, indeed! All society's dearest symbols, or nearly all—including some for which we would have sacrificed our lives yesterday with hardly a second thought—have been emptied of meaning. And now the question is not whether we will be able to live without them as landmarks and beacons to light our way, but whether we will be able to live and think peacefully. All intellectual concepts are distorted or destroyed. That science on which we as laymen relied without even having been aware of it, which was a haven and a new reason for living to the nineteenth century, has altered brutally from one day to the next and been reborn to a different existence. It is to us now honored but unstable, constantly in flux, inaccessible, and it seems certain that we will never again have the time or the opportunity to reestablish a working dialogue with it. All the social sciences, history amongst them, have changed likewise, in a less spectacular manner but no less decisively. It is a new world, so why not a new history?

But all the same let us dwell for a moment, tenderly, perhaps even a trifle irreverently (may we be forgiven!), on our past mentors. Behold the slim volume by Charles-Victor Langlois and Charles Seignobos, their *Introduction aux études historiques*, which appeared in 1978. It has no relevance for us today, but yesterday and for years it was a most authoritative work. And that in itself is a fact sufficiently amazing to give us pause. It is not too hard to discern in this venerable book, crammed with principles and minor recommendations, a particular image of the historian as conceived in the early years of this century. Think of an artist, a landscape painter. Before him there are trees, houses, hills, roads, an entire peaceful landscape. Such for the historian is the reality of the past—a reality which has been carefully verified, dusted off, and reconstructed. The landscape painter must leave nothing out, not a shrub, not a puff of smoke. Nothing must be left out except, of course, that the painter himself must be overlooked. For the ideal is to suppress the observer, as if reality were something to be surprised without frightening it off, as if history somehow existed outside our reconstructions, in a raw state of pure fact. The observer is a source of error, and criticism must be on its guard against him. "The natural instinct of a man in the water," wrote Charles-Victor Langlois in all seriousness, "is to do all he can to drown himself; learning to swim is a question of repressing those spontaneous movements and performing others instead. In the same way, a critical attitude is not a natural one; it must be learned, and becomes a part of oneself only through repeated practice. Thus the historian's work is above all a work of criticism; should one go into it without previously being on one's guard against instinct, one must surely drown."

There is nothing to be said against the criticism of historical documents and materials. The historical spirit is fundamentally a critical one. But above and beyond an obvious scrupulousness, it consists in reconstruction, as Charles Seignobos with his perceptive mind contrived to state on two or three occasions. But after all those cautions and warnings, was that really sufficient to maintain the vigor and the impetus necessary to history?

Of course if we were to go further back, if we were to turn this time to really great minds, to a Cournot, a Paul Lacombe, our illustrious forefathers—or to really great historians, to a Michelet above all, or to a Ranke, a Jacob Burckhardt, a Fustel de Coulanges, their genius would forbid us to smile. And yet—except perhaps for Michelet once again, the greatest of them all, whose genius is so charged with illumination and foresight—it would nonetheless be true to say that their answers would hardly fit our questions: we historians of today have the sense of belonging to a different age, to a different adventure of the intellect. Above all, our profession no longer seems to us to be a calm, secure undertaking, with just rewards automatically awarded to hard work and patience. It no longer gives us that secure feeling of having the whole of history surrounded, so that if only we apply ourselves courageously it will surrender itself to us. Surely no remark rings more strangely in our ears than that of the young Ranke in 1817, when in an enthusiastic address to Goethe he spoke fervently of "the solid ground of history."

## II

It is a hard task—doomed from the start—to try and relate in a few words just what it is that has changed in the area of our studies, and above all how and why that change came about. Thousands of details clamor for our attention. Albert Thibaudet claimed that truly radical upheavals are always essentially simple to comprehend. So, where is that simple little fact, that effective signal of renewal? Certainly not in the long-expected failure of philosophy of history, whose ambitious and hasty conclusions had lost all credibility even before the turn of the century. Nor in the bankruptcy of a scientific history that had, in any case, hardly begun to be sketched out. There could be no science, so they used to say, without the ability to predict: it had to be prophetic, or nothing. Today we would say that no social science, history included, can be prophetic, and thus by the old rules of the game none of them can lay claim to the fine title of a science. Besides, note well that there can be no science without historical continuity, and that is something which sociologists, but not all historians, call violently into question. But what is the point of arguing about this troublesome word science and the factitious problems which derive from it? We would do as well to become involved in the more classic but even more sterile debate about objectivity and subjectivity in history, a debate from which we will never be free so long as philosophers, by force of habit perhaps, care to linger over it, and so long as they lack the courage to ask themselves whether even those sciences which claim to be real are not themselves both objective and subjective at the same time. Those of us who have no difficulty in not believing in the necessity of antithesis will be happy to dispense with our customary discussions on method for this debate. The problem of history is not to be found in the relationship between painter and painting, nor even, though some have thought such a suggestion excessively daring, in the relationship between the painting and the landscape. The problem is right in the landscape, in the heart of life itself.

Just like life itself, history seems to us to be a fleeting spectacle, always in movement, made up of a web of problems meshed inextricably together, and able to assume a hundred different and contradictory aspects in turn. How should one tackle such a complex, living entity and break it up so as to be able to lay hold of it, or at least of some part of it? Numerous failed attempts are there to deter us even before we begin.

So we can no longer believe in the explanation of history in terms of this or that dominant factor. There is no unilateral history. No one thing is exclusively dominant: neither the conflict between races, whose collisions or reconciliation supposedly shaped the whole of man's past; nor powerful economic rhythms, creators of progress or ruin; nor constant social tensions; nor that diffused spiritualism that those like Ranke see as the sublimation of the individual and of the whole vast body of history; nor the reign of technology; nor the demographic expansion, that vegetable expansion with all its eventual consequences for the life of communities. Man's complexity is yet other.

Nevertheless these attempts to reduce the diverse to the simple or the nearly simple have meant an unprecedented enrichment of our historical studies for more than a century. They have set us progressively farther along the path of transcending the individual and the particular event, a transcendence long foreseen, foreshadowed, glimpsed, but fully accomplished only in our time. *That* perhaps is the decisive step, implying and summarizing all other transformations. We do not, for all that, seek to deny the reality of events or the role of individuals; to do so would be puerile. But it must be said that, in history, the individual is all too often a mere abstraction. In the living world there are no individuals entirely sealed off by themselves; all individual enterprise is rooted in a more complex reality, an "intermeshed" reality, as sociology calls it. The question is not to deny the individual on the grounds that he is the prey of contingency, but somehow to transcend him, to distinguish him from the forces separate from him, to react against a history arbitrarily reduced to the role of quintessential heroes. We do not believe in this cult of demigods, or to put it even more simply, we are against Treitschke's proud and unilateral declaration: "Men make history." No, history also makes men and fashions their destiny—anonymous history, working in the depths and most often in silence, whose domain, immense and uncertain as it is, we must now approach.

Life, the history of the world, and all individual histories present themselves to us as a series of events, in other words of brief and dramatic acts. A battle, an encounter between statesmen, an important speech, a crucial letter are instants in history. I remember a night near Bahia, when I was enveloped in a firework display of phosphorescent fireflies; their pale lights glowed, went out, shone again, all without piercing the night with any true illumination. So it is with events; beyond their glow, darkness prevails. Another memory will enable me to render my argument even more succinctly. Twenty years or so ago, in America, a much-heralded film caused an unparalleled sensation. It was claimed to be neither more nor less than the first authentic film on the Great War, now known, sadly enough, as the first World War. For over an hour we were privileged to witness the official hours of the conflict, to attend fifty military reviews, some before King George V of England, some before the King of the Belgians or the King of Italy, others before the Emperor of Germany or before our own president, Raymond Poincaré. We were privileged to be there at the exits from the great military and diplomatic conferences, to see a whole procession of illustrious, forgotten people, made even more ghostly and unreal by the jerkiness of the films of those far-off days. As for the real war, it was depicted by three or four special effects and a few sham explosions: background.

Doubtless the example is overstated, like any example intended to instruct. But nonetheless you must admit that it often is just such meager images that chronicles, traditional history, the narrative history so dear to the heart of Ranke offer us of the past and of the sweat of men. A gleam but no illumination; facts but no humanity. Note that this narrative history always claims to relate "things just as they really happened." Ranke deeply believed in this statement when he made it. In fact, though, in its own covert way, narrative history consists in an interpretation, an authentic philosophy of history. To the narrative historians, the life of men is dominated by dramatic accidents, by the actions of those exceptional beings who occasionally emerge, and who often are the masters of their own fate and even more of ours. And when they speak of "general history," what they are really thinking of is the intercrossing of such exceptional destinies, for obviously each hero must be matched against another. A delusive fallacy, as we all know. Or perhaps we should say, more justly, a vision of too narrow a world, a world made familiar by dint of having been so much explored and evoked, a world in which the historian may delight in consorting with princes—above all a world, torn from its context, where one might believe in all good faith that history is nothing but a monotonous game, always changing yet always the same, like the thousand combinations of pieces in a game of chess—a game constantly calling forth analogous situations and feelings which are always the same, with everything governed by the eternal, pitiless recurrence of things.

It is precisely our task to get beyond this first stage of history. The social realities must be tackled *in themselves and for themselves.* By social realities I mean all the major forms of collective life, economies, institutions, social structures, in short and above all, civilizations—all aspects of reality which earlier historians have not exactly overlooked, but which with a few outstanding exceptions they have all too often regarded as a backdrop, there only to explain or as if intended to explain the behavior of the exceptional individuals on whom the historian so complacently dwells.

This necessarily entails enormous errors of perspective and of reasoning, for what they are thus attempting to reconcile, to fit into the same framework, are in fact movements which have neither the same duration, nor the same direction, some belonging to the time of men, of our own brief, transient lives, others partaking of the time of societies, for whom a day, a year hold hardly any meaning, for whom, sometimes, a whole century lasts but a moment. Though we must of course be clear that social time does not flow at one even rate, but goes at a thousand different paces, swift or slow, which bear almost no relation to the day-to-day rhythm of a chronicle or of traditional history. Thus I believe in the reality of a particularly slow-paced history of civilizations, a history of their depths, of the characteristics of their structure and layout. Of course, the most precious flowerings of any civilizations are mortal; of course, they shine out and are then extinguished, to bloom again in other forms. But these breaks occur more rarely and farther apart than one might expect. And even more importantly they do not destroy everything equally. By which I mean that within the domain of a particular civilization, the social content can renew itself almost completely without ever reaching certain deep-seated structural characteristics which distinguish it sharply from neighboring civilizations.

There is, besides, a history slower still than the history of civilizations, a history which almost stands still, a history of man in his intimate relationship to the earth which bears and feeds him; it is a dialogue which never stops repeating itself, which repeats itself in order to persist, which may and does change superficially, but which goes on, tenaciously, as though it were somehow beyond time's reach and ravages.

## III

If I do not mistake, historians today are beginning to be aware of an entirely new history, a ponderous history whose time cannot be measured by any of our long-established instruments. Nor is it a history which offers itself to them as an easy discovery. In fact each form of history demands an appropriate erudition. I might even go as far as to say that all those who deal with the economic destinies, the social structures, and the various, often minor problems of civilization find themselves faced with a task of research beside which the labors of the most learned and well-known scholars of the eighteenth and nineteenth centuries seem amazingly easy. In order to have a new history a whole vast body of documentation must be brought to light so as to be able to answer the new questions. In fact, I am by no means sure the historian's traditional craft is equal to our present ambitions. Given the danger that this represents and the difficulties which its solution implies, there can be no salvation unless we work together in teams.

There is a whole past to be reconstructed. Endless tasks rear up and demand our attention, if we are to deal with even the simplest realities of these collective lives, such as, for instance, the short-lived economic rhythms of a particular conjuncture. Look, for example, at the fairly severe recession which led to a clearly identifiable crisis in Florence between 1580 and 1585, a recession which quickly grew in strength and which as quickly disappeared. Researches in and around Florence offer indications of it by such sure signs as the repatriation of the Florentine merchants who left France and Germany at that time, and who sometimes, even more significantly, sold their shops in order to buy land in Tuscany. But this crisis, which appears so clear-cut at first sight, must be more precisely diagnosed, it must be established scientifically by a coherent sequence of prices. This is still local work, but immediately the question arises whether the crisis was peculiar to Tuscany, or whether it was in fact a general crisis. Quickly we find traces of it in Venice, and without much difficulty in Ferrara. But just how far afield did it make itself felt? Without knowing its exact scope, we are unable to define its nature. Does this mean that the historian must set off to search every archive in Europe, seeking out series of prices which scholarship usually overlooks? It is an endless journey! the whole task still lies before him. And to top it all, a historian interested in China and India and believing that the Far East dominated the circulation of precious metals, and thus the rhythm of economic life throughout the world in the sixteenth century, will soon note that there were years of instability in the Far East for the trade in pepper and spices corresponding almost exactly to these years of difficulty in Florence. This trade, slipping from the feeble hands of the Portuguese, was seized by the cunning Moorish merchants, longtime denizens of the Indian Ocean and the Sunda Strait, and passed on to the caravaneers of India, to be finally swallowed up in Central Asia and China. Even in pursuit of such a simple topic, the research has just taken us around the world.

At this very time, I myself together with some young historians am concerned in studying the general conjuncture of the sixteenth century, and I hope that I may shortly be able to speak to you on the subject. It hardly needs saying that in dealing with such a subject we find the whole world claiming our attention. The conjuncture of the sixteenth century consists not only of Venice or Lisbon, Antwerp or Seville, Lyons or Milan, but also the complex economy of the Baltic, the ancient rhythms of the Mediterranean, the major currents of the Atlantic and the Iberian Pacific, Chinese junks, and even now I am omitting things. And it must be added that the conjuncture of the sixteenth century is also the fifteenth century on one side and the seventeenth century on the other. It consists not only in the movement of prices in their entirety, but also the diversity of these prices and how they compare with each other, with some increasing more or less than others. It is doubtless likely that the prices of wine and of real estate led all others in their regular development. That would seem to explain the way in which the land soaked up, so to speak, attracted, immobilized the wealth of the *nouveaux riches*. And therein lies a whole social drama in itself. It would also explain that invasive civilization obsessed with wines and wine-making: the prices dictated it, so the fleets grew, those ships loaded with casks, flooding toward the north from Seville, from the coasts of Portugal, or from the Gironde; so too grew the tides of carioles *(carretoni)* which took the new Friulian and Venetian wines to Germany every year by way of the Brenner—those cloudy wines which Montaigne himself would have drunk on the spot, with such relish.

Even the history of technological developments, the simple history of technology (leaving aside for one moment the uncertain minutiae of researches constantly interrupted, when all too often the thread breaks between our fingers, or rather the documents we are examining have a sudden omission) the history of technology too offers too wide a vista, poses problems which are too vast. In the sixteenth century, the Mediterranean taken as a whole was the scene of a whole series of dramatic technological developments. It was then that artillery was installed on the narrow decks of its ships, though this was something which happened only very gradually. It was then that its secrets made their way to the countries along the upper reaches of the Nile and into the interior of the Near East. With dire consequences ensuing every time... In another, more silent drama, it was then that there came about a strange slow diminution in marine tonnages. Hulls became increasingly small and lightweight. Venice and Ragusa were the homes of the large cargoes: their merchant ships weighed up to a thousand tonnes and more. They were the great floating bodies of the sea. In a short time, though, one can see everywhere the success of the small sailing-ships, whether Greek, Provençal, Marseillais, or from the North, against these giants of the sea. In Marseilles it was the hour of the tartane, the saic, the minutest barques. You could hold one of these skiffs in the palm of your hand, they rarely went over a hundred tonnes. But should the need arise, these pocket sailing ships could prove their worth. The lightest wind was sufficient to propel them; they could get into any port; they could load in a few days, a few hours, as opposed to the weeks and months required by the Ragusan ships to swallow their loads.

When one of these Ragusan ships happened by chance to seize a small Marseilles boat, took possession of its load and, throwing the entire crew into the water, made all trace of the rival vessel disappear in an instant, that incident captures in miniature the whole struggle on the sea between the large ships and the small. But it would be wrong to believe this conflict confined to the Central Sea. Great and small were running up against each other and destroying each other on all the seven seas. On the Atlantic their struggle was the greatest struggle of the age. Would the Iberians invade England? That was the crucial question before, during, and after the Invincible Armada. The Northmen savage the peninsula and there you have the expedition against Cadiz, or they savage the Iberian Empire and you have Drake and Cavendish and a host of others. The English hold the Channel; the Iberians, Gibraltar. Which of these would prove most advantageous? Even more crucial, though, was the question of who would prevail between the heavy Portuguese caraques, the ponderous Spanish galleons, and the diminutive Northern ships, a thousand tonnes on the one hand, two hundred, one hundred, sometimes not more than fifty on the other? It was often an unequal struggle, as those contemporary engravings illustrate, showing one of the Iberian giants surrounded by a cloud of Lilliputian barques. The little boats harrassed the big ones, riddling them with shot. When they seized one, they would take the gold, the precious stones, a few bales of spices, then they would set the huge, useless carcass on fire. But is what I have summarized here rather too neatly all that history has to say on the subject? For if Iberian resistance continued, it was because convoys of galleons persisted in getting through, more or less unscathed, guided by the hand of God, so the Genoese said, and made their way to the Antilles, to return laden with silver; it was because the mines of the New World remained in Iberian control. The history of ships is not a self-contained history. It must be put back into the context of the other kinds of history which surround and support it. So once again the truth, while not denying itself to us, yet manages to retreat before us.

I repeat, there is no problem which does not become increasingly complex when actively investigated, growing in scope and depth, endlessly opening up new vistas of work to be done. I will have occasion to mention this again when discussing the imperial vocation in the sixteenth century, which is what I shall be speaking to you about this year, and which is not, as you will have suspected, entirely to be ascribed to the sixteenth century itself. There is never any problem, ever, which can be confined within a single framework.

Should we quit the domain of economics, of technology, for the realm of civilizations, should we dare to contemplate those insidious, almost invisible cracks which become deep rifts within a century or two, beyond which the whole life and character of man is changed, should we consider these amazing, internal revolutions, then slowly the whole vista becomes distinguishable, revealing with increasing intensity yet wider views and further complications. There is a young Italian historian who had the feeling after careful prospecting that the idea of death and the depiction of death in art changed utterly around the middle of the fifteenth century. A deep rift came into being: instead of a celestial death, calm, turned toward the beyond—a wide-open door through which the whole man (his soul and almost his entire body) could pass without too much trepidation—instead of such a serene death, we find a human death, the first inkling of reason. But this new death, so slow to reveal its true aspect, first comes to light, or seems first to come to light in the complex countries of the Rhine, and the direction of the inquiry accordingly follows the path thus dictated, and we are put in touch with that most silent but most imperious history of civilizations. So we proceed beyond the usual décor of the Reformation, feeling our way with infinite care and patient study. We will have to read books of devotion and wills, to collect iconographic documents, to consult, in towns like Venice which have kept their archives well, the papers of the *Inquisitori contra Bestemmie,* those "black archives" on the control of moralism which now prove to be of such indescribable value.

But, you know, it is not enough to take refuge in this indispensible prospecting of new material. All this material must be scrutinized methodically. Doubtless these methods, or some of them at least, may change drastically from one day to the next. In ten years or twenty, our methods in economics, in statistics, stand every chance of being challenged and our results cast aside: the fate of relatively recent studies tells us that this is so. All this information, this material, must be taken up and reconsidered in the light of man himself, and one must try if possible, to rediscover, beyond all the details, life itself: how its forces combine, how they knit or conflict, how too, frequently, their rushing waters mingle. Everything must be recaptured and relocated in the general framework of history, so that despite the difficulties, the fundamental paradoxes and contradictions, we may respect the unity of history which is also the unity of life.

It is too great a task, you may say. It is always the difficulties of our profession which engage our attention; but without wishing in any way to deny them, would it not be possible for once to point out its irreplaceable advantages? Can we not, on a first examination of a historical situation, perceive which feature is crucial in terms of future development?

Of all the forces in play, we know which will prevail, we can make out beforehand the important events, "those which will bear fruit," to whom the future will finally be delivered. What an immense privilege! From amongst all the jumbled facts of our present lives, who could distinguish equally surely the lasting from the ephemeral? Now, this distinction lies at the very heart of the work of the social sciences, at the heart of knowledge, at the heart of the destiny of man, within the domain of his most crucial problems. As historians, we have no difficulty in joining in the discussion. Who, for instance, would deny that the great question of the continuity or discontinuity of our social destiny, which the sociologists are so busy discussing, is essentially, a question of history? If great rifts break up the destiny of humanity, if everything has been put in a new light the day after they appear, and neither yesterday's tools nor yesterday's thoughts apply any more—the reality of these breaks is a question for history to decide. Is there or is there not an exceptional and short-lived coincidence between all the different times of the life of men? That is the great question which is ours to answer. All progressions, however slow, are one day accomplished, and the age of true revelations is also the age in which things come to bloom.

## IV

History has been led to these possibly dangerous shores by life itself. As I have said before, it is life which is our school. But history has not been alone in attending life's lessons and in drawing their consequences once having understood them. In fact, history is above all indebted to the victorious progress of the still-young human sciences, with their superior sensitivity to the conjunctures of the present. During the past fifty years we have witnessed the birth, rebirth, and growth of a series of imperialistic human sciences, and each time their development has entailed for us, as historians, an initial shock, complications, and then an enormous enrichment. History may perhaps be the greatest beneficiary of all from these recent developments.

Is it necessary to dwell on its debt to geography, or to political economy or, yet again, to sociology? One of the most influential works as far as history is concerned, perhaps the most influential of all, must surely have been that by Vidal de la Blache, historian by training and geographer by vocation. I would freely declare that the *Tableau de la géographie de la France,* published in 1903, just before Ernest Lavisse's great history of France, is a major work not only of geography but also in the canon of the French school of history. In the same way, it would take but a word or two to demonstrate how much history owes to François Simiand's outstanding work—a philosopher turned economist, whose voice, sadly, was heard here at the Collège for all too brief a time. The discoveries he made concerning the crises and rhythms which occur in the material lives of men made possible the dazzling work of Ernest Labrousse, which has surely been the most original contribution to history of the past twenty years. Look too at what the history of civilizations has been able to retain of the distinguished teaching of Marcel Mauss, who was one of the real glories of the Collège de France. Who better taught us, historians, the art of studying civilizations in their exchanges with each other and at their crumbling edges, beyond the confines wherein yesterday's history, the slave to every overnight celebrity, has indulged itself too long and too exclusively? Finally, on a more personal note, need I mention what the sociology of Georges Gurvitch, his books and still more his dazzling conversation, have done for me in encouraging me to think afresh and to take new directions?

There is no need to multiply these examples to explain how history has in recent years been enriched by acquisitions and nourishment drawn from its neighbors. It has used them to rebuild itself in a genuinely new form.

Nonetheless historians themselves, handicapped by their training and sometimes by their predilections, remained to be convinced. It often happens that a whole generation, influenced by strong and rich traditions, can traverse the fertile period of an intellectual revolution without ever being affected by it. Happily it can also happen, and almost always does, that some men are more sensitive than others, more able to perceive the new streams of thought which have arisen in their time. It is clear that it was a decisive moment for French history when the *Annales d'histoire économique et sociale* was founded by Lucien Febvre and Marc Bloch in Strasbourg in 1929. I will, I hope, be allowed to speak of this publication with due admiration and gratitude, since it has accrued twenty years' worth of riches in hard work and success, and I myself am but a laborer come recently to the vineyard.

Today there is nothing easier than to emphasize and convince people of the vigorous originality of the movement at its inception. Lucien Febvre wrote at the start of his new review: "While historians are applying their tried and true methods to the documents of the past, greater and greater numbers of men are devoting their energies, though not, on occasion, without a certain feverishness, to the study of contemporary societies and economies. . . . Of course, clearly nothing could be better than that each scholar, while pursuing his own legitimate specialty, busily cultivating his own garden, should nonetheless make the effort to follow his neighbor's work. But often the walls are so high that they cut off the view. Yet what a wealth of precious suggestions on method and on the interpretation of facts, what cultural gains, what a step forward in intuition if intellectual exchanges between these diverse groups were more frequent. The future of history . . . is at stake here and also a true understanding of the events which will be history tomorrow. It is against these formidable divisions that we would pit ourselves."

I would like to reemphasize these words today, words which, while not having entirely won over each individual historian, have nonetheless, willy-nilly, had an effect on the entire younger generation. "Willy-nilly," because *Annales* has been received, like any other outstanding thing, with both violent enthusiasm and obstinate antipathy. But, for all that, it has had and still has the logic of our profession on its side, the evidence of events and the incomparable privilege of being in the forefront of research, however bold that research may be.

I have no need to speak here, before an audience of historians, of the vicissitudes of this long-standing struggle. Nor do I need to mention the abundance and diversity and wealth of the work of my illustrious predecessor. Everyone is familiar with Lucien Febvre's *Philippe II et la Franche-Comté*, his *La Terre et l'évolution humaine, Le Rhin, Luther*, his splendid *Rabelais et l'incroyance religieuse au XVIe siècle* and, last of all, that subtle study *Marguerite de Navarre*. On the other hand, I would like to emphasize the numberless articles and innumerable letters which I would not hesitate to say are his major intellectual and human contribution to the thought and the debates of his time. It was in these that he freely tackled all subjects, all theses, all points of view, with that delight in discovery and in sharing his discoveries which has had its effect on all who have ever really tried to approach him. No one could ever draw up an exact account of the ideas thus lavished, of all the seeds thus sown, nor have we always been able to follow him on his keen-minded journeyings.

Surely no one but he would have been able to fix our course amid the conflicts and reconciliations between history and the neighboring social sciences. None was better placed to restore our confidence in our profession and in its usefulness. "Vivre l'histoire," ("To live history"), such was the title of one of his articles, a fine title and a fine program. History for him was never a game of sterile learning, a sort of art for art's sake, of learning sufficient unto itself. It always seemed to be concerned above all with the explanation of man and society in terms of that one precious, subtle, complex gauge—time—which we as historians alone know how to handle, and without which neither the societies nor the individuals of either past or present ever regains the appearance and warmth of life.

Doubtless it was providential for French history that Lucien Febvre, while being particularly sensitive to the whole, to the total history of man in all its aspects, while having clearly understood the new possibilities of history, nonetheless remained able both to feel with the refined culture of a humanist and to express vividly whatever was particular and unique in each individual adventure of the spirit.

The dangers of a social history are clear to us all, and in particular the danger of forgetting, in contemplation of the deep currents in the lives of men, each separate man grappling with his own life and his own destiny; the danger of forgetting, perhaps even of denying, the inimitable essence of each individual. For to challenge the enormous role that has sometimes been assigned to certain outstanding men in the genesis of history is by no means to deny the stature of the individual as individual and the fascination that there is for one man in poring over the fate of another.

I said earlier that men, even the greatest, do not seem as free to us as to our predecessors in history, but the fascination of their lives is in no way diminished because of this, quite the contrary. And the problem is not that of reconciling, on the level of principles, the need for individual history and for social history. The problem is to remain sensitive to both at one and the same time and, fired with enthusiasm for one, not to lose sight of the other. It is a fact that French history, set by Lucien Febvre along the path of collective destinies, has nonetheless never ceased to be interested in the pinnacles of intellect and attainment. Lucien Febvre studied the lives of Luther, Rabelais, Michelet, Proudhon, and Stendhal with a close and passionate interest. It was a mark of his originality that he never relinquished the company of these true princes. I am thinking particularly of the most brilliant of his books, *Luther*, in which I suspect he wished for a moment to envisage to himself a truly free man in command of his destiny and of the destiny of history. If so, it was only during the early years of his rebellious and creative life, before the destiny of Germany and of his age implacably closed over him.

I do not believe that this intense interest in the minds of men entailed any contradiction for Lucien Febvre. History remained an immensely open undertaking for him. He always managed to resist the perfectly natural desire to tie all his new riches together. For to construct something must always mean to limit oneself, must it not? And that is why, if I am not mistaken, all the great historians of our generation, the greatest and therefore the most instinctively individual, have felt at ease in the illumination and scope of his thinking. I have no need to emphasize the different contrasts between the major works of Marc Bloch, Georges Lefebvre, Marcel Bataillon, Ernest Labrousse, Andrè Piganiol, and Augustin Renaudet. Isn't it extraordinary that without an effort they can all reconcile themselves to that history which was first glimpsed and then consciously worked out more than twenty years ago?

Perhaps it is this diversity of possibilities which lends the French school of history its present strength. French school? A Frenchman hardly dares utter the phrase, and beset with a sense of all the internal divergences, he hesitates to repeat it. And yet, viewed from abroad, our situation does not appear so complicated. A young English history teacher wrote recently: "If a new inspiration is to make its way into our historical work, then it is more than likely that it will come from France." Is there any need to say that such an assessment cannot but be a source of encouragement and pride for us? Yet it also gives us the feeling that we bear the burden of an exceptional responsibility, and an anxious sense of not being worthy.

This anxiety, which may seem to have cropped up almost by chance in the closing moments of my lecture, is in fact, as you must know, a sensation which has been with me before ever I uttered a word of it. Who would not feel anxious within himself at taking his place amongst you? Happily, custom comes to one's aid with good advice, holding out at least three possible points of refuge. To start with, reading one's lecture, and I assure you that this is the first time in my life that I have sunk to doing so. Is that not sufficient indication of my nervousness? Then, hiding behind a program, sheltering behind one's most precious ideas—though that is a screen which does not provide much cover. Finally, evoking one's friendships and sympathies so as to feel less alone. I remember these friendships and sympathies with gratitude: the active sympathy of my colleagues in the Hautes Études, to which I was nominated nearly fifteen years ago, and of my fellow historians, amongst both my elders and my contemporaries, who have never failed me, particularly at the Sorbonne where I take such pleasure in getting to know our younger generation. Others, very dear ones, watch over me here.

I was brought into this institution by the very great kindness of Augustin Renaudet and Marcel Bataillon. Doubtless because despite my failings I belong to the small band of students of the sixteenth century, and because I have loved and continue to love the Italy of Augustin Renaudet and the Spain of Marcel Bataillon with a whole heart. They bear no grudge against me because compared to them I am a night caller; the Spain of Philip II is no longer the Spain of Erasmus, the Italy of Titian and of Caravaggio no longer has the unforgettable brilliance of the Florence of Lorenzo the Magnificent and Michelangelo to illuminate it. The twilight of the sixteenth century! Lucien Febvre used to speak of the unhappy men who came after 1560. Unhappy men, certainly, those men exposed to every blow, to each surprise, to all the treachery that other men or fate could engineer, exposed to every bitter turn of fate, to every useless rebellion. Around them and within them, what unassuageable wars... Alas! those unhappy men resemble us like brothers!

Thanks to you, my dear colleagues, the fabric of the history of modern civilizations, restored in 1933, has been preserved, and the honor of ensuring its continuity has fallen to me. It is a very heavy honor. Friendship, sympathy, goodwill, one's own enthusiasm for the task, none of these can dissipate the apprehension which one cannot but feel, in all conscience and without false modesty, at being called on to succeed a man on whom the enormous task defined in the margins of his books, in the very stamp of his untiring intellect, depends even today. I mean our dear, great Lucien Febvre in whom, for many years, to the greater glory of this Institution, could be heard again the voice of Jules Michelet, a voice one might have thought forever stilled.

Part 2

*History and the Other
Human Sciences*

# History and the
# Social Sciences

## The *Longue Durée*

There is a general crisis in the human sciences: they are all overwhelmed by their own progress, if only because of the accumulation of new knowledge and the need to work together in a way which is yet to be properly organized. Directly or indirectly, willingly or unwillingly, none of them can remain unaffected by the progress of the more active among them. But they remain in the grip of an insidious and retrograde humanism no longer capable of providing them with a valid framework for their studies. With varying degrees of clear-sightedness, all the sciences are preoccupied with their own position in the whole monstrous agglomeration of past and present researches, researches whose necessary convergence can now clearly be seen.

Will the human sciences solve these difficulties by an extra effort at definition or by an increase in ill temper? They certainly seem to think so, for (at the risk of going over some very well trodden ground and of raising a few red herrings), today they are engaged more busily than ever in defining their aims, their methods, and their superiorities. You can see them vying with each other, skirmishing along the frontiers separating them, or not separating them, or barely separating them from their neighbors. For each of them, in fact, persists in a dream of staying in, or returning to, its home. A few isolated scholars have managed to bring things together: Claude Lévi-Strauss[1] has pushed "structural" anthropology toward the procedures of linguistics, the horizons of "unconscious" history, and the youthful imperialism of "qualitative" mathematics. He leans toward a science which would unite, under the title of communications science, anthropology, political economy, linguistics ... But is there in fact anyone who is prepared to cross the frontiers like this, and to realign things in this way? Given half a chance, geography would even like to split off from history!

But we must not be unfair. These squabbles and denials have a certain significance. The wish to affirm one's own existence in the face of others is necessarily the basis for new knowledge: to deny someone is already to know him. Moreover, without explicitly wishing it, the social sciences force themselves on each other, each trying to capture society as a whole, in its "totality." Each science encroaches on its neighbors, all the while

*Annales E.S.C.*, no. 4 (October–December 1958), Débats et combats, pp. 725–53.

96045

believing it is staying in its own domain. Economics finds sociology closing in on it, history—perhaps the least structured of all the human sciences—is open to all the lessons learned by its many neighbors, and is then at pains to reflect them back again. So, despite all the reluctance, opposition, and blissful ignorance, the beginnings of a "common market" are being sketched out. This would be well worth a trial during the coming years, even if each science might later be better off readopting, for a while, some more strictly personal approach.

But the crucial thing now is to get together in the first place. In the United States this coming together has taken the form of collective research on the cultures of different areas of the modern world, "area studies" being, above all, the study by a team of social scientists of those political Leviathans of our time: China, India, Russia, Latin America, the United States. Understanding them is a question of life and death! But at the same time as sharing techniques and knowledge, it is essential that each of the participants should not remain buried in his private research, as deaf and blind as before to what the others are saying, writing, or thinking! Equally, it is essential that this gathering of the social sciences should make no omissions, that they should all be there, that the older ones should not be neglected in favor of the younger ones that seem to promise so much, even if they do not always deliver it. For instance, the position allotted to geography in these American exercises is almost nil, and that allowed to history extremely meager. Not to mention the sort of history it is!

The other social sciences are fairly ill informed as to the crisis which our discipline has gone through in the past twenty or thirty years, and they tend to misunderstand not only the work of historians, but also that aspect of social reality for which history has always been a faithful servant, if not always a good salesman: social time, the multifarious, contradictory times of the life of men, which not only make up the past, but also the social life of the present. Yet history, or rather the dialectic of duration as it arises in the exercise of our profession, from our repeated observations, is important in the coming debate among all the human sciences. For nothing is more important, nothing comes closer to the crux of social reality than this living, intimate, infinitely repeated opposition between the instant of time and that time which flows only slowly. Whether it is a question of the past or of the present, a clear awareness of this plurality of social time is indispensable to the communal methodology of the human sciences.

So I propose to deal at length with history, and with time in history. Less for the sake of present readers of this journal, who are already specialists in our field, than for that of those who work in the neighboring human sciences: economists, ethnographers, ethnologists (or anthropologists), sociologists, psychologists, linguists, demographers, geographers, even social mathematicians or statisticians—all neighbors of ours whose experiments and whose researches we have been following for these many years because it seemed to us (and seems so still) that we would thus see history itself in a new light. And perhaps we in our turn have something to offer them. From the recent experiments and efforts of history, an increasingly clear idea has emerged—whether consciously or not, whether excepted or not—of the multiplicity of time, and of the exceptional value of the long time span. It is this last idea which even more than history itself—history of a hundred aspects—should engage the attention and interest of our neighbors, the social sciences.

History and Time Spans

All historical work is concerned with breaking down time past, choosing among its chronological realities according to more or less conscious preferences and exclusions. Traditional history, with its concern for the short time span, for the individual and the event, has long accustomed us to the headlong, dramatic, breathless rush of its narrative.

The new economic and social history puts cyclical movement in the forefront of its research and is committed to that time span: it has been captivated by the mirage and the reality of the cyclical rise and fall of prices. So today, side by side with traditional narrative history, there is an account of conjunctures which lays open large sections of the past, ten, twenty, fifty years at a stretch ready for for examination.

Far beyond this second account we find a history capable of traversing even greater distances, a history to be measured in centuries this time: the history of the long, even of the very long time span, of the *longue durée*. This is a phrase which I have become accustomed to for good or ill, in order to distinguish the opposite of what François Simiand, not long after Paul Lacombe, christened *"l'histoire événementielle,"* the history of events. The phrases matter little; what matters is the fact that our discussion will move between these two poles of time, the instant and the *longue durée*.

Not that these words are absolutely reliable. Take the word *event:* for myself I would limit it, and imprison it within the short time span: an event is explosive, a *"nouvelle sonnante"* ("a matter of moment") as they said in the sixteenth century. Its delusive smoke fills the minds of its contemporaries, but it does not last, and its flame can scarcely ever be discerned.

Doubtless philosophers would tell us that to treat the word thus is to empty it of a great part of its meaning. An event can if necessary take on a whole range of meanings and associations. It can occasionally bear witness to very profound movements, and by making play, factitiously or not, with those "causes" and "effects" so dear to the hearts of the historians of yore, it can appropriate a time far greater than its own time span. Infinitely extensible, it becomes wedded, either freely or not, to a whole chain of events, of underlying realities which are then, it seems, impossible to separate. It was by adding things together like this that Benedetto Croce could claim that within any event all history, all of man is embodied, to be rediscovered at will. Though this, of course, is on condition of adding to that fragment whatever it did not at first sight appear to contain, which in turn entails knowing what is appropriate—or not appropriate—to add. It is the clever and perilous process which some of Jean-Paul Sartre's recent thinking seems to propose.[2]

So, to put things more clearly, let us say that instead of a history of events, we would speak of a short time span, proportionate to individuals, to daily life, to our illusions, to our hasty awareness—above all the time of the chronicle and the journalist. Now, it is worth noting that side by side with great and, so to speak, historic events, the chronicle or the daily paper offers us all the mediocre accidents of ordinary life: a fire, a railway crash, the price of wheat, a crime, a theatrical production, a flood. It is clear, then, that there is a short time span which plays a part in all forms of life, economic, social, literary, institutional, religious, even geographical (a gust of wind, a storm), just as much as political.

At first sight, the past seems to consist in just this mass of diverse facts, some of which catch the eye, and some of which are dim and repeat themselves indefinitely. The very facts, that is, which go to make up the daily booty of microsociology or of sociometry (there is microhistory too). But this mass does not make up all of reality, all the depth of history on which scientific thought is free to work. Social science has almost what amounts to a horror of the event. And not without some justification, for the short time span is the most capricious and the most delusive of all.

Thus there is among some of us, as historians, a lively distrust of traditional history, the history of events—a label which tends to become confused, rather inexactly, with political history. Political history is not necessarily bound to events, nor is it forced to be. Yet except for the factitious panoramas almost without substance in time which break up its narrative,[3] except for the overviews inserted for the sake of variety, on the whole the history of the past hundred years, almost always political history centered on the drama of "great events," has worked on and in the short time span. Perhaps that was the price which had to be paid for the progress made during this same period in the scientific mastery of particular tools and rigorous methods. The momentous discovery of the document led historians to believe that documentary authenticity was the repository of the whole truth. "All we need to do," Louis Halphen wrote only yesterday,[4] is allow ourselves to be borne along by the documents, one after another, just as they offer themselves to us, in order to see the chain of facts and events reconstitute themselves almost automatically before our eyes." Toward the end of the nineteenth century, this ideal of history "in the raw," led to a new style of chronicle, which in its desire for exactitude followed the history of events step by step as it emerged from ambassadorial letters or parliamentary debates. The historians of the eighteenth and early nineteenth centuries had been attentive to the perspectives of the *longue durée* in a way in which, afterwards, only a few great spirits—Michelet, Ranke, Jacob Burckhardt, Fustel— were able to recapture. If one accepts that this going beyond the short span has been the most precious, because the most rare, of historiographical achievements during the past hundred years, then one understands the preeminent role of the history of institutions, of religions, of civilizations, and (thanks to archeology with its need for vast chronological expanses) the ground-breaking role of the studies devoted to classical antiquities. It was only yesterday that they proved the saviors of our profession.

The recent break with the traditional forms of nineteenth-century history has not meant a complete break with the short time span. It has worked, as we know, in favor of economic and social history, and against the interests of political history. This has entailed upheavals and an undeniable renewal, and also, inevitably, changes in method, the shifting of centers of interest with the advent of a quantitative history that has certainly not exhausted all it has to offer.

But above all, there has been an alteration in traditional historical time. A day, a year once seemed useful gauges. Time, after all, was made up of an accumulation of days. But a price curve, a demographic progression, the movement of wages, the variations in interest rates, the study (as yet more dreamed of than achieved) of productivity, a rigorous analysis of money supply all demand much wider terms of reference.

A new kind of historical narrative has appeared, that of the conjuncture, of the cycle, and even of the "intercycle," covering a decade, a quarter of a century and, at the outside, the half-century of Kondratiev's classic cycle. For instance, if we disregard any brief and superficial fluctuations, prices in Europe went up between 1791 and 1817, and went down between 1817 and 1852. This unhurried double movement of increase and decrease represents an entire intercycle measured by the time of Europe, and more or less by that of the whole world. Of course these chronological periods have no absolute value. François Perroux[5] would offer us other, perhaps more valid, dividing lines, measured with other barometers, those of economic growth, income, or the gross national product. But what do all these current debates matter! What is quite clear is that the historian can make use of a new notion of time, a time raised to the level of explication, and that history can attempt to explain itself by dividing itself at new points of reference in response to these curves and to the very way they breathe.

Thus Ernest Labrousse and his students, after their manifesto at the last Rome Historical Congress (1955), set up a vast inquiry into social history in quantitative terms. I do not think I am misrepresenting their intention when I say that this inquiry must necessarily lead to the determination of social conjunctures (and even of structures) that may not share the same rate of progress, fast or slow, as the economic conjuncture. Besides, these two distinguished gentlemen—the economic conjuncture and the social conjuncture,—must not make us lose sight of other actors, though their progress will be difficult if not impossible to track, for lack of a precise way of measuring it. Science, technology, political institutions, conceptual changes, civilizations (to fall back on that useful word) all have their own rhythms of life and growth, and the new history of conjunctures will be complete only when it has made up a whole orchestra of them all.

In all logic, this orchestration of conjunctures, by transcending itself, should have led us straight to the *longue durée*. But for a thousand reasons this transcendence has not been the rule, and a return to the short term is being accomplished even now before our very eyes. Perhaps this is because it seems more necessary (or more urgent) to knit together "cyclical" history and short-term traditional history than to go forward, toward the unknown. In military terms, it has been a question of consolidating newly secured positions. Ernest Labrousse's first great book, published in 1933, was thus a study of the general movement of prices in France during the eighteenth century,[6] a movement lasting a good hundred years. In 1943, in the most important work of history to have appeared in France in twenty-five years, this very same Ernest Labrousse succumbed to this need to return to a less cumbersome measure of time when he pinpointed the depression of 1774 to 1791 as being one of the most compelling sources, one of the prime launching pads of the French Revolution. He was still employing a demi-intercycle, a large measure. In his address to the International Congress in Paris in 1948, *Comment naissent les révolutions?* ("How are revolutions born?"), he attempted this time to link a new-style pathetic fallacy (short-term economic) to a very old style pathetic fallacy (political, the "revolutionary days"). And behold us back up to our ears in the short time span. Of course, this is a perfectly fair and justifiable procedure, but how very revealing! The historian is naturally only too willing to act as theatrical producer. How could he be expected to renounce the drama of the short time span, and all the best tricks of a very old trade?

Over and above cycles and intercycles, there is what the economists without always having studied it call the secular tendency. But so far only a few economists have proved interested in it, and their deliberations on structural crises, based only on the recent past, as far back as 1929, or 1870 at the very most,[7] not having had to withstand the test of historical verification, are more in the nature of sketches and hypotheses. They offer nonetheless a useful introduction to the history of the *longue durée*. They provide a first key.

The second and far more useful key consists in the word *structure*. For good or ill, this word dominates the problems of the *longue durée*. By *structure*, observers of social questions mean an organization, a coherent and fairly fixed series of relationships between realities and social masses. For us historians, a structure is of course a construct, an architecture, but over and above that it is a reality which time uses and abuses over long periods. Some structures, because of their long life, become stable elements for an infinite number of generations: they get in the way of history, hinder its flow, and in hindering it shape it. Others wear themselves out more quickly. But all of them provide both support and hindrance. As hindrances they stand as limits ("envelopes," in the mathematical sense) beyond which man and his experiences cannot go. Just think of the difficulties of breaking out of certain geographical frameworks, certain biological realities, certain limits of productivity, even particular spiritual constraints: mental frameworks too can form prisons of the *longue durée*.

The example which comes most readily to mind is once again that of the geographical constraint. For centuries, man has been a prisoner of climate, of vegetation, of the animal population, of a particular agriculture, of a whole slowly established balance from which he cannot escape without the risk of everything's being upset. Look at the position held by the movement of flocks in the lives of mountain people, the permanence of certain sectors of maritime life, rooted in the favorable conditions wrought by particular coastal configurations, look at the way the sites of cities endure, the persistence of routes and trade, and all the amazing fixity of the geographical setting of civilizations.

There is the same element of permanence or survival in the vast domain of cultural affairs. Ernst Robert Curtius's magnificent book,[8] which has at long last appeared in a French translation, is a study of a cultural system which prolonged the Latin civilization of the Byzantine Empire, even while it distorted it through selections and omissions. This civilization was itself weighed down by its own ponderous inheritance. Right up to the thirteenth and fourteenth centuries, right up to the birth of national literatures, the civilization of the intellectual élite fed on the same subjects, the same comparisons, the same commonplaces and catchwords. Pursuing an analogous line of thought, Lucien Febvre's study

*Rabelais et le problème de l'incroyance au XVIᵉ siècle,*[9] is an attempt to specify the mental tools available to French thought at the time of Rabelais. Febvre was concerned to define the whole body of concepts which regulated the arts of living, thinking, and believing well before Rabelais and long after him, and which profoundly limited the intellectual endeavors of the freest spirits from the very outset. Alphonse Dupront's subject[10] too appears as one of the freshest lines of research within the French school of history. In it the idea of the crusade is examined in the West after the fourteenth century, that is, well after the age of the "true" crusade, in the continuity of an attitude endlessly repeated over the *longue durée,* which cut across the most diverse societies, worlds, and psyches, and touched the men of the nineteenth century with one last ray. In another, related field, Pierre Francastel's book *Peinture et société,*[11] demonstrates the permanence of "geometric" pictorial space from the beginnings of the Florentine Renaissance until cubism and the emergence of intellectual painting at the beginning of our own century. In the history of science, too, all the many model universes are just as many incomplete explanations, but they also regularly last for centuries. They are cast aside only when they have served their turn over a long period. The Aristotelian concept of the universe persisted unchallenged, or virtually unchallenged, right up to the time of Galileo, Descartes, and Newton; then it disappeared before the advent of a geometrized universe which in turn collapsed, though much later, in the face of the Einsteinian revolution.[12]

In a seeming paradox, the main problem lies in discerning the *longue durée* in the sphere in which historical research has just achieved its most notable successes: that is, the economic sphere. All the cycles and intercycles and structural crises tend to mask the regularities, the permanence of particular systems that some have gone so far as to call civilizations[13]—that is to say, all the old habits of thinking and acting, the set patterns which do not break down easily and which, however illogical, are a long time dying.

But let us base our argument on an example, and one which can be swiftly analyzed. Close at hand, within the European sphere, there is an economic system which can be set down in a few lines: it preserved its position pretty well intact from the fourteenth to the eighteenth century or, to be quite sure of our ground, until about 1750. For whole centuries, economic activity was dependent on demographically fragile populations, as was demonstrated by the great decline in population from 1350 to 1450, and of course from 1630 to 1730.[14] For whole centuries, all movement was dominated by the primacy of water and ships, any inland location being an obstacle and a source of inferiority. The great European points of growth, except for a few exceptions which go only to prove the rule (such as the fairs in Champagne which were already on the decline at the beginning of the period, and the Leipzig fairs in the eighteenth century), were situated along the coastal fringes. As for other characteristics of this system, one might cite the primacy of merchants; the prominent role of precious metals, gold, silver, even copper, whose endless vicissitudes would only be damped down, if then, by the decisive development of credit at the end of the sixteenth century; the repeated sharp difficulties caused by seasonal agricultural crises; let us say the fragility of the very basis of economic life; and finally the at first sight utterly disproportionate role accorded to one or two external trade routes: the trade with the Levant from the twelfth to the sixteenth century and the colonial trade in the eighteenth century.

These are what I would define, or rather suggest in my turn following many others, as being the major characteristics of mercantile capitalism in Western Europe, a stage which lasted over the *longue durée*. Despite all the obvious changes which run through them, these four or five centuries of economic life had a certain coherence, right up to the upheavals of the eighteenth century and the industrial revolution from which we have yet to emerge. These shared characteristics persisted despite the fact that all around them, amid other continuities, a thousand reversals and ruptures totally altered the face of the world.

Among the different kinds of historical time, the *longue durée* often seems a troublesome character, full of complications, and all too frequently lacking in any sort of organization. To give it a place in the heart of our profession would entail more than a routine expansion of our studies and our curiosities. Nor would it be a question of making a simple choice in its favor. For the historian, accepting the *longue durée* entails a readiness to change his style, his attitudes, a whole reversal in his thinking, a whole new way of conceiving of social affairs. It means becoming used to a slower tempo, which sometimes almost borders on the motionless. At that stage, though not at any other—this is a point to which I will return—it is proper to free oneself from the demanding time scheme of history, to get out of it and return later with a fresh view, burdened with other anxieties and other questions. In any case, it is in relation to these expanses of slow-moving history that the whole of history is to be rethought, as if on the basis of an infrastructure. All the stages, all the thousands of stages, all the thousand explosions of historical time can be understood on the basis of these depths, this semistillness. Everything gravitates around it.

I make no claim to have defined the historian's profession in the preceding lines—merely one conception of that profession. After the

storms we have been through during recent years, happy not to say naïf
the man who could believe that we have hit upon true principles, clear
limits, the Right School. In fact, all the social sciences find their tasks
shifting all the time, both because of their own developments and because of the active development of them all as a body. History is no
exception. There is no rest in view, the time for disciples has not yet
come. It is a long way from Charles-Victor Langlois and Charles Seignobos to Marc Bloch. But since Marc Bloch, the wheel has not stopped
turning. For me, history is the total of all possible histories—an as-
semblage of professions and points of view, from yesterday, today, and
tomorrow.

The only error, in my view, would be to choose one of these histories
to the exclusion of all others. That was, and always will be, the cardinal
error of historicizing. It will not be easy, we know, to convince all historians of the truth of this. Still less, to convince all the social sciences, with
their burning desire to get us back to history as we used to know it
yesterday. It will take us a good deal of time and trouble to accommodate
all these changes and innovations beneath the old heading of history.
And yet a new historical "science" has been born, and goes on questioning and transforming itself. It revealed itself as early as 1900, with the
*Revue de synthèse historique,* and with *Annales* which started to come out in
1929. The historian felt the desire to concentrate his attention on *all* the
human sciences. It is this which has given our profession its strange
frontiers, and its strange preoccupations. So it must not be imagined that
the same barriers and differences exist between the historian and the
social scientist as existed yesterday. All the human sciences, history included, are affected by one another. They speak the same language, or
could if they wanted to.

Whether you take 1558 or this year of grace 1958, the problem for
anyone tackling the world scene is to define a hierarchy of forces, of
currents, of particular movements, and then tackle them as an entire
constellation. At each moment of this research, one has to distinguish
between long-lasting movements and short bursts, the latter detected
from the moment they originate, the former over the course of a distant
time. The world of 1558, which appeared so gloomy in France, was not
born at the beginning of that charmless year. The same with our own
troubled year of 1958. Each "current event" brings together movements
of different origins, of a different rhythm: today's time dates from yesterday, the day before yesterday, and all former times.

## The Quarrel with the Short Time Span

These truths are of course banal. Nonetheless, the social sciences seem little tempted by such remembrance of things past. Not that one can draw up any firm accusation against them and declare them to be consistently guilty of not accepting history or duration as dimensions necessary to their studies. The "diachronic" examination which reintroduces history is never absent from their theoretical deliberations.

Despite this sort of distant acknowledgment, though, it must be admitted that the social sciences, by taste, by deep-seated instinct, perhaps by training, have a constant tendency to evade historical explanation. They evade it in two almost contradictory ways: by concentrating overmuch on the "current event" in social studies, thanks to a brand of empirical sociology which, disdainful of all history, confines itself to the facts of the short term and investigations into "real life"; by transcending time altogether and conjuring up a mathematical formulation of more or less timeless structures under the name of "communications science." This last and newest way is clearly the only one which can be of any substantial interest to us. But there are enough devotees of the current event to justify examining both aspects of the question.

We have already stated our mistrust of a history occupied solely with events. To be fair, though, if there is a sin in being overconcerned with events, then history, though the most obvious culprit, is not the only guilty one. All the social sciences have shared in this error. Economists, demographers, geographers are all balanced (and badly balanced) between the demands of yesterday and of today. In order to be right they would need to maintain a constant balance—easy enough, and indeed obligatory, for the demographer, and almost a matter of course for geographers (particularly ours, reared in the Vidalian school)—but rare for economists, held fast to the most short lived of current events, hardly looking back beyond 1945 or forecasting further in advance than a few months, or at most a few years. I would maintain that all economic thinking is trapped by these temporal restrictions. It is up to historians, so economists say, to go back further than 1945, in search of old economies. Economists thus voluntarily rob themselves of a marvelous field of observation, although without denying its value. They have fallen into the habit of putting themselves at the disposal of current events and of governments.

The position of ethnographers and ethnologists is neither so clear nor so alarming. Some of them have taken great pains to underline the impossibility (but intellectuals are always fascinated by the impossible) and the uselessness of applying history within their profession. Such an authoritarian denial of history would hardly have served Malinowski and his disciples. Indeed, how could anthropology possibly not have an interest in history? History and anthropology both spring from the same impulse, as Claude Lévi-Strauss[15] delights in saying. There is no society, however primitive, which does not bear the "scars of events," nor any society in which history has sunk completely without trace. This is something there is no need to complain about or to insist on further.

On the other hand, where sociology is concerned, our quarrel along the frontiers of the short term must necessarily be a rather bitter one. Sociological investigations into the contemporary scene seem to run in a thousand different directions, from sociology to psychology to economics, and to proliferate among us as they do abroad. They are, in their own way, a bet on the irreplaceable value of the present moment, with its "volcanic" heat, its abundant wealth. What good would be served by turning back toward historical time: impoverished, simplified, devastated by silence, reconstructed—above all, let us say it again, *reconstructed*. Is it really as dead, as reconstructed, as they would have us believe, though? Doubtless a historian can only too easily isolate the crucial factor from some past age. To put it in Henri Pirenne's words, he can distinguish without difficulty the "important events," which means "those which bore consequences." An obvious and dangerous oversimplification. But what would the explorer of the present-day not give to have this perspective (or this sort of ability to go forward in time), making it possible to unmask and simplify our present life, in all its confusion—hardly comprehensible now because so overburdened with trivial acts and portents? Claude Lévi-Strauss claims that one hour's talk with a contemporary of Plato's would tell him more than all our classical treatises on the coherence or incoherence of ancient Greek civilization.[16] I quite agree. But this is because for years he has heard a hundred Greek voices rescued from silence. The historian has prepared his way. One hour in modern Greece would tell him nothing, or hardly anything, about contemporary Greek coherence or incoherence.

Even more to the point, the researcher occupied with the present can make out the "fine" lines of a structure only by himself engaging in *reconstruction*, putting forward theories and explanations, not getting embroiled in reality as it appears, but truncating it, transcending it. Such maneuvers allow him to get away from the given situation the better to control it, but they are all acts of reconstruction. I would seriously question whether sociological photography of the present time is any more "true" than the historical portrayal of the past, more particularly the more it tries to get any further away from the *reconstructed*.

Philippe Ariès[17] has emphasized the importance of the unfamiliar, of surprise in historical explanation: you are in the sixteenth century, and you stumble upon some peculiarity, something which seems peculiar to you as a man of the twentieth century. Why this difference? That is the question which one then has to set about answering. But I would claim that such surprise, such unfamiliarity, such distancing—these great highways to knowledge—are no less necessary to an understanding of all that surrounds us and which we are so close to that we cannot see clearly. Live in London for a year and you will not know much about England. But by contrast, in light of what has surprised you, you will suddenly have come to understand some of the most deep-seated and characteristic aspects of France, things which you did not know before because you knew them too well. With regard to the present, the past too is a way of distancing yourself.

In this way historians and social scientists could go on forever batting the ball back and forth between dead documents and all-too-living evidence, the distant past and the too-close present. But I do not believe that this is a crucial problem. Past and present illuminate each other reciprocally. And in exclusively observing the narrow confines of the present, the attention will irresistibly be drawn toward whatever moves quickly, burns with a true or a false flame, or has just changed, or makes a noise, or is easy to see. There is a whole web of events, as wearisome as any in the historical sciences, which lies in wait for the observer in a hurry, the ethnographer dwelling for three months with some Polynesian tribe, the industrial sociologist delivering all the clichés of his latest investigation, or who truly believes that he can thoroughly pin down some social mechanism with cunningly phrased questionnaires and combinations of punched cards. Social questions are more cunning game than that.

In fact, what possible interest can we take, we the human sciences, in the movements of a young girl between her home in the sixteenth arrondissement, her music teacher, and the Ecole des Sciences-Po, discussed in a sound and wide-ranging study of the Paris area?[18] They make up a fine-looking map. But if she had studied agronomy or gone in for water-skiing, the whole pattern of her triangular journeys would have been altered. It is nice to see on a map the distribution of all domiciles belonging to employees in a large concern. But if I do not have an earlier map, if the lapse of time between the two maps is not sufficient to allow the tracing of a genuine movement, then precisely where is the problem without which any inquiry is simply a waste of effort? Any interest in inquiries for inquiry's sake is limited to the collection of data at best. But even then these data will not all be *ipso facto* useful for future work. We must beware of art for art's sake.

In the same way I would question whether any study of a town, no matter which, could be the object of a sociological inquiry in the way that Auxerre[19] was, or Vienne in the Dauphiné,[20] without being set in its historical context. Any town, as an extended social entity with all its crises, dislocations, breakdowns, and necessary calculations, must be seen in relation to the whole complex of districts surrounding it, as well as in relation to those archipelagos of neighboring towns which Richard Häpke, the historian, was one of the first to discuss. Similarly, it must also be considered in relation to the movement, more or less distant in time, sometimes extremely distant, which directs this whole complex. It cannot be of no interest, it must rather surely be crucial to note down particular urban/rural exchanges, particular industrial or mercantile competition, to know whether you are dealing with a movement in the full flush of its youth, or at the end of its run, with the beginnings of a resurgence or a monotonous repetition.

One last remark: Lucien Febvre, during the last ten years of his life, is said to have repeated: "History, science of the past, science of the present." Is not history, the dialectic of time spans, in its own way an explanation of society in all its reality? and thus of contemporary society? And here its role would be to caution us against the event: do not think only of the short time span, do not believe that only the actors which make the most noise are the most authentic—there are other, quieter ones too. As if anybody did not know that already!

## Communication and Social Mathematics

Perhaps we were wrong to linger on the tempestuous borders of the short time span. In actual fact, that debate proceeds without any great interest, certainly without any useful revelations. The crucial debate is elsewhere, among our neighbors who are being carried away by the newest experiment in the social sciences, under the double heading of "communications" and mathematics.

But this will be no easy brief to argue. I mean it will be by no means easy to prove that there is no sort of social study which can avoid historical time, when here is one which, ostensibly at least, has its being entirely outside it.

In any case, the reader who wishes to follow our argument (either to agree or to dissociate himself from our point of view) would do well to weigh for himself, one after another, the terms of a vocabulary which, though certainly not entirely new, have been taken up afresh and rejuvenated for the purposes of these new debates. There is nothing more to be said here, obviously, about events, or the *longue durée*. Nor a great deal about *structures*, though the word—and the thing—is by no means entirely free from uncertainty and debate.[21] Nor would there be any point in dwelling on the words *synchronous* and *diachronous:* they are self-defining, though their function in the actual study of social questions might be less easy to make out than it appears. In fact, as far as the language of history is concerned (insofar as I conceive it) there can be no question of perfect synchrony: a sudden halt, in which all time spans would be suspended, is almost an absurdity in itself, or, and this comes to the same thing, is highly factitious. In the same way, a descent following the onward stream of time is conceivable only in terms of a multiplicity of descents, following the innumerable different rivers of time.

These brief summaries and warnings must suffice for now. But one must be more explicit when dealing with *unconscious history, models,* and *social mathematics*. Besides, these commentaries will, I hope, without too much delay, link together what is problematic in all the social sciences.

*Unconscious history,* is, of course, the history of the unconscious elements in social development. "Men make their own history, but they do not know that they are making it."[22] Marx's formula pinpoints the problem, but does not explain it. In fact it is the same old problem of short time span, of "microtime," of the event, that we find ourselves confronted with under a new name. Men have always had the impression, in living out their time, of being able to grasp its passage from day to day. But is this clear, conscious history delusory, as many historians have agreed? Yesterday linguistics believed that it could derive everything from words. History was under the illusion that it could derive everything from events. More than one of our contemporaries would be happy to believe that everything is the result of the agreements at Yalta or Potsdam, the incidents at Dien Bien Phu or Sakhiet-Sidi-Youssef, or again from that other event, important in a different way it is true, the launching of the sputniks. Unconscious history proceeds beyond the reach of these illuminations and their brief flashes. One has, then, to concede that there does exist, at some distance, a social unconscious. And concede, too, that this unconscious might well be thought more rich, scientifically speaking, than the glittering surface to which our eyes are accustomed. More rich scientifically, meaning simpler, easier to exploit—not easier to discover. But the step from bright surface to murky depths—from noise to silence—is difficult and dangerous. Equally let it be said that "unconscious" history, belonging half to the time of conjunctures and wholly to structural time, is clearly visible more frequently than one would willingly admit. Each one of us can sense, over and above his own life, a mass history, though it is true he is more conscious of its power and impetus than of its laws or direction. And this consciousness is not only of recent date (like the concerns of economic history), although today it may be increasingly sharp. The revolution, for it is an intellectual revolution, consisted in confronting this half darkness head on, and giving it a greater and greater place next to, and even to the detriment of, a history purely of events.

History is not alone in this prospecting (quite the reverse, all it has done has been to follow others into the area, and adapt the perspectives of the new social sciences for its own use), and new instruments of knowledge and research have had to be created: hence *models*, some more or less perfected, some still rather rough and ready. Models are only hypotheses, systems of explanations tied solidly together in the form of an equation, or a function: this equals that, or determines the other. Such and such a reality never appears without that one, and constant and close links are revealed between the one and the other. The carefully constructed model will thus allow us to inquire, throughout time and space, into other social environments similar to the observed social environment on the basis of which it was originally constructed. That is its constant value.

These systems of explanation vary infinitely according to the temperament, calculations, and aims of those using them: simple or complex, qualitative or quantitative, static or dynamic, mechanical or statistical. I am indebted to Lévi-Strauss for this last distinction. A mechanical model would be of the same dimensions as directly observed reality, a reality of limited dimensions, of interest only to very small groups of people (this is how ethnologists proceed when dealing with primitive societies). When dealing with large societies, where great numbers come in, the calculation of the average becomes necessary: this leads to the construction of statistical models. But what do these sometimes debatable distinctions really matter!

In my opinion, before establishing a common program for the social sciences, the crucial thing is to define the function and limits of models, the scope of which some undertakings seem to be in danger of enlarging inordinately. Whence the need to confront models, too, with the notion of the time span; for the meaning and the value of their explanations depend fairly heavily, it seems to me, on their implied duration.

To be more clear, let us select our examples from among historical models,[23] by which I mean those constructed by historians. They are fairly rough and ready as models go, not often driven to the rigor of an authentic scientific law, and never worried about coming out with some revolutionary mathematical language—but models nonetheless, in their own way.

Above we have discussed mercantile capitalism between the fourteenth and the eighteenth centuries: one model which, among others, can be drawn from Marx's work. It can be applied in full only to one particular family of societies at one particular given time, even if it leaves the door open to every extrapolation.

There is already a difference between this and the model which I sketched out in an earlier book,[24] of the cycle of economic development in Italian cities between the sixteenth and eighteenth centuries. These cities became in turn mercantile, "industrial," and finally specialists in banking, this last development being the slowest to grow and the slowest to die away. Though in fact less all-embracing than the structure of mercantile capitalism, this sketch would be much the more easily extended in time and space. It records a phenomenon (some would say a dynamic structure, but all structures in history have at least an elementary dynamism) capable of recurring under a number of common circumstances. Perhaps the same could be said of the model sketched out by Frank Spooner and myself[25] which dealt with the history of precious metals before, during, and after the sixteenth century: gold, silver, copper—and credit, that agile substitute for metal—all play their part too. The "strategy" of one weighs on the "strategy" of another. It would not be particularly difficult to remove this model from the special and particularly turbulent world of the sixteenth century, which happened to be the one we selected for our observations. Have not economists dealing with the particular case of underdeveloped countries attempted to verify the old quantitative theory of money, which was, after all, a model too in its own fashion.[26]

But the time spans possible to all these models are brief compared with those of the model conceived by the young American social historian Sigmund Diamond.[27] Diamond was struck by the double language of the dominant class of great American financier contemporaries of Pierpont Morgan, consisting of a language internal to their class, and an external language. This last, truth to tell, was a brand of special pleading with public opinion to whom the success of the financier is presented as the typical triumph of the *self-made man,* the condition necessary for the nation's prosperity. Struck by this double language, Diamond saw in it the customary reaction of any dominant class which feels its prestige waning and its privileges threatened. In order to camouflage itself, it is necessary for it to confuse its own fate with that of the City or the Nation, its own private interests with the public interest. Sigmund Diamond would willingly explain the evolution of the idea of dynasty or of empire, the English dynasty or the Roman empire, in the same way. The model thus conceived clearly has the run of the centuries. It presupposes certain conditions, but these are conditions with which history is abundantly supplied: it follows that it is valid for a much longer time span than either of the preceding models, but at the same time it puts into question much more precise and exact aspects of reality.

At the limit, as the mathematicians would say, this kind of model is kin to the favorite, almost timeless models of sociological mathematicians. Almost timeless, in actual fact, traveling the dark, untended byways of the extreme *longue durée.*

The preceding explanations must of necessity provide only an inadequate introduction to the science and theory of models. And historians are far from standing in the forefront. Their models are hardly more than bundles of explanations. Our colleagues are more ambitious and advanced in research, attempting to establish links between the theories and languages of information or communications theory or of qualitative mathematics. Their merit—and it is a great one—is in absorbing the subtle language of mathematics into their domain, though this runs the risk, should our attention flag even slightly, of its escaping from our control and running off, Heaven only knows where! Information and communications theory, qualitative mathematics, all come together under the already substantial patronage of social mathematics. And we must try, as far as we are able, to light our lantern by their flame too.

Social mathematics[28] is made up of at least three languages, and there is still scope for them to mingle and develop more. Mathematicians have not yet come to the end of their inventiveness. Besides, there is not *one* mathematics, *the* mathematics (or, if there is, it is only as an assertion, not a fact): "one should not say algebra, geometry, but an algebra, a geometry" (Th. Guilbaud)—which does not make our problems, or theirs, any easier. Three languages, then: that of necessary facts (a given fact, and its consequence), which is the domain of traditional mathematics; the language of contingent facts, dating from Pascal, which is the domain of the calculation of probabilities; and finally the language of conditioned facts, neither determined nor contingent but behaving under certain constraints, tied to the rules of a game, to the "strategic" axis in the games of Von Neumann and Morgenstern,[29] those triumphant games which have gone on developing on the basis of their inventors' first bold principles. Game theory, with its use of wholes, of groups, and of the calculation of probabilities, opens the way to "qualitative" mathematics, and from that moment the move from observation to mathematical formulation does not have to be made along the painful path of measurements and long statistical calculations. One can pass directly from an observation of social reality to a mathematical formulation, to the calculating machine, so to speak.

Of course, the machine's diet has to be prepared in advance, since there are only certain kinds of food which it can cope with. Besides, the science of information has evolved as a function of true machines and their rules of functioning, in order to promote *communication* in the most material sense of the word. The author of this article is by no means a specialist in these complex fields. The research toward creating a translating machine, which I followed from afar but nonetheless followed, has left me and many others deep in thought. All the same, two facts remain:

(1) such machines, such mathematical possibilities, do exist; and (2) society must prepare itself for social mathematics, which is no longer our old accustomed mathematics of price curves and the graphs of birthrates.

Now, while the workings of the new mathematics may often elude us, the preparation of social reality for its use, fitting it out and trimming it appropriately, is a task we can well cope with. The preliminary treatment has up till now been almost always exactly the same: choose some unified limited object of observation, such as a "primitive" tribe or a demographic "isolate," in which almost everything can be seen and touched directly, then establish all possible relationships, all possible games among the elements thus distinguished. Such relationships, rigorously worked out, provide the very equations from which mathematics will be able to draw all possible conclusions and projections in order to come up with a *model* which sums them all up, or rather takes them all into account.

Obviously a million openings for research exist in these areas. But one example is worth any amount of prolonged explanation. We have Claude Lévi-Stauss as an excellent guide, let us follow him. He can introduce us to one area of these researches, call it that of a science of *communications.*[30]

"In any society," writes Lévi-Strauss,[31] "communication operates on at least three levels: communication of women, communication of goods and services, communication of messages." Let us agree that these are, at their different levels, different *languages,* but languages nonetheless. If that is so, are we not entitled to treat them as languages, or even as *language,* and to associate them, whether directly or indirectly, to the sensational progress made by linguistics, and even more by phonemics, which "will certainly play the same renovating role with respect to the social sciences that nuclear physics, for example, has played for the physical sciences" ?[32] That is saying a lot, but sometimes one has to say a lot. Just as history is caught in the trap of events, linguistics, caught in the trap of words (the relation between word and object, the historical evolution of words), was set free by the phonemic revolution. It became aware, beneath the word, of the unit of sound which is the phoneme, at that point paying no attention to its sense, but carefully noting its placing, the sounds accompanying it, the grouping of these sounds, the infraphonemic structures, and the whole underlying *unconscious* reality of language. On the basis of the few dozen phonemes which occur in every language in the world, the new mathematical calculations set to work, and in so doing set linguistics, or at least one aspect of linguistics, free from the realm of social studies to scale the "heights of the physical sciences."

To extend the meaning of language to elementary structures of kinship, myths, ceremonial, economic exchanges is to attempt that difficult but worthwhile route to the summit. Claude Lévi-Strauss showed this sort of courage initially when dealing with matrimonial exchanges—that first language, so essential to all human communication that there is no society, whether primitive or not, in which incest, marriage within the nuclear family, is not forbidden. Thus, a language. And beneath this language he sought the one basic element which would, so to speak, correspond to the phoneme. That element, that "atom" of kinship, was put forward by our guide in its most simple format in his thesis of 1949:[33] the man, his wife, their child, and the child's maternal uncle. On the basis of this quadrangular element and of all known systems of marriage within these primitive worlds—and they are many—the mathematicians were enabled to work out all possible combinations and solutions. With the help of the mathematician André Weill, Lévi-Strauss was able to translate the observations of the anthropologist into mathematical terms. The resulting model should provide proof of the validity and stability of the system, and point out the solutions which it implies.

The procedure of this research is clear: to get past superficial observation in order to reach the zone of unconscious or barely conscious elements, and then to reduce that reality to tiny elements, minute identical sections, whose relations can be precisely analyzed. It is at this "micro-sociological [of a certain kind, I would add] stage that one might hope to discover the most general structural laws, just as the linguist discovers his at the infra-phonemic level or the physicist at the infra-molecular or atomic level."[34] This is of course an activity which can be pursued in a good many other directions. Thus, what could be more instructive than to see Lévi-Strauss coming to grips, this time, with myths, and in a light-hearted way with cooking. Myths he reduced to a series of individual cells, or *mythemes;* the language of cookbooks he reduced (none too seriously) to *gustemes.* Each time, he has sought the deepest, least conscious layers. I am not concerned, while I speak, with the phonemes in my speech; nor, unless very exceptionally, when I am at the table, do I concern myself with "gustemes," if gustemes in fact exist. And yet, each time, the subtle and precise interplay of relationships is there, keeping me company. As far as these simple, mysterious relationships go, will the final act of sociological research be to grasp them where they lie beneath all languages, in order to translate them into one Morse code that is the universal language of mathematics? That is the prime ambition of the new social mathematics. But that, if I may say so, is another story.

But let us get back to the question of time spans. I have said that models are of varying duration: they are valid for as long as the reality with which they are dealing. And for the social observer, that length of time is fundamental, for even more significant than the deep-rooted structures of life are their points of rupture, their swift or slow deterioration under the effect of contradictory pressures.

I have sometimes compared models to ships. What interests me, once the boat is built, is to put it in the water to see if it will float, and then to make it ascend and descend the waters of time, at my will. The significant moment is when it can keep afloat no longer, and sinks. Thus the explanation which Frank Spooner and I proposed for the interplay of precious metals seems to me to have little validity before the fifteenth century. Earlier than that, the competition between metals was of a violence quite unparalleled in previous observations. It was up to us then to find out why. Just as, going downstream this time, we had to find out why the navigation of our over-simple craft became first difficult and then impossible in the eighteenth century with the unprecedented growth of credit. It seems to me that research is a question of endlessly proceeding from the social reality to the model, and then back again, and so on, in a series of readjustments and patiently renewed trips. In this way the model is, in turn, an attempt at an explanation of the structure, and an instrument of control and comparison, able to verify the solidity and the very life of a given structure. If I were to construct a model on the basis of the present, I would immediately relocate it in its context in reality, and then take it back in time, as far back as its origins, if possible. After which, I would project its probable life, right up to the next break, in accordance with the corresponding movement of other social realities. Unless I should decide to use it as an element of comparison, and take it off through time and space, in search of other aspects of reality on which it might shed new light.

Would I be wrong to believe that the models put forward by qualitative mathematics, at least insofar as they have been shown to us up till now,[35] would lend themselves ill to such excursions, above all because they are committed to traveling along only one of time's many possible highways, that of the extreme *longue durée*, sheltered from all accidents, crises, and sudden breaks? I will refer, once again, to Claude Lévi-Strauss, because his experiments in this field seem to me the most well thought out, the clearest, and the most securely rooted in the social experience which any such undertaking should be based on and return to. Let us note that each time he is concerned with questioning a phenomenon which develops only very slowly, almost timelessly. All kinship systems persist because there is no human life possible beyond a certain ratio of consanguinity, so that, for a small group of people to survive, it must open onto the outside world: the prohibition of incest is a reality of the *longue durée*. Myths too, developing slowly, correspond to structures of an extremely long duration. Without even bothering to pick out the oldest, one could collect together all the versions of the Oedipus story, so that classified according to their different variations, they might throw light on the underlying impulse which shapes them all. But let us suppose for a moment that our colleague was not interested in myths, but in, say, the images projected by, and succeeding interpretations of, "Machiavellianism," and that he was seeking the basic elements in this fairly straightforward and very widespread doctrine, which came into being in the middle of the sixteenth century. Everywhere here he would find rifts and reversals, even in the very structure of Machiavellianism, for it is not a system which has the theatrical, sempiternal solidity of myth. It is sensitive to any action and reaction, to all the various inclemencies of history. In a word, it does not have its being solely within the calm, monotonous highways of the *longue durée*. Thus the process recommended by Lévi-Strauss in the search for mathematizable structures is valid not only on the level of microsociology, but also in confronting the infinitely small and the extreme *longue durée*.

Does this mean that this revolutionary qualitative mathematics is condemned to follow only the paths of the extreme *longue durée*? In which case, after a hard struggle, all we find ourselves with are truths built rather too much on the dimensions of eternal man. Elementary truths, aphorisms amounting to no more than mere common sense, are what the disappointed might be inclined to say. To which would come the reply, fundamental truths, able to cast new light on the very bases of all social life. But that is not the whole question.

I do not in fact believe that these experiments—or analogous experiments—cannot be conducted outside the scope of the very *longue durée*. The stuff of qualitative social mathematics is not figures but links, relationships, which must be fairly rigorously defined before they can be rendered into a mathematical symbol, on the basis of which one can study all the mathematical possibilities of these symbols, without having to trouble oneself any more about the social reality which they represent. Thus the entire value of the conclusions is dependent upon the value of the initial observation, and on the selection of essential elements within the observed reality and the determination of their relationships. One can thus see why social mathematics has a preference for what Claude Lévi-Strauss calls mechanical models, that is to say, models based on fairly narrow groups in which each individual can, so to speak, be directly observed, and in which a highly homogeneous social organization enables a secure definition of human relationships, in a simple and concrete way, and with few variations.

So-called statistical models, on the other hand, deal with large and complex societies, in which observation can be carried out only according to averages, or in other words according to traditional mathematics. But once the averages have been arrived at, should the observer be able to establish, on the scale of groups rather than of individuals, those basic relationships which we have been discussing and which are necessary to the formulation of qualitative mathematics, then there would be nothing to stop him from making use of them again. So far as I know, there have not been any attempts made along these lines. But these are early days for such experiments. For the moment, whether one is dealing with psychology, economics, or anthropology, all the experiments have been carried out in the way I discussed when speaking of Lévi-Strauss. But qualitative social mathematics will not have proved itself until it has confronted a modern society with involved problems and different rates of development. I would wager that this venture will tempt one of our sociologist-mathematicians; I would wager equally that it will prompt a necessary revision of the methods according to which the new mathematics has operated so far, penned up in what I would call, in this instance, the excessive *longue durée*. It must rediscover the diversity of life—the movement, the different time spans, the rifts and variations.

## Time for the Historian, Time for the Sociologist

And here I am, after an incursion into the timeless realms of social mathematics, back at the question of time and time spans. And incorrigible historian that I am, I stand amazed yet again that sociologists have managed to avoid it. But the thing is that their time is not ours: it is a great deal less imperious and less concrete and is never central to their problems and their thoughts.

In truth, the historian can never get away from the question of time in history: time sticks to his thinking like soil to a gardener's spade. He may well dream of getting away from it, of course. Spurred on by the anguish of 1940, Gaston Roupnel [36] wrote words on this subject that will make any true historian suffer. Similar is the classic remark made by Paul Lacombe who was also a historian of the grand school: "Time is nothing in itself, objectively, it is only an idea we have." [37] But do these remarks really provide a way out? I myself, during a rather gloomy captivity, struggled a good deal to get away from a chronicle of those difficult years (1940–45). Rejecting events and the time in which events take place was a way of placing oneself to one side, sheltered, so as to get some sort of perspective, to be able to evaluate them better, and not wholly to believe in them. To go from the short time span, to one less short, and then to the long view (which, if it exists, must surely be the wise man's time span); and having got there, to think about everything afresh and to reconstruct everything around one: a historian could hardly not be tempted by such a prospect.

But these successive flights cannot put the historian definitively beyond the bounds of the world's time, beyond historical time, so imperious because it is irreversible, and because it flows at the very rhythm of the earth's rotation. In fact, these different time spans which we can discern are all interdependent: it is not so much time which is the creation of our own minds, as the way in which we break it up. These fragments are reunited at the end of all our labors. The *longue durée,* the conjuncture, the event all fit into each other neatly and without difficulty, for they are all measured on the same scale. Equally, to be able to achieve an imaginative understanding of one of these time spans is to be able to understand them all. The philosopher, taken up with the subjective aspect of things, interior to any notion of time, never senses this weight of historical time, of a concrete, universal time, such as the time of conjuncture that Ernest Labrousse[38] depicts at the beginning of his book like a traveler who is constantly the same and who travels the world imposing the same set of values, no matter the country in which he has disembarked, nor what the social order with which it is invested.

For the historian everything begins and ends with time, a mathematical, godlike time, a notion easily mocked, time external to men, "exogenous," as economists would say, pushing men, forcing them, and painting their own individual times the same color: it is, indeed, the imperious time of the world.

Sociologists, of course, will not entertain this oversimplified notion. They are much closer to the *dialectique de la durée* as put forward by Gaston Bachelard.[39] Social time is but one dimension of the social reality under consideration. It is within this reality just as it is within a given individual, one sign of particularity among others. The sociologist is in no way hampered by this accommodating sort of time, which can be cut, frozen, set in motion entirely at will. Historical time, I must repeat, lends itself less easily to the supple double action of synchrony and diachrony: it cannot envisage life as a mechanism that can be stopped at leisure in order to reveal a frozen image.

This is a more profound rift than is at first apparent: sociologists' time cannot be ours. The fundamental structure of our profession revolts against it. Our time, like economists' time, is one of measure. When a sociologist tells us that a structure breaks down only in order to build itself up afresh, we are happy to accept an explanation which historical observation would confirm anyway. But we would wish to know the precise time span of these movements, whether positive or negative, situated along the usual axis. An economic cycle, the ebb and flow of material life, can be measured. A structural social crisis should be equally possible to locate in time, and through it. We should be able to place it exactly, both in itself and even more in relation to the movement of associated structures. What is profoundly interesting to the historian is the way these movements cross one another, and how they interact, and how they break up: all things which can be recorded only in relation to the uniform time of historians, which can stand as a general measure of all these phenomena, and not in relation to the multiform time of social reality, which can stand only as the individual measure of each of these phenomena separately.

Rightly or wrongly, the historian cannot but formulate such opposed ideas, even when entering into the welcoming, almost brotherly realm of Georges Gurvitch's sociology. Did not a philosopher[40] define him recently as the one "who is driving sociology back into the arms of history"? But even with him, the historian can recognize neither his time spans nor his temporalities. The great social edifice (should one say *model?*) erected by Georges Gurvitch is organized according to five basic architectural aspects:[41] the deeper levels; the level of sociability; the level of social groups; the level of global societies; and the level of time. This final bit of scaffolding, temporalities, the newest and the most recently built, is as if superimposed on the whole.

Georges Gurvitch's temporalities are various. He distinguishes a whole series of them: the time of the *longue durée* and slow motion, time the deceiver and time the surpriser, time with an irregular beat, cyclic time running in place, time running slow, time alternating between running slow and fast, time running fast, explosive time.[42] How could a historian believe in all this? Given such a range of colors, he could never reconstitute a single, white light—and that is something he cannot do without. The historian quickly becomes aware, too, that this chameleon-like time barely adds any extra touch, any spot of color to the categories which had been established earlier. In the city that our friend has built, time, the last to arrive, cohabits quite naturally with all the other categories. It fits itself to the dimensions of their homes and their demands, according to the "levels," sociabilities, groups, and global societies. It is a different way of rewriting the same equations without actually changing them. Each social reality secretes its own peculiar time, or time scale, like common snails. But what do we historians get out of all this? The vast edifice of this ideal city remains static. History is nowhere to be seen. The world's time, historical time is there, but imprisoned, like Aéolus in his goat's skin. It is not history which sociologists, fundamentally and quite unconsciously, bear a grudge against, but historical time—which is a reality that retains its violence no matter how one tries to bring it to order and to break it down. It is a constraint from which the historian is never free, while sociologists on the other hand almost always seem to manage to avoid it, by concentrating either on the instant, which is always present as if suspended somewhere above time, or else on repeated phenomena which do not belong to any age. So they escape the two contradictory movements of the mind, confining them within either the narrowest limits of the event or the most extended *longue durée*. Is such an evasion justifiable? That is the crux of the debate between historians and sociologists, and even between historians of differing persuasions.

I do not know whether this rather excessively cut and dried article, relying overmuch, as historians have a tendency to do, on the use of examples, will meet with the agreement of sociologists and of our other neighbors. I rather doubt it. Anyway, it is never a good thing, when writing a conclusion, simply to repeat some insistently recurrent leit-motif. Should history by its very nature be called upon to pay special attention to the span of time and to *all* the movements of which it may be made up, the *longue durée* appears to us, within this array, as the most useful line to take toward a way of observing and thinking common to all the social sciences. Is it too much to ask our neighbors that, at some stage in their reasoning, they might locate their findings and their research along this axis?

For historians, not all of whom would share my views, it would be a case of reversing engines. Their preference goes instinctively toward the short term. It is an attitude aided and abetted by the sacrosanct university courses. Jean-Paul Sartre, in recent articles,[43] strengthens their point of view, when he protests against that which is both oversimplified and too ponderous in Marxism in the name of the biographical, of the teeming reality of events. You have not said everything when you have "situated" Flaubert as bourgeois, or Tintoretto as petty bourgeois. I entirely agree. But in every case a study of the concrete situation—whether Flaubert, Valéry, or the foreign policies of the Gironde—ends up by bringing Sartre back to its deep-seated structural context. His research moves from the surface to the depths, and so links up with my own preoccupations. It would link up even better if the hourglass could be turned over both ways—from event to structure, and then from structure and model back to the event.

Marxism is peopled with models. Sartre would rebel against the rigidity, the schematic nature, the insufficiency of the model, in the name of the particular and the individual. I would rebel with him (with certain slight differences in emphasis) not against the model, though, but against the use which has been made of it, the use which it has been felt proper to make. Marx's genius, the secret of his long sway, lies in the fact that he was the first to construct true social models, on the basis of a historical *longue durée*. These models have been frozen in all their simplicity by being given the status of laws, of a preordained and automatic explanation, valid in all places and to any society. Whereas if they were put back within the ever-changing stream of time, they would constantly reappear, but with changes of emphasis, sometimes overshadowed, sometimes thrown into relief by the presence of other structures which would themselves be susceptible to definition by other rules and thus by other models. In this way, the creative potential of the most powerful social analysis of the last century has been stymied. It cannot regain its youth and vigor except in the *longue durée*. Should I add that contemporary Marxism appears to me to be the very image of the danger lying in wait for any social science wholly taken up with the model in its pure state, with models for models' sake?

What I would like to emphasize in conclusion is that the *longue durée* is but one possibility of a common language arising from a confrontation among the social sciences. There are others. I have indicated, adequately, the experiments being made by the new social mathematics. The new mathematics draws me, but the old mathematics, whose triumph is obvious in economics—perhaps the most advanced of the human sciences—does not deserve to be dismissed with a cynical aside. Huge calculations await us in this classic field, but there are squads of calculators and of calculating machines ready too, being rendered daily yet more perfect. I am a great believer in the usefulness of long sequences of statistics, and in the necessity of taking calculations and research further and further back in time. The whole of the eighteenth century in Europe is riddled with our workings, but they crop up even in the seventeenth, and even more in the sixteenth century. Statistics going back an unbelievably long way reveal the depths of the Chinese past to us through their universal language.[44] No doubt statistics simplify the better to come to grips with their subject. But all science is a movement from the complex to the simple.

And yet, let us not forget one last language, one last family of models, in fact: the necessary reduction of any social reality to the place in which it occurs. Let us call it either geography or ecology, without dwelling too long on these differences in terminology. Geography too often conceives of itself as a world on its own, and that is a pity. It has need of a Vidal de la Blache who would consider not time and place this time, but place and social reality. If that happened, geographical research would put the problems of all the human sciences first on its agenda. For sociologists, not that they would always admit it to themselves, the word ecology is a way of not saying geography, and by the same token of dodging all the problems posed by place and revealed by place to careful observation. Spatial models are the charts upon which social reality is projected, and through which it may become at least partially clear; they are truly models for all the different movements of time (and especially for the *longue durée*), and for all the categories of social life. But, amazingly, social science chooses to ignore them. I have often thought that one of the French superiorities in the social sciences was precisely that school of geography founded by Vidal de la Blache, the betrayal of whose thought and teachings is an inconsolable loss. All the social sciences must make room "for an increasingly geographical conception of mankind." [45] This is what Vidal de la Blache was asking for as early as 1903.

On the practical level—for this article does have a practical aim—I would hope that the social sciences, at least provisionally, would suspend their constant border disputes over what is or is not a social science, what is or is not a structure... Rather let them try to trace those lines across our research which if they exist would serve to orient some kind of collective research, and make possible the first stages of some sort of coming together. I would personally call such lines mathematization, a concentration on place, the *longue durée*... But I would be very interested to know what other specialists would suggest. For it goes without saying that this article has not been placed under the rubric *Débats et Combats*[46] by pure chance. It claims to pose, but not resolve, the obvious problems to which, unhappily, each one of us, when he ventures outside his own specialty, finds himself exposed. These pages are a call to discussion.

## Notes

1. Claude Lévi-Strauss, *Structural Anthropology*, trans. Claire Jacobson and Brooke Grundfest Schoepf (London: Allen Lane, The Penguin Press, 1968), 1:300 and passim.
2. Jean-Paul Sartre, "Questions de méthode," *Les Temps Modernes* nos. 139 and 140 (1957).
3. "Europe in 1500," "The World in 1880," "Germany on the Eve of the Reformation," and so on.
4. Louis Halphen, *Introduction à l'histoire* (Paris: P.U.F., 1946), p. 50.
5. See his *Théorie générale du progrès économique*, Cahiers de l'I.S.E.A., 1957.
6. *Esquisse du mouvement des prix et des revenus en France au XVIIIe siècle*, 2 vols. (Paris: Dalloz, 1933).
7. Considered in René Clémens, *Prolégomènes d'une théorie de la structure économique* (Paris: Domat-Montchrestien, 1952); see also Johann Akerman,

"Cycle et structure," *Revue économique*, no. 1 (1952).

8. Ernst Robert Curtius, *Europäische Literatur und lateinisches Mittelalter* (Berne, 1948).

9. Paris, Albin Michel, 1943; 3d ed., 1969.

10. "Le mythe de croisade: Essai de sociologie religieuse," thesis, Sorbonne.

11. Pierre Francastel, *Peinture et société: Naissance et destruction d'un espace plastique, de la Renaissance au cubisme* (Lyon: Audin, 1951).

12. Other arguments: I would like to suggest those forceful articles which all of them advance a similar thesis, such as Otto Brunner's (*Historische Zeitschrift*, vol. 177, no. 3) on the social history of Europe; R. Bultmann's (ibid., vol. 176, no. 1), on humanism; Georges Lefebvre's (*Annales historiques de la Révolution française*, no. 114 [1949]) and F. Hartung's (*Historische Zeitschrift*, vol. 180, no. 1), on enlightened despotism.

13. René Courtin, *La Civilisation économique du Brésil* (Paris: Librairie de Médicis, 1941).

14. As far as France is concerned. In Spain, the demographic decline was visible from the end of the sixteenth century.

15. Claude Lévi-Strauss, *Structural Anthropology*, p. 23.

16. "Diogène couché," *Les Temps Modernes*, no. 195, p. 17.

17. *Les Temps de l'histoire* (Paris: Plon, 1954), especially p. 298 *et seq.*

18. P. Chombart de Lauwe, *Paris et l'agglomération parisienne* (Paris: P.U.F., 1952), 1:106.

19. Suzanne Frère and Charles Bettelheim, *Une Ville française moyenne: Auxerre en 1950*, Cahiers de Sciences Politiques, no. 17 (Paris: Armand Colin, 1951).

20. Pierre Clément and Nelly Xydias, *Vienne su-le-Rhône: Sociologie d'une cité française*, Cahiers des Sciences Politiques, no. 71 (Paris: Armand Colin, 1955).

21. See the Colloquium on Structures, 6th section of the École Pratique des Hautes Études, typed summary, 1958.

22. Quoted by Claude Lévi-Strauss, *Structural Anthropology*, vol. 1, p. 23.

23. It would be tempting to make room here for the "models" created by economists, which have, in fact, been a source of inspiration to us.

24. *The Mediterranean and the Mediterranean World in the Age of Philip II*, trans. Sian Reynolds, 2 vols. (New York: Harper & Row, 1972–74).

25. Fernand Braudel and Frank Spooner, *Les Métaux monétaires et l'économie au XVIe siècle*, Rapports au Congrès international de Rome 4 (1955): 233–64.

26. Alexandre Chabert, *Structure économique et théorie monétaire*, Publications du Centre d'Études économiques (Paris: Armand Colin, 1956).

27. Sigmund Diamond, *The Reputation of the American Businessman* (Cambridge, Mass., 1955).

28. See, in particular, Claude Lévi-Strauss, *Bulletin internationale des sciences sociales*, UNESCO, vol. 6, no. 4, and in general the whole of this very interesting issue, entitled *Les Mathématiques et les sciences sociales*.

29. *The Theory of Games and Economic Behavior* (Princeton, 1944). See also the brilliant summary by Jean Fourastié, *Critique*, no. 51 (October 1951).

30. All the following quotations are drawn from his most recent work, *Structural Anthropology*.

31. Ibid., 1:296.

32. Ibid., 1:33.

33. *Les Structures élémentaires de la parenté* (Paris: P.U.F., 1949). See *Structural Anthropology*, 1:36–51.

34. *Structural Anthropology*, 1:35.

35. I am careful to say qualitative mathematics, according to games strategy. As far as classic models and those used by economists are concerned, a different sort of discussion would be called for.

36. *Histoire et destin* (Paris: Bernard Grasset, 1943), p. 169 and passim.

37. *Revue de synthèse historique* (1900), p. 32.

38. Ernest Labrousse, *La Crise économique française à la veille de la Révolution française* (Paris: P.U.F., 1944), Introduction.

39. *Dialectique de la durée*, 2d ed., (Paris: P.U.F., 1950).

40. Gilles Granger, *Événement et structure dans les sciences de l'homme*, Cahiers de l'Institut de Science Économique Appliquée, Série M., no. 1, pp. 41–42.

41. See my doubtless too polemical article "Georges Gurvitch et la discontinuité du social," *Annales E.S.C.* 3 (1953): 347–61.

42. Cf. Georges Gurvitch, *Déterminismes sociaux et liberté humaine* (Paris: P.U.F., 1955), pp. 38–40 and passim.

43. Ibid. See also Jean-Paul Sartre, "Fragment d'un livre à paraître sur le Tintoret," *Les Temps Modernes* (November 1957).

44. Otto Berkelbach, Van der Sprenkel, "Population Statistics of Ming China," B.S.O.A.S., 1953; Marianne Rieger, "Zur Finanz- und Agrargeschichte der Ming Dynastie, 1368–1643," *Sinica*, 1932.

45. P. Vidal de la Blache, *Revue de synthèse historique* (1903), p. 239.

46. Well-known rubric of *Annales E.S.C.*

# Unity and Diversity
# in the Human Sciences

At first sight the human sciences—at least to anyone who has played however small a part in their development—are striking not for their unity, which is difficult to formulate and to promote, but for their long-standing, confirmed, fundamental, indeed almost *structural* diversity. They are first and foremost narrowly themselves, putting themselves forward as so many different countries, so many languages, and, less justifiably, so many competing race-tracks, each with its own rules, its own scholarly enclosures, its commonplaces comprehensible only to itself.

Of course an image is not an argument, but it has a way of substituting itself for any true explanation in order to curtail difficulties and mask weaknesses. So let us assume, to be brief, that all the human sciences are interested in one and the same landscape: that of the past, present, and future actions of man. Let us also suppose that such a landscape is coherent, an assumption which would of course have to be demonstrated. With regard to this panorama, the human sciences could be seen as being so many observation points, each with its particular views, its different perspectives, coloring, chronicles. Unhappily, the sections of landscape which each has cut out do not join together, do not refer to each other, in the way that the pieces of a child's puzzle demand the whole image and are valid only in relation to that preestablished image. Each time, from each observation point, man appears different. And each time the portion thus discerned is promoted to the status of being the whole landscape, even if the observer is careful, and he usually is. But his own explanations continually lead him astray, insidiously, unconsciously. An economist looks at the economic structures and imagines the noneconomic structures that surround them, support them, or constrain them. This might seem perfectly harmless and justifiable, but what it means is that at a stroke he has assembled the puzzle to conform to his own vision. The demographer is no different, claiming that his criteria alone can control and explain everything. He has his own customary, efficient tests: and these are sufficient for him to grasp man in his entirety, or at least, to put forward that aspect of man which he does grasp

*Revue de l'enseignement supérieur*, no. 1 (1960), pp. 17–22.

as being the integral or essential man. Sociologists, historians, geographers, psychologists, ethnographers are often even more naïf. There is, in short, one obvious fact: each social science is imperialistic, however much it may deny it. Each tends to present its conclusions as being a total vision of man.

An observer acting in good faith, assumed moreover to be without previous experience in the field and therefore free of all bias, could not fail to ask what relationships could be established among the different views available to each science, among the explanations being pressed on him, among the theories—those superexplanations—being forced on him. And what if this innocent witness, with his fresh outlook, should actually be able to go and look over this landscape for himself! He would work it out somehow. But the "reality" dealt with by the human sciences is not the landscape we have been speaking of, for want of a better metaphor, or at least is a landscape which has been recast, just like the landscapes of the natural sciences. Reality in the raw is nothing but a mass of observations needing to be set in order.

Besides, if one were to leave the observation points of the individual human sciences, it would mean abandoning a major undertaking, and condemning oneself to doing it all over again by oneself. But who could walk alone in that obscurity, who is there today who could of his own strength reformulate all acquired knowledge, so as to be able to go beyond it, so as to be able to hold it at arm's length, imbue it with life, and impose a single language on it—and a scientific language at that? It is not so much the knowledge to be acquired that would make such an enterprise so formidable, but its application. He would need all the appropriate skills and energy which each of us has acquired, for what it may be worth, but acquired only within the confines of our individual professions, and often only at the price of a long apprenticeship. Life is too short to allow any one of us to acquire the mastery of such a variety of fields. The economist must stay an economist, the sociologist a sociologist, the geographer a geographer, and so on. The wise will say that it is doubtless better so, with each speaking his mother tongue, discussing the things he knows: his own shop, his own trade.

Perhaps. But the human sciences, as they extend and perfect their own controls, are progressively better placed to ascertain their weaknesses. The more they pretend to efficiency, the more they run up against a hostile social reality. Each of their failures in the realm of practical application becomes thus a way of checking their validity, perhaps even their very reason for existence. Besides, if these sciences were perfect they would automatically join together, by the very fact of their own progress. The tendential rules which they lay down, their calculations, the forecasts which they think to base on them, all these explanations should add together to clarify the same essential lines, the same deep-seated movements, the same tendencies within the huge mass of human facts. But we know only too well that this is by no means the case, that the society which surrounds us remains scarcely known, baffling, and largely unpredictable in the vast majority of its actions.

Nothing goes further to prove the way the human sciences cannot at present be reduced one to another than the dialogues which have been attempted now and then across the frontiers. I believe that history lends itself readily to this sort of meeting and discussion. A certain kind of history, that is, not the traditional kind which dominates our teaching and will continue to dominate it for a long while yet, because of an inertia which still exists though we may rail against it, because of the support of aged scholars, and because of the institutions which open their embracing arms to us when we ourselves cease to be dangerous revolutionaries and become good bourgeois—for there is a terrible bourgeoisie of the intellect. History certainly lends itself to these dialogues. It is not rigidly structured, and is open to all its neighboring sciences. But these dialogues often reveal themselves in practice to be entirely useless. Is there a sociologist who would not be apt to make a hundred and one false assertions about history? He has Lucien Febvre before him, and challenges him as if he were dealing with Charles Seignobos. To them, history is what it was yesterday, that small-scale science of contingence, of the specific narrative, of reconstructed time, and for all these reasons and others, rather more than half absurd as a "science." If history claims to be a study of the present by means of the past, a speculation on the nature of time, or rather of time spans, then sociologists and philosophers simply shrug their shoulders and smile. But to do that is to disregard all the tendencies of contemporary history and the important precursors of these tendencies without giving them a second chance, and to forget how much historians have got away from this sort of facile and limited interest erudition in the past twenty or thirty years. That there has been a thesis presented at the Sorbonne entitled *Le Mythe de croisade: Essai de sociologie religieuse* (by Alphonse Dupront) must in itself go a long way toward demonstrating that research into social psychology, into the underlying realities, the "deeper levels," in short, into that history which some would call "unconscious," is more than simply a theoretical program.

And we could name other achievements, other innovations, any number of other proofs! All the same, we should not complain too much. It is not, I repeat, a question of attempting to formulate some sort of a definition of history despite those who choose not to see it as we would like them to, or of drawing up a list of grievances against them. Besides, the wrongs are by no means all on one side. The "reciprocity of perspectives" is much in evidence.

For we historians also tend to see our neighboring sciences in our own way, with distortions and an obvious time lag. And so, from one neighbor to the next down the road, misunderstandings multiply. In fact, any worthwhile understanding of these diverse fields would call for a prolonged familiarity with them and active participation in them, and an abandonment of all prejudices and previous habits of mind. It is asking a lot. Nor would it really be enough, in order to succeed, to slip for a moment into some avant garde aspect of sociological or political economy research—which would, after all, be easy enough. One would have to see how such research related to the whole and expressed its new directions—and that is not a task within everybody's reach. It is not enough simply to read Alphonse Dupront's thesis; it has to be related to Lucien Febvre, to Marc Bloch, to the Abbé Bremond, among others. It is not enough to be able to follow the authoritative thinking of François Perroux, without also being able to place it immediately in its context, to recognize its origins and by what sequence of agreement and rebuttal it is integrated into the whole still-changing body of economic thinking.

I have previously raised my voice in all good faith against social investigations working directly on "real life," captives of an unreal present—unreal because too short. On the same occasion, I also protested against a political economy which paid insufficient attention to the *"longue durée,"* because it was too wedded to government tasks equally confined to the doubtful reality of the present.[1] I was told in reply, perfectly justifiably, that this sort of sociology direct from life was by no means in the forefront of sociological research, and in their turn W. Rostow and W. Kula assure me that economics, in its most recent and valuable research, has been attempting to include the problems of the long time span, and that they are even a major part of its diet. So it is a general difficulty. If we are not careful, despite appearances these discussions held over our fences will not be conversations conducted between contemporaries, because of omissions and oversimplifications, coupled with a slowness in mutual understanding. Our conversations and discussions, and even our highly problematical agreements run slower than the time of the mind. We must either put our watches right or else resign ourselves to useless and unreal exchanges. Or just gossip.

Anyway, I do not believe that if a common market of the human sciences can be established, it can be on the basis of a series of bilateral agreements, or of partial customs unions applicable to a gradually widening circle. Two closely similar sciences repel each other, as if they both carried the same electrical charge. The "university" union of geography and history, which yesterday redounded to their double glory, has ended in a necessary divorce. You may hold discussions with a historian or a geographer, but if you are an economist or a sociologist all it does is to make you feel more of one than you ever did before. In fact, these limited unions make too many specific demands. The wise path would be for us to lower our usual customs duties all together. The free circulation of ideas and techniques would be encouraged by such a move, and though they would certainly be modified in passing from one human science to another, they would also at least begin to sketch out the makings of a common language. One great step would be if certain words might have virtually the same resonance and meaning from one small territory to another. It is both history's advantage and its weakness to use common speech—by which I mean literary language. It is a privilege which Henri Pirenne has often recommended that it retain. Our discipline is therefore the most literary, the most readable of all the human sciences, and the most accessible to the public at large. But scientific research in common would demand a certain "basic" vocabulary. This could be obtained by allowing, to a greater extent than we do today, our phrases, our formulas, and even our slogans to pass from one discipline to another.

In this way Claude Lévi-Strauss has attempted to show what the incursion of social (or qualitative) mathematics could do for the human sciences, an incursion at one and the same time of a different language, a different mentality, and different techniques. Doubtless tomorrow we will have to take a new overview to distinguish what can be set in mathematical terms, and what cannot as far as the human sciences are concerned, and there is no guarantee that we would not have to make a choice between the two paths.

But let us choose a less important and, truth to tell, less dramatic example. In today's political economics there can be no doubt that the crucial thing is "modeling," the construction of "models." The important thing is to distinguish the simple strands of the fairly constant relations among structures from the complex web of the present. The precautions taken at the outset are so numerous that, however simplified, the model plunges into the real, sums up its connections, and justifiably transcends its particular contingencies. This is what Léontieff and his imitators have done. Given this, nothing could seem more justifiable than to set your reasoning within the framework of the model, making use of the methods of pure mathematics. Though it goes under a new name, the model is nothing but a tangible form of the most classic methods of reasoning. We have all made use of models without being aware of it, just as Molière's M. Jourdain always talked in prose. In fact, the model turns up in all the human sciences. A geographical map is a model. Psychoanalysts' "grids," of the kind that young literary critics are only too happy to slip under the works of our great literary figures (see Roland Barthes's precise, perfidious little piece on Michelet), are models. The varied sociology of Georges Gurvitch is thronged with models. And history has its models too—how could it keep them out? I have recently been reading a splendid article by our colleague from Nuremberg,

Hermann Kellenbenz, on the history of the "entrepreneur" in southern Germany between the fifteenth and the eighteenth centuries—an article following along the same lines as the Center for Business Studies which Arthur Cole's strong and generous spirit has inspired at Harvard. In fact, this article and the varied achievements of Arthur Cole are nothing but historians' versions of Schumpeter's model. For Schumpeter, the entrepreneur, in the best sense of the word, is "a craftsman, the creative element in economic progress, bringing into being new combinations of capital, land, and labor." And he has been so throughout history. "Schumpeter's definition," notes Kellenbenz, "is above all a model, an idealized figure." Now in dealing with a model, the historian delights in constantly referring it back to the specific contingency from which it was drawn, and floating it like a ship on the waters of a particular time. The entrepreneurs of southern Germany were, predictably enough, of different types and natures between the fifteenth and the eighteenth centuries. But the historian, engaged in this pastime, constantly destroys the benefits of "modeling" by breaking up the ship. He would not be able to get back to any kind of general rule unless he rebuilt the ship, or built another one, or *related* the different models with all their distinct peculiarities to each other, and then functioning along historical lines proceeded to explain them all together in terms of their chronological succession.

Modeling would thus draw our discipline away from its taste for the particular and the limitations which that implies. The very movement of history is one vast explanation. Should there be a discussion, for instance, between literary critics, historians, and sociologists on the subject of psychoanalysts' grids, would we not be tempted to ask: are these grids valid for *all* eras or not? And is their evolution, if there is such a thing, an equally important line of research as the grid itself?

Recently, at the Faculté des lettres at Lyons, I was present at the defense of a thesis on *The School and Education in Spain, 1874–1902*,[2] and thus on that great religious conflict around schooling which is a legacy of the nineteenth century. Spain offers one example among others of this varied and essentially religious conflict. Everything would seem to be in favor of the modelization of this group of discussions. Suppose the thing done and the elements securely in place: the need to educate the masses; vivid blindly warring passions; the Church, the State, the budget... This whole theoretical construct will better enable us to understand the unity of this prolonged crisis, a crisis which is certainly not over yet. If then, armed with this model, we return to Spain between 1874 and 1902, our first care as historians would be to particularize the model, to take the mechanism apart and add new parts at leisure, thus bringing it closer to all the diversity and individuality of life and removing it from the sphere of scientific simplification. But how much better off one would be if one could then dare to return to the model, or to the various models, so as to be able to discern what development there had been, if any!

Let us stop there, the demonstration has been made. The model is certainly able to make its way usefully throughout all the human sciences, even in places which did not a priori appear to suit it.

Similar examples proliferate. But they are only minor methods of coming together. At the very most they represent only a few threads knotted together here and there. But, still in terms of the human sciences in their entirety, it is possible to do more, to organize movements of the whole, convergences which do not disrupt everything but which could deeply modify problematics and approaches.

Our Polish colleagues designate these concerted movements by the useful term "complex studies." "By this," Aleksander Gieysztor goes on to specify, "we mean the work of different specialists on a subject definable by one, two, or even three principles of the classification of social phenomena: geographic, chronological, or whatever the particular nature of the subject might be." In this way the area studies of our American colleagues are also "complex studies," their principle being to bring together several human sciences so as to study and define great *cultural areas* of the contemporary world, and in particular the monsters of Russia, China, the Americas, India, and I hardly dare say Europe.

So in the vast domain of the human sciences there have already been meetings and coalitions and joint works. Such attempts are not even particularly new. At least, I can see an important precedent for them in the *Semaines de synthèse* put out by Henri Berr, who has proved yet again to be a genuine precursor of contemporary movements. Anyway, what does it matter if they are old or new! They are experiments which must be made, and since their success—at least in their task of uniting the social sciences—is always highly debatable, repeated again and again, after the closest possible study. There are certainly a few important rules which can be laid down even now, rules which dominate the whole discussion right from the start.

At the outset one must accept the possibility that these attempts may one day displace frontiers, may move the centers of gravity, alter the problematics and the traditional shape of the fields. And this is the case for all the human sciences without exception. Which means that any "nationalist" spirit anywhere would have to be relinquished. Then we must recognize that we cannot go putting in surveying rods just anywhere as the whim takes us; they have to be aligned, and in the very act of aligning them we have our axes of assembly and regrouping, those reductions to time and place of which Gieysztor was speaking, and also reductions in numbers and to the biological.

Finally, and most importantly, it must be *all* the human sciences which are examined like this, the most classic, the oldest, and the newest. These last would rather call themselves social sciences, and would like to form the four or five "major" sciences in our world. Now I would maintain that in order to build up a unity, all research has a contribution to make, Greek epigraphy just as much as philosophy, or Henri Laugier's biology, or public opinion polls if carried out by an intelligent man such as Lazarsfeld. It seems that we too need to hold an ecumenical council.

The failure of area studies—in the normative domain, be it understood, for the works which they have inspired or themselves carried out have been by no means inconsiderable—must be a lesson to us. Perhaps our colleagues at Harvard, at Columbia, the members of the bold team in Seattle have not sufficiently widened the circle of their convocations. Hazarding themselves within the narrow confines of the present, in their studies on India or China they have only rarely appealed to historians for help, and never to my knowledge have they turned to geographers. Can sociologists, economists (in the widest sense), psychologists, linguists really, by themselves, mobilize the entire forces of the human sciences? I think not. But, I would repeat, such a general mobilization is the only way which will work, at least at the moment.

I have already advanced this thesis several times before, and I have here taken advantage of the platform offered me by the *Revue de l'enseignement supérieure* to put it forward again. France has neither the best economists, nor the best historians, nor the best sociologists in the world. But we do have one of the best groups of researchers. What is more, the benefits of the policy of the Centre National de là Recherche Scientifique are, at one point at least, indisputable: we have at our disposal, in nearly every discipline, young men who by training and ambition are entirely dedicated to research. That is the one thing which it would be completely impossible to improvise. Soon the Maison des Sciences de l'Homme will bring all the centers of research and all the laboratories together in Paris that are valuable in this huge field. All this fresh vigor, all the new methods are within arm's reach, while at the same time we have the indispensable framework of all the classic human "sciences," which is more precious than anything and doubtless unique in the world, and without which no decisive action can be possible. Let us then set in motion the movement toward unity which is being sketched out the world over, and if need be, as soon as intellectually possible and profitable let us press on with it, as quickly as we can. Tomorrow is already too late.

## Notes

1. See my article "Histoire et sciences sociales: La longue durée," *Annales E.S.C.* (1958), and the replies made by Rostow and Kula, ibid. (1959 and 1960).
2. Thesis by Yvonne Turin (Paris: Presses Universitaires de France).

# History and Sociology

A few preliminary remarks will serve, I hope, to place the present chapter in its context. By *sociology* I mean, more often than not, indeed almost always, that global science which Emile Durkheim and François Simiand intended right at the beginning of the century. Sociology is not yet that science, but it is constantly tending toward it, even if it is destined never fully to achieve it. By *history* I mean research conducted scientifically; at a pinch I might even call it a *science,* but a complex one: there is no *one* history, *one* profession of historian, but many professions, many kinds of history, a whole list of inquiries, points of view, possibilities, a list to which yet more lines of inquiry, points of view, possibilities will be added tomorrow. But in order to be understood by the sociologist—who, like philosophers, has a tendency to see history as a discipline whose rules have been defined utterly and once and for all—would I do better to say that there are as many debatable and debated ways of coming to grips with the past as there are attitudes to the present? And that history can even be considered as in some sense a study of the present?

This said, no one must expect to find here an answer, or indeed an attempt at an answer, to the usual questions on the relationship between history and sociology, or a sequel to the constantly recurring, constantly changing argument between these neighbors who seem able neither to ignore nor to understand each other, and who define themselves in their quarrels in an entirely one-sided way. There are false arguments, just as there are false problems. Anyway, there is hardly ever any real dialogue between sociologist and historian. When François Simiand quarrels with Charles Seignobos, he thinks he is speaking with history, whereas in fact he is speaking only with a certain kind of history, that which Henri Berr christened *l'histoire historisante* ("historicizing history").[1] When at about the same date he engages Henri Hauser, he is faced with doubtless the most brilliant historian of his generation, but too brilliant, too subtle a dialectician, entrenched behind early successes and the ancient rules of his profession. He should have addressed himself to Paul Lacombe in order to have had an adversary his own size. But then perhaps he might

Chapter 4 of the Introduction to the *Traité du sociologie,* published under the general editorship of Georges Gurvitch, 2 vols. (Paris: P.U.F., 1958–60).

have run the risk of finding himself in agreement with him, might he not?

Now, argument is possible only if the adversaries give themselves up to it, and are ready to "take up the sword," [2] in the phrase an irritated and amused historian, none other than Paul Lacombe himself in fact, used long ago now, in 1900, in answering a critic. I imagine that in his passionate desire for a "scientific history," this devotee of history could easily have reached an understanding with the sociologist François Simiand. A little close reading would have sufficed. In his desire to free himself from the frustrations and insoluble difficulties of our profession, did not Paul Lacombe even go so far as to avoid time? "Time!" he wrote. "It is nothing in itself, objectively, it is only an idea we have." [3] Unhappily, François Simiand dealt with Paul Lacombe's theories only in passing, and chose to charge against other, irreducible adversaries. In fact, there is always *a* history which can be in agreement with *a* sociology—or, obviously, which can on the other hand be made to collide with it. Georges Gurvitch,[4] in his article of historicosociological debate, the most recent of its kind—at least, that I know of—cannot agree with Henri Marrou, but finds it much easier to agree with me... If we look even more closely, perhaps we will find that between historian and sociologist there can never be either true agreement, or perfect accord.

I

A first, essential precaution: let us try and give a rapid picture of history, as it appears in its most recent definitions, for all sciences are constantly redefining and reexamining themselves. Each historian is necessarily aware of the changes which he himself must precipitate, however involuntarily, in a flexible profession which evolves of itself because of the weight of new knowledge, new aims, new enthusiasms, as well as because of the general development of the human sciences. All the social sciences infect each other, and history is just as much a prey to these epidemics as any of the others. Whence come its changes in function, or method, or appearance.

If we begin our retrospective with this century, we should have at least ten analyses at our disposal, and a thousand different visions of history, without counting the positions implicit in the works of historians themselves, who like to believe that their particular interpretations and points of view are better conveyed by their work than by being set forth in any precise and formal discussion (whence the amused reproach brought by philosophers that historians never quite know what sort of history it is they are writing).

At the beginning of the series, let us put the classic *Introduction aux sciences historiques* by Charles-Victor Langlois and Charles Seignobos,[5] since everybody still does so. Beside this, let us call attention to the youthful article written by the young Paul Mantoux (1903).[6] Then, much later, after Raymond Aron's classic *Introduction à la philosophie de l'histoire*,[7] which represents a philosopher's vision of history, we come to *Métier d'historien* by Marc Bloch,[8] an incomplete posthumous publication (doubtless fairly different from what its author would have finally produced, had he not died with such tragic suddenness). We arrive next at Lucien Febvre's scintillating *Combats pour l'histoire*, a collection of articles which he put together himself.[9] Do not let us overlook, as we pass, Louis Halphen's brief essay,[10] or Philippe Ariès's lively book,[11] or Éric Dardel's existentialist treatise,[12] or the articles of André Piganiol,[13] nor Henri Marrou's interesting and subtle discussion,[14] though this last is perhaps overly limited, for my taste, to the events of ancient history, and too deeply entrenched in the thinking of Max Weber, with the consequence that it is quite disproportionately obsessed with the problem of objectivity. This problem of objectivity and subjectivity in social questions fired the nineteenth century, the discoverer of the scientific method, but is it really of such prime importance today? In any case it is not our problem alone. There is a weakness in the scientific approach which can be overcome, as Henri Marrou so rightly says, only by redoubling our care and honesty. But please, do not exaggerate beyond all bounds the role of the Historian, even written with a capital H!

Though abridged, incomplete, and deliberately limited to citing only the French literature on the subject, this extremely short bibliography nonetheless makes it possible to take stock of the arguments that have been put forward: it follows them fairly closely. But on the other hand, the chosen books and articles are far from indicating the profound variety of contemporary history—and yet that is the most important thing of all. Unless I am much mistaken, the fundamental movement of history today is not one of choosing between this or that path, or different point of view, but of accepting and absorbing all the successive definitions in which, one after another, there have been attempts to confine it. For all the different kinds of history belong to us.

At the beginning of this century, people were only too happy to claim, following Michelet, that history consisted in the "resurrection of the past." A fine phrase, and a fine program! The "task of history is to commemorate the past, all of the past," wrote Paul Mantoux in 1908. Indeed: and what, in fact, was retained of this past? Our young historian answered readily, in 1903: "The particular, whatever occurs only once is the domain of history."[15] It is the classic answer, the image of history that philosophers and sociologists readily put forward, to the exclusion of any other. When we were on a boat together on our way to Brazil in 1936, Émile Bréhier, the historian of philosophy, would not waver from this point of view during our friendly discussions on the subject. According to him, anything which recurred in the past belonged to the domain of sociology, to the neighboring concern. So the whole of the past did not belong to us. But let us not prolong the debate. Like any historian, I am attracted to the unique event, which blooms for but a single day and then fades, never again to be held between one's fingers. Moreover, I believe that in any society there must always be thousands upon thousands of such unique occurrences. And above all, I believe that if one should ever manage to grasp such a society in its entirety, it would be quite right to assert that it would never wholly be repeated: it consists of a provisional *balance,* original and unique unto itself.

So I would agree with Philippe Ariès for structuring his history on the basis of a recognition of the differences between periods and social realities. But history does not consist only in differences, in the unique and the novel—whatever will not happen twice. Besides, the novel is never entirely new. It goes hand in hand with the recurrent and the regular. Talking of the battle of Pavia (24 February 1525) and even more of Rocroi (19 May 1643), Paul Lacombe remarked that certain incidents in these battles "derived from a system of armaments, tactics, customs, and traditions of warfare which can also be found in a good many other battles of the age."[16] In one way Pavia marks the beginning of modern warfare; it is an event, but an event occurring within the context of a whole family of other events. And really, how could one believe in a history confined exclusively to the unique occurrence? Quoting Paul Lacombe approvingly, François Simiand[17] added on his own account the historian's assertion that "there is no fact in which one cannot discern one entirely individual aspect, and another deriving from its social context, one aspect a consequence of contingency, and another of recurring factors." Thus, from the very beginning of the century there has been a protest or at least some doubt about a history entirely confined to individual events, and because of this noteworthy fact, about this "linear," "contingent" history, *l'histoire événementielle,* the history of events, as Paul Lacombe was to end by calling it.

To transcend the event means transcending the short time span in which it is set, the time span of the chronicle, or of journalism—the brief moments of awareness whose traces give us such a vivid sense of the events and lives of the past. It means asking if over and above the passage of events, there is not an unconscious, or rather a more or less conscious, history which to a great extent escapes the awareness of the actors, whether victors or victims: they make history, but history bears them along.

This search for a history outside the confines of the event was imposed imperiously by contact with the other human sciences,. an inevitable contact (as the running arguments will testify). In France it dates from as early as 1900, with Henri Berr's marvelous *Revue de synthèse historique* which is so moving to read in retrospect, followed in 1929 by the vigorous and most effective campaign carried out in Lucien Febvre and Marc Bloch's *Annales.*

From that time on, history busied itself in dealing with recurrent events as well as individual occurrences, conscious and unconscious realities alike. From that time on, the historian has wanted to be, and has become, an economist, sociologist, anthropologist, demographer, psychologist, linguist. These new meetings of the mind were at the same time meetings of friends and of feelings. The friends of Lucien Febvre and Marc Bloch, the founders and the inspiration of *Annales,* made up a permanent colloquium on the human sciences, ranging from Albert Demangeon and Jules Sion, the geographers, to Maurice Halbwachs, the sociologist, Charles Blondel and Henri Wallon, the psychologists, and François Simiand, the philosopher-sociologist-economist. With their help, whether well or ill but certainly with determination, history laid hold of all the human sciences. Along with its guides, it wanted somehow to become an impossible universal science of man. In so doing it gave itself up to a kind of juvenile imperialism, but only for the same reasons and in the same way as nearly all the human sciences at that time, which, small nations though they truly were, all dreamed of devouring, overthrowing, dominating everything else in the field.

From that time on, history has gone on along the same lines, feeding off the other human sciences. The movement has not stopped, though it has changed, as one might have expected it would. There is a great distance[18] between Marc Bloch's testament, *Métier d'historien,* and the postwar *Annales,* managed in fact under the sole direction of Lucien Febvre. All too little attentive to method and orientation, historians are hardly aware of this. Nevertheless, after 1945, the question posed itself afresh: what were the position and the usefulness of history? Was it, should it be, simply an exclusive study of the past? If, during the past years, it had thrown itself into tying together the whole bundle of the human sciences, would this not have inevitable consequences as far as its nature was concerned? Within its own sphere, it might be all the human sciences. But where does the past end?

Everything is history, they say jokingly. Claude Lévi-Strauss wrote only recently: "For everything is history, what was said yesterday is history, what was said a minute ago is history."[19] I would amend this to whatever was said, thought, acted, or merely lived. But if history, omnipresent history, raises questions about society as a whole, it always does so on the basis of that very movement of time which carries life ceaselessly along, and at the same time steals it away, extinguishing and rekindling its flames. History is a dialectic of the time span; through it, and thanks to it, history is a study of society, of the whole of society, and thus of the past, and thus equally of the present, past and present being inseparable. In a remark he repeated again and again during the last ten years of his life, Lucien Febvre put it this way: "History, science of the past, science of the present."

It will be understood that the author of this chapter, heir to the *Annales* of Marc Bloch and Lucien Febvre, feels himself in a particularly favored position to encounter, "sword in hand," the sociologist who would reproach him either with not thinking like him, or else with thinking too much like him. History seems to me to be a dimension of social science; they are both aspects of one and the same thing. In fact, time, the passage of time, history impose themselves, or should impose themselves on all the human sciences. Their tendency is not to oppose, but to coalesce.

## II

I have already written,[20] in part against Georges Gurvitch, that sociology and history made up one single intellectual adventure, not two different sides of the same cloth but the very stuff of that cloth itself, the entire substance of its yarn. Such an assertion is of course debatable, and could hardly be maintained to the letter. But it satisfies a desire, even an imperious desire I have for unification among the different human sciences, so that they might submit themselves less to a common market than to a common problematic. This would free them from a host of false problems and useless knowledge and after all the necessary pruning and rearrangement the way would be prepared for a new future divergence which would be both fertile and creative. For we need a new impetus for the human sciences.

It can hardly be denied that history and sociology come together, identify with each other, and merge often enough. The reasons are straightforward. On the one hand there is the inflated imperialism of history, on the other the similarity in their two natures: history and sociology alike are the only two *global* sciences, given to extending their inquiries into any aspect of social reality whatever. Insofar as it consists in all the human sciences in the vast domain of the past, history is a synthesizer, an orchestrator. And if the study of time *in all its manifestations* opens up for it, as I believe, all the doors to an understanding of the present, then it has got a finger in every pie on the table. And it finds itself regularly sharing the dish with sociology, which is also a synthesizer by vocation, and which the dialectic of the time span forces to turn toward the past—whether it would or no.

Even if one should see sociology according to the old formula as the "science of those facts which taken together go to make up the collective life of man," even if one should regard it as the search for new structures arising amid all the heat and confusion of contemporary life—will not all of social life lie within the range of its inquiry and assessment? Collective life cannot be seen except by contrast with the life of the individual, or as an aspect of the life of an individual: it is a constantly recurring dichotomy. There is a renewal, but it can exist only in relation to what is old and is not always ready to be consumed within the fires of the present, which burn everything, new wood and old alike, the one as fast as the other.

So the sociologist should not feel himself a stranger around the workshops of history: he will find there his own materials, his own tools, his own vocabulary, his own problems, even his own uncertainties. Of course, the likeness is not total and is often misleading: there is the whole business of education, apprenticeship, career, inheritance, the feel of the profession, the different techniques of information demanded by a whole range of documentary sources (but this last is true even within history itself: the study of the Middle Ages and the study of the nineteenth century call for quite different attitudes to documents). History, one might say, is one of the least structured of the social sciences, and so one of the most flexible and open. The social sciences are perhaps present in us even more frequently than in sociology, even though its mission is to contain them all. There is an economic history whose richness must shame, I am sure, the poverty-stricken anemia of economic sociology. There is a wonderful geographic history and a vigorous historical geography which can hardly be compared with the *pointilliste* ecology of the sociologists. There is a demographic history (either it is history, or it does not exist) in the light of which social morphology seems a thing of straw. There is even a social history, which though mediocre would hardly find itself enriched through contact with the rather thin studies of typological sociology (to avoid the pleonastic social sociology). And it is more than likely that quantitative history, following the lines set out by Ernest Labrousse and his students (Rome Historical Congress, 1955) will prove decisively more advanced in the domain of the study of social classes than abstract sociology, which in my view is overly preoccupied with the concept of social classes propounded by Marx and his disciples.

But let us call a halt there. It would be too easy to make what sociologists are attempting and what we historians are engaged in seem to correspond, term for term. The sociology of knowledge and the history of ideas; microsociology and sociometry on the one hand, the history of surface happenings, so-called *histoire événementielle,* on the other, that microhistory which juxtaposes the most casual news item and the most shattering, explosive sociodrama affecting a nation or a whole world... There even comes a point when I cannot draw any clear distinction between such immediate activities as the sociology of art and the history of art, the sociology of work and the history of work, literary sociology and literary history, or between religious history at Henri Bremond's level and religious sociology on the exceptionally brilliant level of Gabriel Le Bras and his followers. And where differences exist, could they not be overcome by an alignment of the less brilliant partner with the more brilliant? In this way the historian can be seen as not being sufficiently attentive to social signs and symbols, to constant underlying social functions. But numerous examples demonstrate that it would not take much to enable the historian to bring these problems within the range of his own particular focus. It is a question of displacements and oversights, not of professional imperatives and exclusions.

There is another sign of this brotherly correspondance: the vocabulary tends to be the same between one science and the next. The historians' term for "structural crisis" is *crise structurale,* while economists speak of a *crise structurelle,* and Lévi-Strauss has returned, to *structurale* in his latest book, *Structural Anthropology.*[21] Similarly, should we say *conjunctural,* which sounds awkward, or *conjoncturel?* And *événementiel,* which was coined by Paul Lacombe (though he hesitated, as I have said, between *éventuel* and *événementiel*) and was taken up by François Simiand, was bounced back to the historians ten years ago, whereupon it took up a common orbit. The word *level ("palier")* emerged from Georges Gurvitch's thinking and for better or worse we are getting used to it. We say that there are not only levels of historical reality, but also levels of historical explanation, and thence possible levels of historicosociological understanding or conflict: one can move from conflict into agreement, just by making a change of levels.

But enough of this game, which would be only too easy to continue. It would be far better now to show where its interest lies. The vocabulary is the same, or is becoming the same, because the problematic is becoming increasingly the same, under the convenient heading of the currently dominant two words *model* and *structure.* The model has made its appearance within the living waters of history as a "workman's tool," but in the service of the most ambitious undertakings. Structure, or structures, beset us everywhere: we hear only too much of them, even, as Lucien Febvre observed in one of his last writings, in *Annales.*[22] In fact, whatever the cost, social science must construct a model, a general and particular explanation of social life, and substitute for a disconcerting empirical reality a clearer image, and one more susceptible to scientific application. We have to choose, cut short, reconstitute, measure, accept, and indeed almost deliberately seek out contradictions. Does social life in fact possess this multileveled structure, is it "laminated," to take up Dr. Roumeguère's term,[23] or not? Does reality change with every stage or level? If it does, then it is "vertically" discontinuous. Is it structured throughout, or is only a certain stratum structured? Outside the rigid envelope of structures, are there free, unorganized zones of reality? The structured and the unstructured, the flesh and bones of social reality. But is the movement which carries society along structured too, according to the plan of a, so to speak, "dynamic" structure? Or, if you prefer, is there any regularity, any phases which necessarily recur in all phenomena of historical evolution? The "movement of history" would not be going blindly on.

In fact, these problems meet and overlap, or should meet and mesh. By a seeming paradox the historian here appears more of a simplifier than the sociologist. In the final analysis, it is all very well for him to claim that the present too falls within his sphere when, for a thousand reasons that need no elaboration, he continues to study it less well and less often than the simplified and decanted society of the past. The present, by contrast, is a recall to the multiple, the complex, the "multidimensional." Perhaps the historian hears and perceives the call less well than the sociologist, the observer of contemporary ferment?

## III

Considering the overall view like this, one tends to get a fairly strong impression of analogy and identity. The two professions, taken in their entirety, have the same boundaries, the same circumference. It hardly matters that the historical sector should be better worked in ours, the sociological in theirs: a little care, a little more work, and our domains would be more like each other, and with little difficulty would be able to share the same achievements.

This analogy would be put in question only should the sociologist not wish the historian to trespass into the present, if then. But would it really be possible, in that case, to turn all our oppositions into a dubious contrast between today and yesterday? Of the two neighbors, one delves into the past, which after all is not strictly speaking his domain, and does so in the name, so to speak, of repetition; the other neighbor makes forays into the present, in the name of a time span creator of construction and destruction, of permanence also. On the one hand repetition and comparison, on the other, duration and dynamism, two ways of coming to grips with reality, both tools each one can use. What clear boundary is there between what has been lived and what is being or will be lived? The early sociologists knew very well that the present made up only part of their construct. Which means, said François Simiand, that we must "seek for facts and cases in the narrative of the past of humankind."[24]

I believe even less in any real opposition of styles. Can history be seen as more continuous, sociology more discontinuous? Such a position has been maintained, but how badly the question is put! In order to get any clear notion, we would have to confront the works themselves, and see whether such oppositions were internal or external to our respective professions. Nor must we forget that discontinuity, today, is only just moving into historical thought. When Marc Bloch posed the problem prematurely, just before the Second World War, all he did was to unleash one of the vainest debates that historians ever undertook.

In fact, each historian and each sociologist has his own style. Georges Gurvitch is almost excessive and overscrupulous in his desire for a complex, hyperempirical sociology, in the image of what he not unreasonably sees as an abundant reality. Claude Lévi-Strauss cuts through this abundance and destroys it in order to bring to light the deep-seated, slender line of human continuity. Does one really absolutely have to choose and decide which one of them is *the* sociologist? I say again, it is a question of style and of temperament. Lucien Febvre too was aware of an abundant reality, full of incidents, and his style was a sort of dialogue which lent itself at pleasure, more and better than any other, to tracing these complicated designs. Fustel had a different kind of simplicity, with his anxiety to trace a line through events with a single sweep of the hand. Michelet exploded into a variety of lines. Pirenne, Marc Bloch were a good deal more continuous than Lucien Febvre. But do they not owe this as much to the nature of what they were contemplating as to their own temperaments? They beheld in the West a Middle Ages shorn of documents. The fifteenth century, and still more the sixteenth, contain a thousand voices which cannot make themselves heard earlier. The great dialogues of the present age have their beginnings then. In short, for me there does not seem to be any single style of history, to which it must remain bound. Any more than there is a single style of sociology. Durkheim has an authoritarian, linear simplicity. Halbwachs, too, classing things once and for all. Marcel Mauss is more various, but we hardly read him anymore—and with good reason: we hear his thought re-echoed by his disciples, and thus joining still-living in the line of contemporary research.

To sum up, the differences we seek in our joint ownership are not of the order of such easy formulas and distinctions. The debate must be carried right into the heart of history (or rather, our inquiry must be carried, for we do not wish to reanimate a debate). We must look first at all the levels of knowledge and historical work—then, along the line of the time span, the times and temporalities of history.

## IV

History exists at different levels, I would even go so far as to say three levels but that would be only in a manner of speaking, and simplifying things too much. There are ten, a hundred levels to be examined, ten, a hundred different time spans. On the surface, the history of events works itself out in the short term: it is a sort of microhistory. Halfway down, a history of conjunctures follows a broader, slower rhythm. So far that has above all been studied in its developments on the material plane, in economic cycles and intercycles. (The masterpiece of this sort of history is Ernest Labrousse's book[25] on the crisis, in fact half an intercycle [1774–91], which formed the launching pad for the French Revolution.) And over and above the "recitatif" of the conjuncture, structural history, or the history of the *longue durée*, inquires into whole centuries at a time. It functions along the border between the moving and the immobile, and because of the long-standing stability of its values, it appears unchanging compared with all the histories which flow and work themselves out more swiftly, and which in the final analysis gravitate around it.

To sum up, there are three series of historical levels, with which sociology unfortunately is not yet in touch. Now, the dialogue with history at these different levels could hardly proceed at the same pace, or at least with the same animation. There surely must be a sociology of history and of historical knowledge for each of these three levels, but they are still waiting to be constructed. We historians can only imagine what they might be like.

A sociology of the history of events would consist in a study of those constant, immediate, nervous mechanisms which record, day by day, the so-called history of the world as it is being made. It is a partially misleading kind of history, in which events cling to each other, affecting each other, and in which great men appear regularly organizing things, like conductors organizing their orchestras. This sociology of the history of events would also take up the old dialogue (between the unique and the recurring). It would, equally, consist in a confrontation between traditional history on the one hand, and microsociology and sociometry on the other. Are these latter two, as I think they are, richer than superficial history, and if so, why? How can one determine the place of this large expanse of history in all the complexity of a society in the grip of time? Unless I am much mistaken, all these questions go further than the old misunderstandings. The incident (if not the event, the sociodrama) exists in repetition, regularity, multitude, and there is no way of saying absolutely whether its level is quite without fertility or scientific value. It must be given closer examination.

If our sociological imagination is working overtime with regard to the event, on the other hand everything remains to be constructed, I was about to say invented, where the *conjuncture,* figure almost entirely overlooked by sociology, is concerned. Is it or is it not sufficiently powerful to have any deep effect on relations, to favor or militate against collective bonds, tightening some, straining and breaking others? François Simiand has only sketched out a possible sociology of conjunctural time according to the expansion and contraction of material conditions. Would an expansion (phase A) and the freedom which it offers, at least in certain sectors, maintain the social relationships and structures, or not? With the contraction of each phase B, material life (and, of course, not only that) would realign itself and seek other balances, inventing them, mobilizing the forces of ingenuity, or at least allowing them full play... But in these areas the research done by historians and economists has not yet built up a sufficient number of working hypotheses or sketched out sufficient viable frameworks to make it possible to resume or extend François Simiand's sketch. Besides, the history of the conjuncture would be complete only if in addition to the economic conjuncture one could have a study of the social conjuncture and all the other concomitant situations of the expansion or contraction. It is the weaving together of a variety of simultaneous conjunctures which would bring about a viable sociology.

As far as the history of the *longue durée* is concerned, history and sociology can hardly be said to meet, or even to rub shoulders. This would be saying too little. What they do is mingle. The *longue durée* is the endless, inexhaustible history of structures and groups of structures. For the historian a structure is not just a thing built, put together; it also means permanence, sometimes for more than centuries (time too is a structure). This great structure travels through vast tracts of time without changing; if it deteriorates during the long journey, it simply restores itself as it goes along and regains its health, and in the final analysis its characteristics alter only very slowly.

I have attempted to show,[26] I would hardly dare say to demonstrate, that all Claude Lévi-Strauss's new research—communications theory and social mathematics together—succeeds only when he launches his models onto the waters of the *longue durée.* Whatever the starting point he has chosen for his journey—be it microsociology or some other level—it is only when he has reached this ground floor of time, which is still half caught in sleep, that the structure becomes clear: primitive relations of kinship, myth, ceremonial, and institutions stand out from the slowest of history's notions. It is the vogue among physicists to speak of weightlessness. A structure is a body removed from gravity, removed from the acceleration of history.

But a historian faithful to the teachings of Lucien Febvre and Marcel Mauss will always wish to grasp the whole, the totality of social life. So he is led to bringing together different levels, time spans, different kinds of time, structures, conjunctures, events. These taken all together go to make up for him a fairly precarious global balance which can be maintained only through a constant series of adjustments, clashes, and slight alterations. In its totality, social reality in flux is ideally, at every instant, *synchronous* with its history, a constantly changing image, although it might repeat a thousand previous details of a thousand previous realities. Who would deny it? That is why the idea of a global structure for society disturbs and embarrasses the historian, even though there must be, of course, a considerable gap between a global structure and a global reality. What the historian would like to rescue from the debate is the uncertainty of the mass movement, its various possibilities for alteration, its freedoms, its particular "functional" explanations, offspring of the moment and the particular. At this stage of "totality"—I hardly like to say "totalization"—in short, at the very moment of uttering the last word, the historian will always revert to the antisociological positions of his teachers. Any society, too, must be unique, even if many of its materials are old. In this way, though it can doubtless be explained outside its own time, yet it can also be explained in the context of its own time. It is indeed a "child of its time," the great expanse of time surrounding it, in the very spirit of Henri Hauser and Lucien Febvre. Each society is a function of that time, and not exclusively of the time spans which it holds in common with other social realities.


V

Have I let myself fall prey to facile illusions? I have shown the historian's profession overstepping its ancient limits, questioning the very basis of social science, or very nearly doing so, and allowing its curiosity free rein in all directions. At the beginning of the century, it turned toward psychology: that was the age during which Werner Sombart claimed that capitalism is primarily a spirit. (Much later, though still along the same lines, Lucien Febvre would speak of mental equipment.) Then, in the thirties, it turned toward the conjunctural political economy which François Simiand revealed to French historians. And for a very long time it has been turned toward geography. It is noticeable how little Marxism has beset our profession in the present century. But its infiltration, its

temptations, its influences have nevertheless been many and marked:
the only thing lacking in this first half of the twentieth century has been a
masterpiece of Marxist history to serve as a model and a rallying point. It
is still awaited. Nonetheless this enormous influence has played its part
among the numerous changes which have taken place in our profession
and have forced the historian to break old habits and acquire new ones,
to make his way out from the legacy of his apprenticeship and even of his
own personal achievements.

All the same, there is an unavoidable, hidden limit to all these migrations and metamorphoses.[27] In truth, the historian can never get away
from the question of time in history: time sticks to his thinking like soil
to a gardener's spade. He may well dream of getting away from it, of
course. Spurred on by the anguish of 1940, Gaston Roupnel[28] wrote
words on this subject that will make any true historian suffer. Similar is
the classic remark made by Paul Lacombe who was also a historian of the
grand school: "Time is nothing in itself, objectively, it is only an idea we
have."[29] But do these remarks really provide a way out? I myself, during
a rather gloomy captivity, struggled a good deal to get away from a
chronicle of those difficult years (1940–45). Rejecting events and the
time in which events take place was a way of placing oneself to one side,
sheltered, so as to get some sort of perspective, to be able to evaluate
them better, and not wholly to believe in them. To go from the short
time span, to one less short, and then to the long view (which, if it exists,
must surely be the wise man's time span); and having got there, to think
about everything afresh and to reconstruct everything around one: a
historian could hardly not be tempted by such a prospect.

But these successive flights cannot put the historian definitively
beyond the bounds of the world's time, beyond historical time, so imperious because it is irreversible, and because it flows at the very rhythm
of the earth's rotation. In fact, these different time spans which we can
discern are all interdependent: it is not so much time which is the
creation of our own minds, as the way in which we break it up. These
fragments are reunited at the end of all our labors. The *longue durée,* the
conjuncture, the event all fit into each other neatly and without difficulty, for they are all measured on the same scale. Equally, to be able to
achieve an imaginative understanding of one of these time spans is to be
able to understand them all. The philosopher, taken up with the subjective aspect of things, interior to any notion of time, never senses this
weight of historical time, of a concrete, universal time, such as the time
of conjuncture that Ernest Labrousse depicts at the beginning of his
book like a traveler who is constantly the same and who travels the world
imposing the same set of values, no matter the country in which he has
disembarked, nor what the social order with which it is invested.

For the historian everything begins and ends with time, a mathematical, godlike time, a notion easily mocked, time external to men, "exogenous," as economists would say, pushing men, forcing them, and painting their own individual times the same color: it is, indeed, the imperious time of the world.

Sociologists, of course, will not entertain this oversimplified notion. They are much closer to the *dialectique de la durée* as put forward by Gaston Bachelard.[30] Social time is but one dimension of the social reality under consideration. It is within this reality just as it is within a given individual, one sign of particularity among others. The sociologist is in no way hampered by this accommodating sort of time, which can be cut, frozen, set in motion entirely at will. Historical time, I must repeat, lends itself less easily to the supple double action of synchrony and diachrony: it cannot envisage life as a mechanism that can be stopped at leisure in order to reveal a frozen image.

This is a more profound rift than is at first apparent: sociologists' time cannot be ours. The fundamental structure of our profession revolts against it. Our time, like economists' time, is one of measure. When a sociologist tells us that a structure breaks down only in order to build itself up afresh, we are happy to accept an explanation which historical observation would confirm anyway. But we would wish to know the precise time span of these movements, whether positive or negative, situated along the usual axis. An economic cycle, the ebb and flow of material life, can be measured. A structural social crisis should be equally possible to locate in time, and through it. We should be able to place it exactly, both in itself and even more in relation to the movement of associated structures. What is profoundly interesting to the historian is the way these movements cross one another, and how they interact, and how they break up: all things which can be recorded only in relation to the uniform time of historians, which can stand as a general measure of all these phenomena, and not in relation to the multiform time of social reality, which can stand only as the individual measure of each of these phenomena separately.

Rightly or wrongly, the historian cannot but formulate such opposed ideas, even when entering into the welcoming, almost brotherly realm of Georges Gurvitch's sociology. Did not a philosopher[31] define him recently as the one "who is driving sociology back into the arms of history"? But even with him, the historian can recognize neither his time spans nor his temporalities. The great social edifice (should one say *model?*) erected by Georges Gurvitch is organized according to five basic architectural aspects:[32] The deeper levels; the level of sociability; the level of social groups; the level of global societies; and the level of time.

This final bit of scaffolding, temporalities, the newest and the most recently built, is as if superimposed on the whole.

Georges Gurvitch's temporalities are various. He distinguishes a whole series of them: the time of the *longue durée* and slow motion, time the deceiver and time the surpriser, time with an irregular beat, cyclic time running in place, time running slow, time alternating between running slow and fast, time running fast, explosive time. How could a historian believe in all this? Given such a range of colors, he could never reconstitute a single, white light—and that is something he cannot do without. The historian quickly becomes aware, too, that this chameleon-like time barely adds any extra touch, any spot of color to the categories which had been established earlier. In the city that our friend has built, time, the last to arrive, cohabits quite naturally with all the other categories. It fits itself to the dimensions of their homes and their demands, according to the "levels," sociabilities, groups, and global societies. It is a different way of rewriting the same equations without actually changing them. Each social reality secretes its own particular time, or time scale, like common snails. But what do we historians get out of all this? The vast edifice of this ideal city remains static. History is nowhere to be seen. The world's time, historical time is there, but imprisoned, like Aeolus in his goat's skin. It is not history which sociologists, fundamentally and quite unconsciously, bear a grudge against, but historical time—which is a reality that retains its violence no matter how one tries to bring it to order and to break it down. It is a constraint from which the historian is never free, while sociologists on the other hand almost always seem to manage to avoid it, by concentrating either on the instant, which is always present as if suspended somewhere above time, or else on repeated phenomena which do not belong to any age. So they escape the two contradictory movements of the mind, confining them within either the narrowest limits of the event or the most extended *longue durée*. Is such an evasion justifiable? That is the crux of the debate between historians and sociologists, and even between historians of differing persuasions.

## VI

I do not believe it is possible to avoid history. Sociologists must take care. Philosophy (where it comes from and where it remains) prepares it only too well not to feel this concrete need for history. The techniques of inquiry into the present threaten only to complete the separation. All these investigators of the living moment, which hurries along and has a tendency to knock over anyone trying to handle it, would do well to beware of a too hasty observation, going only skin deep. A sociology of events clutters up our libraries, the files of governments and businesses. Far be it from me to revolt against the fashion or to declare it useless. But whatever can its scientific value be, if it does not record the direction, the speed or slowness, the ascent or descent of the movement which carries along any social phenomenon, and if it does not attach itself to the movement of history, to the resounding dialectic which runs from the past to the present, and even to the future?

I wish that during their years of apprenticeship young sociologists would take the necessary time to study, even in the most modest of archives, the simplest of historical questions, so that they might at least once have contact outside the sterility of the textbooks with what is essentially a simple profession, but one which can be understood only by practicing it—like any other profession, I have no doubt. There can be no social science, in my meaning of the word, except in a reconciliation and the simultaneous application of our various professions. Setting them up one against the other is easy enough, but it is a quarrel which is danced to a pretty old tune. What we need now are new tunes.

## Notes

1. The famous controversy did nonetheless also arise over a book of Paul Lacombe's, *De l'Histoire considérée comme science* (Paris, 1894). François Simiand's article "Méthode historique et science sociale," *Revue de synthèse historique* (1903): 1–22 and 129–57, is, in fact, subtitled "Étude de critique d'après les ouvrages récents de M. Lacombe et de M. Seignobos." But Paul Lacombe's work is hardly touched on.

2. Xénopol, in *Revue de synthèse historique*, no. 2 (1900), p. 135.

3. "La Science de l'histoire d'après M. Xénopol," *Revue de synthèse historique* (1900), p. 32.

4. "Continuité et discontinuité en histoire et en sociologie," *Annales E.S.C.*, (1957), pp. 73–84.

5. And let us add, Charles Seignobos, *La Méthode historique appliquée aux sciences sociales* (Paris, 1901).

6. "Histoire et sociologie," *Revue de synthèse historique* (1903), pp. 121–40.

7. 2d ed. (Paris, 1948; first edition published 1938).

8. *Apologie pour l'histoire ou métier d'historien* (Paris, 1949). See J. Stengers's perceptive note on this fine book, "Marc Bloch et l'histoire," *Annales E.S.C.* (1953), pp. 329–37.

9. Paris, 1953.

10. *Introduction à l'histoire* (Paris, 1946).

11. *Le Tempe de l'histoire* (Paris, 1954).

12. *Histoire: Science du concret* (Paris, 1946).

13. "Qu'est-ce que l'histoire?" *Revue de métaphysique et de morale* (1955): 225–47.

14. *De la Connaissance historique,* 1954. To be completed by the two excellent bulletins on historiography put out by H.-J. Marrou, *Revue historique* (1953), pp. 256–70, and ibid. (1957), pp. 270–89.

15. Mantoux, "Histoire et sociologie," p. 122.

16. See above, note 3.

17. Simiand, "Méthode historique," p. 18.

18. See how wise, and how from another age, appears Jean Meuvret's article "Histoire et sociologie," *Revue historique* (1938).

19. *Structural Anthropology,* trans. Claire Jacobson and Brooke Grundfest (London: Schoepf, 1968), p. 12.

20. *Annales E.S.C.* (1957), p. 73.

21. Op cit.

22. "And then, what about 'structures'? A highly fashionable word, I know; it can even sometimes be found in *Annales,* rather too often for my taste" (Preface to Huguette and Pierre Chaunu, *Séville et l'Atlantique* [Paris, 1959], vol. 1, p. xi).

23. Colloquium of the École des Hautes Études, 6th section, on structures, typed summary, 1958.

24. Simiand, "Méthode historique," p. 2.

25. *La Crise de l'économie française à la veille de la Révolution* (Paris, 1944).

26. F. Braudel, "Histoire et sciences sociales: La longue durée," *Annales E.S.C.* no. 4 (1958). See above, p. 25.

27. The reader will notice that the following 3 pages reproduce a passage of the article on the *longue durée* (see above, p. 47), published in *Annales* in the same year. It was felt that taking the passage out of either article would disrupt the unity of the reasoning.

28. *Histoire et distin* (Paris, 1943), passim.

29. See above, note 3.

30. *Dialectique de la durée,* 2d ed. (1950).

31. Gilles Granger, "Événement et structure dans les sciences de l'homme," *Cahiers de l'Institut de Science économique appliquée,* Série M, no. 1, pp. 41–42.

32. Georges Gurvitch, *Déterminismes sociaux et liberté humaine* (Paris, 1955), pp. 38–40 and passim.

## Select Bibliography

1. Even more than the books which I have quoted in this article as illustrating the conflict between history and sociology, I would recommend young sociologists to read certain works which could put them directly in touch with history, and, more particularly, with that form of history most closely kin to their own profession.

The titles listed below are only one possible selection out of innumerable others which could be made according to the varying tastes and curiosity of the individual.

Vidal de la Blache, P. *La France: Tableau géographique.* Paris, 1906.

Bloch, M. *Les Caractères originaux de l'histoire rurale française.* Paris-Oslo, 1931.

———. *La Société féodale.* Paris, 1940.

Febvre, L. *Rabelais et les problèmes de l'incroyance au XVIe siècle.* Paris, 1943.

Dupront, A. *Le Mythe de croisade: Étude de sociologie religieuse.* Paris, 1956.

Francastel, P. *Peinture et société.* Lyons, 1941.

Braudel, F. *The Mediterranean and the Mediterranean World in the Age of Philip II,* trans. Sian Reynolds. 2 vols. N.Y.: Harper & Row, 1972–74.

Curtius, E. *Le Moyen age latin.* Paris, 1956.

Huizinga, J. *The Waning of the Middle Ages,* trans. F. Hopman. England, 1924.

Labrousse, E. *La Crise de l'économie française à la veille de la Révolution.* Paris, 1944.

Lefebvre, G. *La Grande Peur.* Paris, 1932.

2. Methodological studies of history are legion, so let us confine ourselves to listing some of those quoted in the preceding article:

Ariès, P. *Le Temps de l'histoire.* Paris, 1954.

Bloch, M. *Métier d'historien.* Paris, 1949.

Braudel, F. "Histoire et sciences sociales: La longue durée," *Annales E.S.C.* no. 4 (1958).

Febvre, L. *Combats pour l'histoire.* Paris, 1954.

Piganiol, A. "Qu'est-ce que l'histoire?" in *Revue de métaphysique et de morale* (1955): 225–47.

Marrou, H.-J. *De la Connaissance historique.* Paris, 1954.

Simiand, F. "Méthode historique et sciences sociale," *Revue de synthèse historique* (1903): 1–22; 129–57.

# Toward a Historical Economics

Are the achievements of economic history already sufficiently substantial for one to be able usefully to transcend them, at least in thought, and to try and distinguish general rules and tendencies over and above individual cases? In other words, could the outline of a historical economics which would pay attention to great units, to the general and the permanent, be of use to economic research, to the solution of present large-scale problems or, which is more to the point, to the formulation of such problems? Physicists from time to time run into difficulties to which only a mathematician, with his particular rules, can find the answer. Could we as historians provide a similar service for our economist colleagues? No doubt the comparison is too flattering. I have an idea that if one wanted a more modest and perhaps more accurate comparison, one could compare us as historians to those travelers who make a note of all the features of the way, the colors of the landscape, and are led by the similarities and parallels to discuss their theories with geographical friends. And in fact, during the course of our journeys through the time of men we do get the feeling of having distinguished economic realities, some stable, others fluctuating, some rhythmical, others not... Are these illusions, useless reconnaissance, or rather work which can already prove worthwhile? It is not something that we alone can judge.

So I believe that a dialogue could and should be initiated between the different human sciences, sociology, history, and economics. Upheavals could follow for all of them. I am ready in advance to accept these upheavals as far as history is concerned, and for this reason it is not a method that I wish or am capable of defining in the few lines which I have agreed, though not without a certain trepidation, to offer to the *Revue économique*. At the very most I would like to point out a few questions which I would like to see considered by economists, so that they might then be offered back to history transformed, clarified, enlarged, or perhaps on the contrary reduced to nothing. But even then there would have been progress, we should have gone a step forward. It goes without saying that I do not claim to pose all the problems or even all the most important problems which would benefit from being confronted with both methods, the historical and the economic. There must be

*Revue économique* (May 1950), pp. 37–44.

thousands more. I would simply like to offer here a few of those which have occupied my own mind, and which I have had occasion to consider while going about my business as a historian. Perhaps they might connect with the preoccupations of some economists, although our points of view seem to me to be still very far apart.

I

The difficulties of the historian's profession are constantly being called to our attention. But without wishing to deny them, would it not be possible for once to point out its irreplaceable conveniences? Can we not at first sight distinguish the crucial factor as far as the future of a given historical situation is concerned? We know which of all the conflicting forces will prevail. We can see in advance which events are important, which ones will have consequences, which ones will affect the future. What an immense privilege! Who else, from among all the jumbled occurrences of contemporary life, would be able to distinguish with any certainty between the lasting and the ephemeral? To those living at the time, incidents unfortunately seem all too often to be all of an equal degree of importance, and the most momentous events, those which will shape the future, make so little noise—arriving with the silent step of a dove, as Nietzsche once said—that one is rarely even aware of their presence. Which is why Colin Clark has tried to add prophetic projections of the future to contemporary economic data, so as to be able to distinguish in advance the main currents shaping and carrying our life along. Everything turned around, a historian's daydream! . . .

So the very first thing the historian sees is the troop of events which have come out on top in the struggle of life. But these events place themselves once again, order themselves within the framework of a variety of contradictory possibilities, among which life finally made its choice. For one possibility which was fulfilled, there were tens, hundreds, thousands, which disappeared, and there are even some which, numberless, never even appear to us at all, too lowly and hidden to impose themselves directly on history. We must nonetheless somehow try to reintroduce them, because these vanishing movements are the multiple material and immaterial forces which have at every moment put the brakes on the great forward impetuses of evolution, slowed down their development, and sometimes put an early end to their existence. It is indispensable that we know them.

So it seems that historians must work against the grain, and react against the advantages of their profession, and study not only progress, the prevailing movement, but also its opposite, that harvest of contrary experiences which fought hard before they went down. Should we call it *inertia,* without giving that word any particular pejorative connotations? In a way, this is the sort of problem which Lucien Febvre deals with in his *Rabelais,* when he asks whether atheism, for which there was to be a great future—specifically, "intellectual" atheism—was possible during the first half of the sixteenth century, whether the intellectual equipment of the age (that is to say, its inertia with regard to atheism) made its conception and clear formulation possible.

We find these problems of inertia, of braking, in the economic field too, and as a rule set out more clearly, even if not any easier to resolve. Beneath the names of capitalism, international economics, *Weltwirtschaft* (with all the difficulties and riches which the word implies in German thought), do we not find descriptions of high points of development, of superlatives, often of exceptions? Alfred Jardé, in his magnificent history of grains in ancient Greece, having considered the "modern" forms of trade in grain, the Alexandrian merchants who controlled the traffic in foodstuffs, pictures to himself such and such a shepherd in the Peloponnese or Epirus, living off his own land, his own olives, on feast days killing off a suckling pig from his own herd... One example of thousands upon thousands of closed or half-closed economies existing outside the sphere of the international economy of their age, and which in their own way inhibit its development and rhythms. Inertias? There are also those imposed on any age by the means at its disposal, its strengths, its different paces, its speed, and even more its relative slowness. Any study of the past must necessarily comprise a minute computation of what at a given moment weighs on it, whether obstacles of geography, of technical development, social obstacles, administrative obstacles... To clarify what I am trying to express, might I go so far as to say that if I undertook the study—which tempts me—of France during the wars of religion, I would start from an impression which might at first sight seem arbitrary, but which I am sure is not. The few forays which I have been able to make into that France have led me to conceive of it as being very like China between the two world wars: a huge country in which men could lose themselves—the more so in that the France of the sixteenth century had nothing like the demographic concentration of the Chinese world. But still the image holds good—a huge expanse of territory dislocated by wars both internal and external. We can find it all: frightened, besieged cities, the dispersal of floating armies between provinces, regional dislocations, reconstructions, miracles, surprises... I would not say that the comparison would stand up very long, that it could be maintained throughout my study. But that is the point to start from, the study of that sort of atmosphere, that immensity, and the countless brakes they would entail if one wished to reach any understanding of the rest, including economics and politics.

These examples do not really set out the problem. But they nonetheless show up some of its salient features. All existence, all experience is imprisoned in an envelope too thick to be broken through at a stroke; there is a limit to the capacity of the existing equipment which makes it impossible to move in certain directions, to hold certain attitudes, to conceive certain ideological innovations. It is a thick layer, at once hopeless and reasonable, good and bad, limiting the development of both the best and the worst, to speak for a moment in moral terms. It almost always functions against the most necessary social progress, but sometimes it also checks the outbreak of a war—I am thinking here of the sixteenth century with its breathless conflicts, broken up by pauses—or makes unemployment impossible, as it also did in the sixteenth century, when the processes of production were broken down into tiny fragments, multitudes of minute organisms which proved extraordinarily resistant to crises.

Such a study of limits and inertias is, or should be, indispensable research for the historian obliged to deal with realities of the past which must be depicted in their true light. Would not such a study also fall within the province of the economist with his more contemporary concerns? Our present economic civilization is also circumscribed by limits and moments of inertia. It is without a doubt difficult for the economist to extricate these problems from either their social or their historical context. But it is up to him, all the same, to tell us how better to formulate them, or else to demonstrate exactly in what way these are false problems, and of no interest. When I recently asked an economist about all this, he replied that he relied above all on historians for any such study of this sort of braking, this viscosity, this resistance. Is that really safe? Are these not, to the contrary, elements that are economically discernible, and which may be measured economically, even if it is only over the long run?

## II

Traditional history is concerned with the short time span of biography, of the event. It is not the sort of time which is of any interest to economic or social historians. Societies, civilizations, economies, political institutions work out their lives at a less headlong pace. Economists will not be surprised, since it is to them in this instance that we owe our methods, if we have in our turn come to speak of cycles, intercycles, and periodic movements with phases lasting for five, ten, twenty, thirty, sometimes even fifty years. But from our point of view even these must seem the wavelets of history, must they not?

Below these small waves, in the domain of the phenomena of tendencies (the century-long tendencies of economists) there stretches out, with almost invisible ups and downs, a history which unravels only slowly, and by that token only slowly reveals itself to our gaze. It is this which, in our imperfect language, we call by the name of *histoire structurale* ("structural history"), less in opposition to the history of events *(événementielle)* than to the history of conjunctures *(conjoncturale)*, to relatively brief waves. One has no idea of the debates[1] and reservations which these few lines could provoke.

But let us imagine that we have got past such debates and have reached if not a definition, then at least an understanding of this history in depth. It is economic history too (demography with its remote-control working across great tracts of time would be a good and one might even go so far as to say an excellent demonstration of it). But it would not be possible to record large-scale structural oscillations of the economy in any valid way without having at our disposal a very long retrospective series of documentation—preferably, statistical. Now we know only too well that this is not the case, and we have to base our work and our speculations on relatively short and particular series, such as the series of prices and incomes. All the same, would there not be some use in working out some sort of systematic vision of a little-known or well-known past made up of units of time of not just years or tens of years, but of whole centuries? Is it a daydream, or a useful concept?

Assuming that there are entities, economic zones with relatively definite boundaries, would not a method of observation based on geographical location prove useful? Rather than describing the social stages of capitalism, for instance, to paraphrase the fine title of a luminous piece by Henri Pirenne, would it not be more interesting to describe the geographical stages of capitalism, or on an even larger scale to set in motion, within our historical studies, systematic research into economic geography—to see, in a word, how the waves and wanderings of history are recorded in a given economic area? Though it is not something I could achieve on my own I have tried to show what Mediterranean life must have been like at the end of the sixteenth century. One of our soundest researchers, M. A. Rémond, is about to round off his studies of France in the eighteenth century and to show how the French economy detached itself from the Mediterranean, despite its increased trade, and turned toward the Atlantic: a turning which entailed important transformations in trade routes, markets, and cities. I am also reminded of the beginning of the nineteenth century,[2] when France consisted of a series of French provinces, each with their own well organized spheres of existence, linked together politically and through their systems of exchange, and behaving toward each other just like national economies, following the rules laid down in our textbooks and making all the consequent currency adjustments to regulate the balancing of their accounts. Do not these geographical considerations, with all the modifications brought about in them by a century rich in innovation, provide a valid field of research as far as France is concerned, and a means, while we await a better one, of attaining those expanses of slowly moving history which spectacular changes and crises otherwise tend to hide from our sight?

Besides, the long perspectives of history suggest, perhaps fallaciously, that economic life is subject to slow-moving rhythms. The splendid cities of medieval Italy, whose decline took gradual shape in the sixteenth century, often began by building their fortunes on the profits from road or sea transport. It was thus with Asti, with Venice, with Genoa. This was followed by mercantile activity, then by industrial development. Finally, the crowning touch, the growth of banking. Inverse proof, the decline affected successively, and sometimes at very great intervals—and not without occasional brief revivals—transport, then commerce, then industry, allowing banking activities to survive long after the others. In the eighteenth century, Venice and Genoa were still centers of finance.

The sketch is oversimplified, and I would not hold it to be perfectly true, but I am more concerned here with suggesting than with demonstrating. To complicate matters and bring them closer to reality, each new activity must be shown to correspond to a break in the barrier, to an obstacle overcome. Equally, these ascents and descents must not be presented as being simple lines; they must be confused by a thousand parasitical interferences. These successive phases, from transport to banking, must also be shown not to have sprung into being through a series of abrupt ruptures. At the very start, like a seed which contains a whole potential plant, each urban economy holds every possible activity within it, though some may still be in embryo. Finally, there is an obvious danger in wishing to deduce a law from one example, and assuming that one might arrive at some conclusion as to the nature of the Italian city-states (a microeconomy?), in using such conclusions a priori to explain contemporary experiences. It is too dangerous a leap not to warrant further consideration.

Nonetheless, could not economists come to our aid yet again? Are we right to see in transport and its associated elements (prices, routes, technical developments) a sort of motor which is decisive in the long term and, to borrow a word from astronomy, is there a precession of some economic movements over others, not only in the narrow time span of cycles and intercycles, but also over very long stretches of time?

## III

There is another problem which seems to be of crucial importance: the problem of the *continuous* and the *discontinuous,* to adopt the language of sociologists. The difficulties which arise can perhaps be attributed to the way in which the plurality of historical time is rarely taken into account. The time which carries us along also carries along, albeit in a different way, societies and civilizations whose reality transcends ours because their life span is a good deal longer than ours and the datum points, the stages along the way to decay are never the same for them and for us. The time which is our time, which we experience and live, which brings back the seasons, makes the roses bloom, and marks our passing years also marks the hours of the existence of a whole variety of social structures, but at quite a different pace. All the same, however slowly they may age, they too must change and die in the end.

Now, what does social *discontinuity* consist in, if not, in the language of history, one of these structural rifts, a profound, silent, and painless break, as we are told. We are born into a particular social arrangement (meaning at once an attitude of mind, frameworks, a civilization, and above all an economic civilization) the same as several generations before us have been familiar with, and then the whole thing can crumble in a lifetime. Whence disturbance and shocks.

This transition from one world to another is the great human drama on which we need to shed light. When Sombart and Sayous argue as to when modern capitalism was born, it is a rift of this sort which they are looking for, even though they do not give it that name and cannot set a precise date for it. I do not seek a philosophy of these catastrophes (or of the falsely typical catastrophe that is the collapse of the Roman world, which one might study just as the German military studied the battle of Cannae), but rather a study in terms of the multiple illumination of discontinuity. Sociologists are already discussing it; historians are uncovering it; might economists consider it? Have they had the chance, as we have had, of coming into contact with the keen mind of Ignace Meyerson? These deep rifts cut through one of the great destinies of mankind, his essential destiny. Everything which forms a part of it at its outbreak goes under, or is at the very least transformed. If, as seems possible, we have just come through one of these decisive zones, then none of the tools, the thoughts and concepts which we used yesterday will apply tomorrow, and any teaching based on an illusory return to old values is out of date. The political economy which we have, after a fashion, assimilated to the lessons of our masters will no longer be any good to us in our old age. But do not economists have anything to say about just this sort of structural discontinuity, even hypothetical? Do they not have anything to say *to us* about it?

It is evident that what seems indispensible to us in any resurgence of the human sciences is less any particular individual venture than the initiation of a great general debate—a debate which could obviously never end, since the history of ideas, including the history of history, is also a living entity, living its own life, independent of the very beings which animate it. Nothing is more tempting, nothing is more profoundly impossible than the illusion of bringing the whole of such a baffling, complicated social reality within the confines of one single explanation. As historians, who along with sociologists are the *only* ones with a right to an overview of *all* that pertains to man, our task and our torment is to reconstitute the fundamental unity of life, with all its different times and different orders of facts. "History is man," according to Lucien Febvre. And when we are attempting to reconstitute man, we must put together all the realities which appear and join up and live at the same pace. If not the puzzle will be out of shape. If we juxtapose structural history and conjunctural history, our explanation will be out of true, or if we turn toward the superficial history of events, we will have to trim our explanation to fit. At every stage, correlations must be sought only from among similar bodies: that must be our first care, the basis of our first researches and our first speculations. Then we can proceed as best we can to reconstruct the edifice.

Notes

1. Would it not have been better, and better grammar, to have said *structurel* and *conjoncturel?*
2. See here the work in progress of a young economist, François Desaunay, assistant at the École des Hautes Études.

# Toward a Serial History

## Seville and the Atlantic,
## 1504–1650

In order to describe Pierre Chaunu's monumental work,[1] one needs an expression that will define both his enterprise and the novelty, deliberately both powerful and restrained, of the kind of history which he is putting forward. Let us call it *serial history,* since that is what Pierre Chaunu himself has recently called it,[2] and since it points up the main perspective of a work in which the reader as he goes along is in danger of letting himself be distracted by the variety of paths offered, and so of losing the thread and getting well and truly lost.

Having read the book a first time and closely, pen in hand, I must admit that I understood the accumulation of approaches and unexpected, deliberate silences better on a second reading. Within the framework of a serial history, this book can find its unity, its justification, and its previously accepted limits.

A work even of such magnificent dimensions must be a question of choices. Serial history, to which Pierre Chaunu confines himself, makes its own demands. It is "less interested in the individual event . . . than in the repeated element, . . . which can be integrated into a homogeneous series capable of then supporting the classic mathematical procedures of series analysis." It has in consequence a language of its own—and an extremely abstract, disembodied language.

This sort of history calls for and absolutely requires the use of *series,* and it is that which gives it its name and its raison d'être. By series is meant a coherent succession, or a succession which has been rendered coherent, of measurements linked one to another, as, say, a function of historical time whose progress has to be patiently established and then its meaning deduced, the more so since its track is sometimes hard to follow and the calculations involved at the beginning never can be sure of determining it automatically in advance.

Function and explanation of historical time? These images and formulas are perhaps not really clear enough. Such a series of figures denoting valid interrelated measurements is like a highway built across our uncertain knowledge, allowing us to travel only along a particular route, but that one a favored one.

The traffic which existed between Seville and the Americas from 1504

*Annales E.S.C.,* no. 3 (May–June 1963), Critical Notes, pp. 541–53.

to 1650, reconstituted as to its original volume and value, such is the historically prestigious series offered to our understanding as a "continuous body of quantified facts." In order to establish it, between 1955 and 1957 Huguette and Pierre Chaunu published seven great volumes of harbor accounts.[3] At one and the same time they have both constructed the series and *invented* it. The crucial thing in their eyes was to establish, long before the beginnings of the eighteenth century and its easily accessible statistics, that solid highway of figures, "to push back in some degree, no matter how small," as Pierre Chaunu has written, "the frontier between measurable economies and those which must be left to a purely qualitative appraisal."

We have known since Earl J. Hamilton that Spanish greatness in the sixteenth century can be measured. We know it even better now. And given the wealth of the Peninsular archives, further progress is yet to be made along the favored approach of the series.

Thus it was only at the end of an enormous labor of innovation that Pierre Chaunu built, single-handedly this time, his huge thesis running to over 3,000 pages. He offers us but a single aspect of Spanish greatness, a single aspect of the world economy, but the axis he chooses is crucial, dominant, bringing an irresistible order to a whole area of thousands of acquired ideas and fragments of knowledge. All historians and economists interested in the beginnings of modernity in the world will find when they read this book that they are called upon to verify and sometimes to throw out the old explanations. When one is enamored of history, there can surely be no finer sight than such a book, so long as one puts it properly in its context and does not ask more of it than it can and, more especially, than it is prepared to deliver.

## Structure and Conjuncture

Despite the obvious resemblances and connections which Pierre Chaunu, with his customary and overgenerous kindness, is good enough to note, I do not believe that the Sevillian Atlantic which he offers us is in any way a repetition or an extension of *The Mediterranean and the Mediterranean World in the Age of Philip II,* a book which came out ten years before his, in 1949. For a start, the Atlantic which he depicts is not considered in its entirety, but is an arbitrary expanse, from the Antilles to the mouth of the Guadalquivir, as the author constantly points out: he is, in his own words, dealing with "a median Atlantic," "the early Atlantic, enclosure of the Iberias," "the Atlantic exclusive to Seville."

It is more a question of a constructed human reality than of an unmodified geographic whole, a question of a system of trade routes end-ing in Seville "where everything comes together. . . in a bottleneck," and from where it all starts off again.

There is another fundamental difference which Pierre Chaunu perceived immediately and which does indeed spring to the eye: the difference between the oldest stretch of sea ever dominated by man—the Mediterranean—with a whole past behind it, and at that time (the sixteenth century) coming to the end of its greatness, and a sea (the Atlantic) with nothing but a borrowed and hastily constructed past.

Doubtless, when he draws a distinction between structure and conjuncture, between stillness and movement, Pierre Chaunu is for a moment following the example which I had set earlier and which seems to have influenced a number of recent theses. So Pierre Chaunu too has let himself be seduced by the useful dialectic between the *longue durée* and the short. But, for all that, his purpose is not at all the same as mine was. In *The Mediterranean* I sought to envisage as best I could a global history, ranging from stillness to the liveliest movements of men. Pierre Chaunu neither claims nor desires to do this. In his book, the description of the main immobile masses (the first part), and then the narrative of the particular conjuncture (the second part) are intended to reconstruct only a certain economic reality, separate from a global history through which it travels but which overwhelms it on all sides. I even suspect that Pierre Chaunu consciously preferred the conjunctural narrative, closer as it is to history as it is lived, and easier to grasp, more scientific if it is enclosed in curves, than structural history, which can be observed only in the abstraction of the *longue durée*.

There were not yet any real structures existing in the Atlantic considered from 1504, the year when the Sevillian primacy took effect and a dozen years after Columbus's voyage. So they had to be imported, to be constructed, in short. Because of this did not Pierre Chaunu see, in the separation of the *longue durée* from the fluctuating, a wonderful opportunity of ridding his conjunctural study from the start—and it is the conjuncture which is the aim of the book and the crux of the undertaking—of anything which got in the way of his ordering of his subject, or which hindered the flow of his commentary? The mathematician does the same in grouping together or casting all his constant terms in one element of an equation.

To put things more clearly, the first volume of Pierre Chaunu's thesis, however rich it may be, is nothing but a preamble to the serial construction which will follow it. If we consider it on its own, we will see in it weaknesses, lacunas, surprising omissions, but these disappear and justify themselves in the general perspective of the work, which corresponds to the architect's intention or rather to the obligation which he has chosen.

The Structuring of the Median Atlantic

Doubtless I tended too much in my initial reaction to Pierre Chaunu's work to think of his first volume as being a book in its own right, which should have then made its own particular demands and above all had its own unity. That the book should go by the ambiguous title of *Les structures géographiques* did not help. This first book is concerned with more than the timeless, and for Pierre Chaunu, as for all historians who have come into contact with Lucien Febvre, geography, however particular its point of view, entails a consideration of the whole lived experience of man, today's as well as yesterday's. In fact, geography is not restrictive here, but on the contrary indicative. It advises and justifies a regional scheme based on proximity in space. An easy scheme, but terribly monotonous and not at all concerned with grouping problems together or with introducing, for the sake of organizing the material, the notion of historical time, though that is here the constructor of structures. From page 164 on, we proceed steadily from one stage to the next according to a program of numbering which could hardly be seriously defended. We will be told that it makes for a pretty impressive array of index cards. True. But what a book might not Pierre Chaunu have written, as the beginning of his oeuvre and in tune with his particular temperament, if he had paid attention to the slow transformation of structures, for they do in fact move and develop. A slow motion film would have been far preferable to the fixity of these magic lantern slides. Besides, on several occasions Pierre Chaunu has multiplied individual histories and, what is more, subordinated them to a typological geography which of itself transcends purely local truths and regroups them, but then he unfortunately proceeds to abandon it on the following page.

The journey, for this first part, consists in a detailed and slow-moving journey, moving from the Old World to the New. In what conditions, historically and geographically speaking, did the Sevillian monopoly on American trade become established, what were its limits and above all its weak points? How, in the shelter of its commanding primacy, did the Iberian world conduct itself, as glimpsed for a moment in its depths and along its coastal fringes? These are the first questions, to which we are given excellent answers. Then Chaunu considers the "islands of Europe," the Canaries (which are extensively studied), Madeira, and the Azores. From these islands, he passes on naturally to those of the New World, Santo Domingo, Puerto Rico, Jamaica, the Bermudas, and the Floridian peninsula. When dealing with the geographical entities offered us by the New World, it was tempting to distinguish between lightweight entities (the "continental islands") and heavyweight entities (the "continents": New Spain and Peru), without forgetting the isth-

muses, especially the Panamanian isthmus, which our author not unreasonably claims to be a "Sevillian isthmus."

On all these questions, whether far-ranging or restricted, this book
frequently manages to cast fresh light. Pierre Chaunu has been lavish
with a whole wealth of learning, and whenever his series of trade figures
allowed to do so in advance, he increased his notation of important
factors, fixed the exchanges, marked the success of major products:
leather, gold, silver, sugar, tobacco. And the result is a whole map of
production forces and areas of production, a whole dictionary stuffed
with facts ready to be consulted. So what are we complaining about?

I say it again, about all that this first book does not go into. More
specifically, about the fact that it falls short of a history of the whole body
of structures, despite all the materials available which it would have been
necessary to use and coordinate. Pierre Chaunu was well enough aware
of this himself in the first hundred or so pages of *Structures* (pp. 40–163),
which curiously are given over to a narrative frequently and above all
concerned with superficial events, in which Columbus occupies a large
place, followed by the stages of the conquest, and concluding with important and original thoughts about the *"conquista"* in terms of place and
of men (pp. 143–59). But this narrative, however useful, is not the
large-scale vista which I seek and which, it seems to me, ought to have
shed light on the slow establishment of the Atlantic structures and the
difficulties involved in laying them down.

The Atlantic and its European and American coasts, the islands in
midocean and along the continental seaboards, the maritime routes
linking all together were empty spaces at the time of the discoveries. Man
was absent from them, or at most rarely and ineffectively present. What
construction there was, here and there, depended on a concentration of
men, whether black, white, or Indian. It meant the transfer and repeated implantation of cultural imports: boats, cultivated plants, domestic animals. Frequently, too, variation in prices was an important factor:
"the low American prices dominated the market," to repeat a remark
made by Ernest Labrousse. The whole was based on particular favored
centers, and founded in the framework of existing structures: religions,
political institutions, administrations, urban organization, and over and
above all of this, an ancient, insidious, supple mercantile capitalism,
already capable of bridging the ocean and subduing it to its will.

Many years ago, André E. Sayous,[4] in his investigations of the notarial
archives in Seville *(Archivo de Protocolos)*, concerned himself with these
great ventures, emphasizing in particular the innovatory and hazardous
undertakings of the Genoese merchants. Since then, a good many
studies of details of these undertakings have appeared. Even now we
are awaiting a definitive work on the subject by Guillermo Lohmann

Villena.[5] But we already have Enrique Otte's original studies,[6] and the letters of the merchant Simón Ruiz[7] (for the second half of the sixteenth century) which are begging to be used,[8] or the priceless papers of Florentine merchants published by Federigo Melis.[9]

So one cannot help being surprised that this long prologue should tell us nothing, except incidentally, about the merchants, the prime movers of Sevillian trade. Nor is there a word about the Iberian cities, matrices for the cities of the New World, or about urban typology on one side of the Atlantic and the other. Nor, in conclusion, is there a word about the very city of Seville itself, truly a "neck" for several different bottles. It led not only to the Indies, but also to the Mediterranean, to the Spanish heartland (as Pierre Chaunu does demonstrate splendidly), and to the northern countries, to Flanders, England, the Baltic, which he does not show at all. It can even be said that it was the coastal navigation around Spain, from Gibraltar to London and Bruges, which prepared the way and finally made possible the great discoveries. It is international capitalist concentration in Seville which goes a long way toward explaining early America.

So Seville *belongs* to other maritime areas, to other routes of shipping, trade, and money than the Seville–Vera Cruz axis alone, and insofar as the "Iberian ocean" was a "dominant" area (in the sense in which François Perroux uses the term in "dominant pole," and "dominant economy"), was it not important to note the forms of "asymmetry," of imbalance, all the visible inferiority complexes which the superiority of the Sevillian ocean brought about in other spheres of oceanic traffic? Yet Pierre Chaunu tells us, when speaking of the Pacific of the distant Philippines,[10] that the Atlantic Ocean annexed it to its own "voracious" existence: so why, when considering geographic structures, did he not turn his gaze toward the North Sea, or toward the Mediterranean of Alicante, of Genoa, and soon to be significant Leghorn? Obviously, in order to clarify these problems he would have needed to widen his archival researches, consulting in Seville the extremely rich *Protocolos*, in Simancas the innumerable papers there on Seville and Flanders. But Pierre Chaunu has chosen of his own free will to remain within the boundaries of his own serial history, without taking any account of other series which might exist.

Seville at any rate had the right to be represented in all its living totality, and not just as a port, below the bridge of boats linking it to the suburb of Triana; to be represented not only in its institutions like the glorious *Casa de la Contratación,* but also in its economic, social, and urban realities, in its hordes of merchants, retailers, money changers, seamen, and insurers—and indeed in all the characteristic jerky rhythm of its life, regulated by the fleets which by turns enriched it and drained it, alternately bringing to the financial markets of the plaza what contemporary documents call the "easiness" and the "tightness" of money. Going through, at Simancas, the *padrón* of Seville, that exhaustive census made of its dwellings and inhabitants in 1561, I was struck by all that Pierre Chaunu denied himself, and denied us.

## The Triumph of the Serial

The two volumes on the conjuncture (volumes 2 and 3 of the work) alarm us at once by their insolent use of the singular. Over and above their concern with the registration of Sevillian traffic, they are in fact concerned with *the* international, universal conjuncture, with the rhythms of a *Weltwirtschaft* extending over all the great civilizations and economies of the world and which Pierre Chaunu sees (though with a good deal of caution, vol. 2, p. 43), as I do myself, as being *one*. Perhaps it was a unity already, long before the close of the fifteenth century, as far as the Old World was concerned, that world apart, with its centuries-long coherence, from Europe to China, India, and Black Africa, thanks to the long-standing dominance of Moslem navigation and caravans. Something which more than one noneconomic historian will have already said many years ago.

All the more reason why there should be a conjuncture in the sixteenth century, when the circles were widening to such a degree and the pace of life quickening at such a rate; and so we read that "the universality of fluctuations . . . seems really to come into being, somewhere between Seville and Vera Cruz." Of course, this worldwide conjuncture does not disrupt everything: "A world economy, in depth, would not be possible until much later, not before the technical and demographic explosion of the nineteenth and twentieth centuries." But in the end, and Pierre Chaunu has said as much in his own defense, the choice of the Atlantic "is a daring choice, it means trying to explain the world." I like this rash pronouncement—it appeals to me.

It is at any rate to this level, that of the world conjuncture, that any criticism of this book should either return or attempt to elevate itself. Pierre Chaunu may say a thousand things (as he already did in his first volume) on the Spanish Empire, but it is not in this context, on which we have a host of other and often more complete information, that we should regard his work. The thing is to move outside the Hispanic universe, and grasp the world conjuncture.

So it was interesting and useful, having dispatched these important but nonetheless secondary explanations, to leave space squarely behind and turn to time, and then to devote himself exclusively to a leisurely account of all its phases, periods, rhythms, and even moments, according to the clock of the arrivals and departures of the Sevillian fleets. We are given an estimate of both the size and the value of cargoes; journeys out and home are examined either separately or cumulatively, and raw curves treated in several different ways (quinquennial averages, the mean over seven or thirteen years).

The record is finally presented as a maze of curves. That these curves have had to be reconstructed, sometimes invented, and often corrected is an indication of the preliminary work necessary to the arrangement of all the serial material. The most difficult obstacle to overcome was the (variable) estimate of the *tonelada;* that alone shows the dangers and risks which had to be accepted, reconnoitered, and in one way or another overcome.

But these considerations on the construction of the book will be of interest only to specialists (are there many of them?). The historian will not be risking much in accepting the author's numerical decisions and conclusions. So he may proceed to join without qualms in the prolonged, certainly tedious, and equally certainly necessary concerns to which Pierre Chaunu calmly devotes himself for at least 2,000 pages. Henri Lapeyre has written recently that our author might have abridged and condensed what he has written.[11] True, but would it have been so easy? And besides, do we actually have to read all these pages with our customary close attention? The most hard pressed among us can simply refer to the atlas accompanying the book, while those with particular concerns need only choose the discussions relevant to them.

Anyway, thank God, the conclusions of the whole thing are both clear and solid.

The *trend* of the centuries describes two great movements: an ascent, which can be called phase A, from 1506 to 1608, and a descent, phase B, from 1608 to 1650.

All the same, Pierre Chaunu prefers to bring his chronology and his observations to a halt at shorter measurements and movements, at periods of from twenty to fifty years at most (though one of them is a good deal shorter than that) and which he calls, in a misleading or at least an ambiguous way, "intercycles," although they are more appropriately half-Kondratievs. But the term hardly matters. It is much easier to forgive Pierre Chaunu his use of "intercycle" than that of "decade," which he persistently employs instead of *decennium.*[12]

So there is a succession of contradictory intercycles, five in all: first, a rise from 1504 to 1550; second, a downward trend from 1550 to 1559–62 (could this be, as I think, a Labroussian intercycle?); third, a rise from 1559–62 to 1592; fourth, a leveling-off from 1592 to 1622; and fifth, a frank decline from 1622 to 1650.

Within these intercycles, analysis owing nothing to chiromancy can find, once again, a succession of cycles lasting a decade. It is even possible to make even shorter fluctuations, "Kitchins."

I do not believe for a moment that the dates and periods thus encapsulated are selected in any way subjectively. On the contrary, they are valid measures with which to gauge the passing of time and its material existence. They do not tell us more about this passage of time than the taking of a temperature tells us about a patient's illness, but that much at least they do tell us, and that is no small help.

So the immense effort which goes to the creation of a serial history results in the fixing of a chronological scale, with all its multiples and submultiples. The main dividing point of this scale comes as no surprise to us. World prosperity splits in two on either side of the watershed of 1608, when the whirlpool of the trend of the century changes direction, though in fact it must be said that the change did not take place in a day, or in a year, but over a long indecisive period of time strewn with illusions and underlying catastrophes. In our necessary periodization (without which there could be no comprehensible general history), some would prefer to choose the preceding years, that is to say the 1590s, and others the concluding years (thus, for Carlo M. Cipolla 1619 or 1620, or for R. Romano 1619–23, or recently for myself 1620).

It is obvious that the debate is by no means closed, and that we are hardly accustomed as yet (even given Earl J. Hamilton's recent work) to discussing the exceptional events which the changes in direction of a secular trend must be. Such an event, of greater intrinsic importance, is much more difficult to explain within the present logic of our profession than the Invincible Armada (about which, as about English piracy, Pierre Chaunu confirms what we already know), or than the beginnings of the so-called Thirty Years' War. It is incontrovertible that the secular trend is by no means a classic subject for discussion yet. At Aix, at the Congress in September of 1962, despite the presence of the author, none of the theses of Mme. J. Griziotti-Kretschmann[13] was discussed, since none of the historians present, with the exception of Ruggiero Romano, Frank Spooner, and myself, had read her extremely rare book.

It is undeniable that a great change did take place between 1590 and 1630, and our imagination if not our reason can let itself go in trying to see to what it can be attributed. It could be the diminishing returns from the American mines (as Ernest Labrousse would readily claim), or the rapid decline of the Indian population in New Spain and doubtless in Peru as well. The old explanations have been abandoned: the absorption of white metal by the growing Hispano-Portuguese economy, or its diversion toward the Philippines and China, or its capture by the increased smuggling toward the Rio de la Plata... Smuggling, stealing have as we know been caught up in the same conjuncture as more normal routes. I would happily suggest, though I am not sure about it, that the crisis of a certain sort of capitalism, rather more financial and speculative than mercantile, had its part to play in the affair. The end of the sixteenth century saw a decline in profits, just as the eighteenth century did toward its end. Whether it is a cause or a consequence, it is nonetheless so!

But the state of our research is still insufficient and the problematic is too desperately meager in these areas for the problem, however well posed, to be properly resolved. Economic thinking, even the most advanced, has not yet furnished us with the necessary explanatory framework.

The problem is too huge, the wise will say. But more restricted problems are not always any clearer to us. This is the case, for instance, to give a good example, with a short intercycle dating from 1550 to 1562 in Seville, which Pierre Chaunu's inquiries have brought to light.

Much more than a warning shot, the transition, fairly dramatic in our eyes, from the age of Charles the Fifth which appears so radiant, to the sad, difficult, and gloomy age of Philip II was a great lurch in the whole "dominant" economy of Seville. In France, the transition from the years of François I to the somber seasons of Henri II... Perhaps tomorrow a historian will tell us that Labrousse's intercycle on the eve of the French Revolution has its equivalent in this "crisis" on the eve of the wars of religion, which like the French Revolution involved the whole of Europe.

This is all the more reason to regret the fact that, on this subject, Pierre Chaunu never ventured outside his Sevillian curves to offer a history of Europe and the world on the scale of the series, or even a descriptive history which would at least have the value of a preliminary sounding: thus the abrupt halt of the movement of English shipping toward the Mediterranean, thus the assured success (even, perhaps, as early as 1530) of Dutch shipping from the North Sea down as far as Seville. Why not seek to find whether the Sevillian cycle was shaped by the American demand or by the potential of the European economy, and how (then and at other times) it projected itself toward the European markets?

### The Stake: The History of Production

It would take pages and pages to give any idea of the riches contained in this endless conjunctural narrative, or to formulate any criticisms or doubts which one might have about it. They are not lacking, but they are all questions of detail. And they are not the crucial concern of Pierre

Chaunu's book. So let us proceed to these crucial concerns, to the last great debate which his book opens up, and which I am amazed not to have seen remarked on by any critics previously.

A curve of the harbor traffic bears witness to the circulation of merchandise and money—but this circulation which has been the prey of a mathematical approach to history for many a long year, doubtless because it lay within our reach, Pierre Chaunu maintains can also give us information about production in Spain and, beyond that, in Europe. Circulation, as the old writers tell us, completes production and follows its momentum. During some recent reading, in particular Gaston Imbert's book,[14] I have been struck by the intrinsic dissimilarity between movements of price and of production. As far as the sixteenth century is concerned, we are familiar with only a few curves of textile production (Hondschoote, Leyden, Venice). They all have the classic appearance of the parabolic curve, meaning in brief that they go up quickly, almost vertically, and then go almost vertically down. The long rise in prices seems to release their swift ascent, but always one step behind prices; when the prices begin to go down slowly, then production drops off sharply, always one step ahead of prices.

Now, it is just the case that there is no exact correlation between Pierre Chaunu's (Sevillian traffic) curves and Hamilton's price curves either. On the whole there is a positive correlation, but there are important differences. "The secular price curve," writes Pierre Chaunu, "has in its entirety from 1504 to 1608 and from 1608 to 1650 . . . a similar orientation, but with three or four times less of a declivity. For the ascendant period, prices multiply themselves by five! trade multiplies by fifteen or twenty. For the descendant phase, on the other hand, trade must be cut by more than two to one, while the prices/metals curve drops by 20% to 30%." All of which, for me, goes some way toward proving, or at least toward beginning to prove, that the Sevillian curves behave like production curves. The demonstration is not complete, but its outlines can be seen.

Am I wrong in thinking that much is at stake here, and that a history of different overlapping cycles within a new dialectic is being mapped out in close accordance with the theoretical and current researches of, say, Geoffrey Moore, for example? And that it would be rewarding not to limit cyclic oscillation to the movement of prices alone, which tends to dominate the thinking of French economic historians? The research done by Felipe Ruiz Martín, our colleague from Bilbao, which is as yet unpublished, though nearing publication, on textile production in Segovia, Cordoba, Toledo, and Cuenca in the sixteenth century will reinforce Pierre Chaunu's work. Broadly speaking, they indicate a characteristic mutation of international capitalism with regard to Spain during the 1580s, at just the time when, a victim as much as an instigator, Spanish imperialism was about to attempt some spectacular undertakings. Let us also note the forthcoming publication in *Annales* of the curve of *asientos* (loans) to the Castillian monarchy, by our colleague from Valencia, Alvaro Castillo.[15] All these series must be put together and coordinated if one wishes to get any overall picture of world history. In short, we must get away from price curves in order to reach other forms of recording, and then perhaps we may be able to measure that production which heretofore has always escaped us because we have had far too many a priori explanations.

### To Write Long or to Write Well?

The great labors of Pierre and, we must not forget, of Huguette Chaunu have been crowned with great success. There can be no question but that that is so. And yet is not this oceanic book too long, too discursive, in sum too hastily written? Pierre Chaunu writes as he speaks; if he had submitted his text to me what arguments we would have had. But every fault has its advantages. By dint of speaking and writing freely, Pierre Chaunu often succeeds in finding some excellent and illuminating formulation.

His text is studded with lucky finds. Here we have (outside Las Palmas) the open unprotected lanes of Grand Canary Island, "only accessible," writes Chaunu, "to boats prepared to go in for microcaboting." Here we are, in the vast continent of New Spain, looking for silver mines at the meeting point of the two Mexicos, the arid and the humid. They are logically sited along the eastern edge of the Sierra Madre: "The mine needs men, but fears water. Flooding is the danger one fears most (as soon as one goes any distance below the surface), since the technical problem of getting rid of the water will not be properly solved before the generalized use of steam pumps in the nineteenth century. Miners found the best safeguard against flooding to be to operate in a subarid climate. They would have gone even farther into the desert if they had not run into other problems: lack of water, food for the men." What could one possibly wish to alter in such a text, or in many others which one could quote from the first volume, in which geography has so often inspired our author to such good effect? "As a recent area of colonization," he writes, "Andalusia (in the sixteenth century) continued to absorb the wealth of northern Spain, and to feed and flourish on it" (1:29). He adds further on, following the same line of thought: "Spain from 1500 to 1600, completing its internal colonization, is a Spain whose weight is shifting toward the south" (1:246). Or yet again, speaking this time of the colonization of the New World: "The first Spanish colonization imported wheat, which necessitated unwieldy and madly expensive communications lines. The second colonization ceased to rely to anything like the same extent on the import of supplies, because between 1520 and 1530, in going from the Greater Antilles toward the continental plateaus, the center of gravity of the Indies had moved from a manioc-producing area to a maize-producing area" (1:518–19). Mediocrity of manioc as support for a culture, magnificence of maize as support for a civilization! Has anyone else ever put it so well? There are particular phrases which I like too, such as "sailing, fossilized in its Mediterranean past." Or this bold phrase: "The deep ground swell of demographic growth since the end of the eleventh century had forced the Christian West toward intelligence and the finding of new solutions." Or this forceful and simple remark: "The great price revolution of the sixteenth century must be placed in its context, and one must not lose sight of the fact that the first phase, running from 1500 to 1550, did no more than fill in the trough of the long and dramatic wave which covered the second half of the fourteenth and all of the fifteenth centuries" (2:51).

If these finds were not buried in a welter of words, if Pierre Chaunu could force himself to write more briefly—which means performing afresh, on the first draft, that labor of elimination and choice which is more than just a question of form—then he would in fact be able to occupy the position in the forefront of young historians to which the force of his work and his passion for history already give him an obvious right.

## Notes

1. *Séville et l'Atlantique, 1550–1650* (Paris: S.E.V.P.E.N., 1959).
2. "Dynamique conjoncturelle et histoire sérielle," *Industrie*, 6 June 1960.
3. Huguette and Pierre Chaunu, *Séville et l'Atlantique*, first part: Statistical Section (1504–1650), 6 vols. (Paris: S.E.V.P.E.N., 1955–56), plus an atlas, *Construction graphique* (1957). Pierre Chaunu's thesis is contained in the second, so-called interpretative section of *Séville et l'Atlantique*, whence the initially rather confusing numbering of his volumes: VIII[1], VIII[2], VIII[2] *bis*.
4. "La Genèse du système capitaliste: La pratique des affaires et leur mentalité dans l'Espagne au XVIe siècle," *Annales d'histoire économique et sociale* (1936), pp. 334–54.
5. *Les Espinosa* (Paris: S.E.V.P.E.N., 1968).
6. "La Rochelle et l'Espagne: L'Expédition de Diego Ingenios à l'Île des Perles en 1528," *Revue d'histoire économique et sociale* vol. 37, no. 1 (1959).
7. Especially those made use of by H. Lapeyre in his thesis *Une Famille de marchands: Les Ruiz*, "Affaires et gens d'affaires" (Paris: S.E.V.P.E.N., 1955).

8. Used by Bennassar, "Facteurs et Sévillans au XVI$^e$ siècle," *Annales E.S.C.*, no. 1 (1957), p. 60; and by F. Braudel, "Réalités économiques et prises de conscience: Quelques témoignages sur le XVI$^e$ siècle," ibid., no. 4 (1959), p. 732.

9. *Il Commercio transatlantico di una compagnia fiorentina stabilita a Siviglia*, 1954.

10. Pierre Chaunu, *Les Philippines et le Pacifique des îles iberiques, XVI$^e$–XVIII$^e$siècles* (Paris: S.E.V.P.E.N., 1960).

11. *Revue historique* (1962), p. 327.

12. *Decade* = ten days (ed.).

13. *Il problema del trend secolare nelle fluttuazioni dei prezzi* (Pavia, 1935).

14. *Des Mouvements de longue durée Kondratieff* (Aix-en-Provence, 1959).

15. "Dette flottante et dette consolidée en Espagne de 1557 à 1600," *Annales E.S.C.* (1963), pp. 745–59.

# Is There a Geography
# of Biological Man?

Maximilien Sorre's fine book, *Les Bases biologiques de la géographie humaine: Essai d'une écologie de l'homme*[1]—to which Lucien Febvre has already directed the attention of our readers in an earlier volume of *Mélanges*—is not, as its title warns us from the beginning, a conclusive or definitive work of human geography. It is a work of cardinal importance, of commanding interest, and one which poses a good many problems, though not all the problems at once. It is an exploration, a limited research exposed in all its detail, a series of trial contacts. This explains its carefulness, its procedures, and the solutions it finds. Rather than an original, solid introduction, as concrete and down-to-earth as possible, to a treatise on general human geography, which is yet to be written, let us call this book an initial operation, the development of an opening theme.

The originality of this introduction derives from a systematic reduction of the problems of man to the level of his biology. Man, here, is not studied in his entirety, but under only one of his aspects, as a living machine, like the plants and animals. Man is treated, to use Maximilien Sorre's own words, as a "naked homeotherm." So man in his essence, living man, comprising a whole collection of beings from social man to *homo faber* to *homo sapiens*—not forgetting man as a self-styled ethnic reality—cannot be at the center of this book. Only one of man's aspects (only one of these zones) is considered: the elementary one of his biological entity, sensitive to heat and cold, to wind, to drought, to lack of sunlight, to insufficient air pressure, an entity unremittingly occupied with seeking and securing food, and finally constrained to defend himself, especially today when he has become aware of the danger, against the diseases which always and everywhere form an impressive retinue around him. Man as studied here is thus brought back to first principles, to the primary conditions of his existence, and is resited as such within the geographic conditions of the wide world.

The author's aim is clear: to narrow his study so as to make it deeper and more effective. Before tackling the complex problems of human geography, though always bearing them in mind as a distant goal, he wished, in order to tackle them better and perhaps even to overcome

*Mélanges d'histoire sociale* 6 (1944): 1–12.

some of their difficulty, to clarify that which, as far as the biological
reality of man is concerned, links him to place, and explains in advance a
considerable part of his geography. What an immense problem!
Although conducted with all the prudence one would expect from a
geographer of the French school, is not this a search for biological
determinism—or at least for the limits and undeniable constraints of
such a determinism?

It cannot be said that such research is entirely new. And yet in a way it
is—since it was never undertaken so systematically before Maximilien
Sorre. Biological man is no stranger, so much is clear. Nor is he a
newcomer in the field of geography, but he has never before been
introduced with this degree of particularity, this taste for scientific exactitude, this care for well-posed problems and clearly conceived inquiries,
conducted as experiments in which everything is subjected to prolonged
and objective description, notation, and explanation. In this lies not only
the originality but also the enormous value of this book.

The problems and object of the inquiry were borrowed, in the beginning, from the books and research of naturalists, biologists, and doctors.
But it was not enough for Maximilien Sorre to summarize the work of
others. He then sought to transpose it and to translate it, in a continuous
way, into geographical terms. This means that whenever possible the
problems were carried over to the map, so that they could be formulated
and studied in a new way, according to the perspectives and laws of
geography which are those of man's space. "Our inquiry," writes
Maximilien Sorre, "comes down in the end to the demarcation and explanation of a particular area of dispersal." I think this short, luminously
simple phrase, which could almost have been taken from some natu-
ralist's study, brings us right to the heart of the matter. It really is, in fact,
what the author hopes to achieve: to discuss the ecology of man as if he
were dealing with the ecology of the olive or the vine. But it is in fact man
he is dealing with, and that makes everything much more complicated.

Can there really be, in fact, an ecology of man as a biological entity, an
elementary basic human geography which could make its way under its
own steam, and which would provide us with the key to complex
problems—in the way that physiologists in earlier days tried to tackle the
problems of classical psychology from behind, and solve them like that?
Even more to the point, could this basic geography be isolated and
detached from its living context? Let us finally add that to be really
useful, it must not only be susceptible of definition to begin with, but also
permit clarification of the whole array of problems of human geography
in the end. Really, what would be the good of breaking down reality if we
run up against the very same obstacles in the end which troubled us in

the beginning? Such is the aim, and I would even go so far as to say, such is the major commitment of this book.

The work is divided into three parts. Biological man is studied successively within the framework of physical geography (book 1), of biogeography (book 2), and in the framework of a geography of infectious diseases (book 3).

These three books work fairly independently of one another, and do not by themselves, let us note, cover the whole of the subject. Maximilien Sorre has not in fact wished to give us an exhaustive study or an academic textbook, whatever the clarity or the didactic quality of his explanations might be. He wished to reach, by three different routes, the fundamental realities of a biological geography. Nothing more, but that is already a great deal. If I am not mistaken, this desire to open up some but not all possible routes often led him to simplify his inquiry, if not always in a particularly explicit manner.

Certainly his method is not a detailed exploration of the limits, the potential, the riches of all the problems posed by his vast subject, taken piece by piece. He deliberately restricts himself to the study of particular special areas, clearly distinct from neighboring zones which he mentions briefly or not at all. Let us add that before undertaking any of these voyages of exploration, Maximilien Sorre—and this is the cardinal characteristic of this book—explains to his reader all that he should know of the scientific conditions of the route to be followed. Which explains the long introductions, and the detailed reiteration of useful ideas whether geographical or not, which sometimes give the feeling of being slightly on the fringe of the inquiry proper, however necessary they may be. Thus we can distinguish three fairly well established operations on the part of the author, and it is these which, by their juxtaposition, give the book its particular character: first stage, simplification (or, let us say, choice of route); second stage, recapitulation of essential ideas; third stage, study of the chosen area. These remarks will better enable us to summarize a work which is fairly resistant, on its own, to any rather simplified inventory.

Here is book 1. It is not devoted to the relationships between man and the physical environment in general, but only to the relationship between man and climate. This is already a considerable simplification (first stage), however much climate must be, on all the evidence, the crucial factor in an ecology of man. Second stage: the biological subject thus stated will not be tackled immediately. Do we not first have to find out exactly what climate consists in?

For the past twenty years or so, climatologists and geographers have been working at renewing such a study of climate, and at getting some sense of its realities outside the theoretical average values which so often distort our understanding. Graphic methods of representation and synthesis have been perfected. So Maximilien Sorre has considered it only proper to summarize this important work in a preface stuffed with facts and useful insights. One can read with profit what he has to say about climographs or climograms, about microclimates and different kinds of weather. His aim is in some sense to come to grips with real climate in its original state, and to do this on the one hand by limiting himself to as narrowly defined a space as possible so as not to have to take account of any local variations, and on the other hand by retaining only one moment or moments—each a separate subject of study—in a climatic history which is in constant motion. It is only after having pinpointed these problems of physical geography that Maximilien Sorre is prepared to go on to study the influence of this *real* climate on biological man.

Here the most important question was to determine the thermal influence of climate—in fact to specify which are the most significant temperatures for the human organism, that homeothermic machine, creator or destroyer of its own internal temperature according to external conditions: creator up to about 61° F, destroyer above about 74° F, acted upon equally in one direction or another between these two temperatures which the author sees, after some discussion, as being the most interesting from a physiological point of view. We have thus a zone of cold beneath 61° F, and a zone of heat above 74° F, presenting us with all the desirable possibilities of referring to a map. Other climatic influences are studied in their turn: the action of atmospheric pressure (particularly as far as altitude is concerned), of light (with all the vast problems posed by skin pigmentation), of humidity in the air, of wind, of atmospheric electricity, and even of meteoropathological complexes as they are more or less understood by us today.

The end of the first book is the great, eminently geographical question of the growth and limits of the *oecumene*.[2] This is the occasion for clarification of the two great barriers which stand in the way of the "natural cosmopolitanism" of man—polar limits on the one hand, limits of altitude on the other. Within this oecumene the variations of human adaptation to climate have been and are very great, the most interesting today being perhaps the adaptations of the white man, since owing to his power and to his triumphs in colonization he can now be found the world over—although at his own physiological risk, not to mention any other possible dangers. Historians would do well to refer to the excellent passage (pp. 94–106) devoted to the acclimatization of the whites in the tropics. The works mentioned in the bibliography allow useful access to the abundant literature on this subject.

The same method is followed in book 2, which tackles the complex problems of biogeography, treated both directly and indirectly. Here, facing man and more or less at his disposal, lies the whole animal and vegetable kingdom: what relationships of strength, conflict, or mutual aid will be established, what geographical links will be tied between this world of living beings and the biology of man? This is how the central problem of the second book can be generally formulated—although it is not dealt with thus by the author, who confines himself in fact to the study of plants and animals cultivated and domesticated by man, to the exclusion of all others (43 animal species according to Geoffroy Saint-Hilaire, 600 plant species according to Vavilof, from a total of 2 million known animal species and of 600,000 plant species). This orientation of the inquiry enables us to have, in the form of a detailed and often highly original introduction, a prolonged study of these living companions of man. When and where did man link so many parallel lives to his own, and we would even ask if it were a question which could ever be given a viable answer, how did he do it? How far did domestication affect beings torn from a free existence? How did man propagate his "associates," for in contrast to natural associations, which have an inbuilt dynamic progression, these associations controlled by man need him to conquer "space" for them?[3] Finally, and it remains a considerable problem, what can threaten or safeguard this "human order," this whole body of man's associations that are constantly in combat with the innumerable forces of life, and therefore constantly being modified by them? These are some of the problems which Maximilien Sorre was able to present with the clarity and competence which informed his earlier work.

Similar explanations have necessarily taken the author a long way in the study of milieus of life in which there are constant battles, often overlapping each other, right to the heart of the geography of this vast struggle conducted on behalf of some life forms (the cotton plant, the vine) against some other life forms—in this case, those of parasites as numerous as they are tenacious. Admirable questions. But it is impossible to sum up the text of the book step by step; it is at this point far too dense. Can the parasitism of man's associations be presented and explained in a few lines, and the history of the great battles which have taken place against the scourges of his crops and against epizootic diseases (just think of what the phylloxera crisis meant for French life)? And what about the whole problem of this "human order" (see pp. 214–15), a biological problem when one considers plants and animals but a *social* one as soon as man is involved, whether one is speaking of his evolution or his present condition. For at this point one finds oneself back with social man—he could hardly be kept out indefinitely, could he? Social man, meaning the old agrarian communities which are so often invoked at the dawn of domestication and agrarian success, meaning the vast modern states and even the whole world, at the present level of speeds and terrible scourges to be fought. A world solidarity watches over, or attempts to watch over, the biological wealth of humanity, and Maximilien Sorre has been able to indicate its enormous importance.

During these long preliminary explanations, biological man has been lost to sight. He quickly resumes his position in the second part of this book, in a passage which I am more than prepared to consider as the most important, though not necessarily the most brilliant, but certainly the richest in insight and in original information of the whole work.

Man must feed himself to the detriment of the living world associated with his existence. What in fact could he ask of the free world of plants and animals and of the mineral world, compared with what his agriculture and his domestic animals supply him with? The study of these alimentary needs poses a variety of questions. Sorre copes with them first by drawing up a list of what the needs are, after which he enumerates the means by which man can satisfy them. This leads to a long passage on the commonest preparations of food (for there is no geography of feasting, which is the exception). It leads, too, to a whole paragraph on the very history of feeding. Having defined the area like this, Sorre then goes on to tackle the heart of the matter, the attempt at a geography of diet (pp. 264–90) which is so very detailed and rich in particular facts that it too plunges right into the problems of real man, and not just of biological man. It is man in all his complexity—in all the density of his history, in all his social cohesion, and with all the constraints imposed by custom and prejudice—that a geography of diet can and does rediscover. How could it be otherwise? For instance, what are those urban diets described on p. 273 et seq. if not a social fact? What is that propagation of the combination of wheat, the olive, and the vine from the Ancient East throughout the Mediterranean (p. 267 et seq.), if not a major fact of cultural history? Is there any need to say to what extent these pages on a geography of diet are original and new? We have to admit that customarily, alas, geographers pay all too little attention to what men eat. Nor, on this point, have contemporary historians in France much to boast about. Perhaps that is why Maximilien Sorre includes many recommendations for the former, which might equally apply to the latter.

Then comes the third and last book, the most brilliant of the entire work. The living environment helps man to live, but it is also in constant conflict with him and putting him constantly in danger. We must expect here the same simplifications, the same manner of approach and the same care as previously. The author chooses among man's antagonists; overlooking the largest, and indeed any which are visible to the naked eye, he reserves his attention for the smallest, which are also incidentally the most dangerous: from the ultraviruses, those inframicrobes, down to various bacteria, right down to certain microscopic fungi, beyond the uncertain frontiers between the animal and the vegetable kingdoms, such as the tribe of *mycobacteriaciae* (whose name is so revealing of our scientific ambiguity) which numbers among its members the carriers of tuberculosis, leprosy, and glanders.

So the illumination of this last book is concentrated on these tiny organisms. They will be presented to us, as they should be, as a whole, and then some of the outstanding ones will be chosen for closer study. In actual fact, these infectious diseases spread in different ways. Thus tuberculosis is directly transmissible from person to person. But as far as a good many other diseases are concerned, the pathogenic agent whether protozoan or fungus associates man with other living beings within its own life cycle, called *vectors* of the disease. Pathogenic agent, vector, man are associated in these *pathogenic complexes* which Maximilien Sorre has placed at the center of his study, for it is these diseases, so-called vector diseases, which he has chosen to study rather than any of the others.[4]

Pathogenic complex? For a specific example, the reader could refer to the case of sleeping sickness (p. 298 et seq.): this links a hematozoon, *Trypanasoma gambiense,* the infinitely small basic element, to the tsetse fly *(Glossina papalis)* and, finally, to man. It is up to the specialists to know how the hematozoon behaves, and at what stage of its development it can be found, and what its characteristics are in each of its different stages and changes of host. It is up to the geographer to map the area in which the disease is endemic. An even clearer example could be found in the even more classic case of the malaria complex (p. 301 et seq.). Here the infecting agents are also hematozoon, but of the genus *Plasmodium,* and the vector is provided by the anopheles mosquito, seventy species of which can be carriers of the paludism. Similar remarks can be made and similar mechanisms observed in the plague, recurrent spirochetosis, leishmaniosis (rickettsiosis), typhus, spotted fever, trachoma, and a quantity of other diseases to be found on the well-stocked shelves of the parasitologist. But there is no need to add to this already lengthy summary to show how, according to the proofs supplied by the author, pathogenic complexes mesh, superimpose upon, and overlap each other, and how they come to evolve. In an appendix to this study, there is a useful table of some of the important nosological groups (p. 231) and a planisphere (fig. 22) showing the localities of some of the major endemic diseases: yellow fever, plague, sleeping sickness, Chagas sickness, tularaemia, and so forth, with their respective areas of extension and their main centers of distribution. The table and map emphasize, if emphasis were needed, the exact nature of the research to which the author has confined himself.

What are the conditions of existence of these pathogenic complexes—what is their ecology, both as far as the agent and the vector are concerned—what too is the action of man upon them: these are yet more of the great questions which Maximilien Sorre exposes with his customary exactitude. Then, in the final chapter (once again, the most important), he sketches out the geography of these infectious diseases, sometimes with highly detailed examples—particularly where the excellent study of the nosology of the Mediterranean (p. 381 et seq.) is concerned.

The preceding analysis is not complete. How could it be with a book so new, so various (in at least three different ways), and so dense? We are no more in a position now to offer detailed criticism of it than we were earlier to analyze it properly step by step. Let us confine ourselves to noting our regret of the intentionally restricted nature of the investigations, while acknowledging that there must be some organizational constraints. If Maximilien Sorre wishes to satisfy us, he would at the very least have to double the large volume he has written.

Would he consider it for a second edition?

I am sorry, too, that in his study of the physical setting in book 1, Sorre restricted himself to questions about climate. Is there not, next to this "climatic complex," a geological complex (soil, subsoil, surface conformation) and also an aquatic complex, especially if one does not confine oneself solely to the direct action of physical factors on the ecology of man? Besides, is not geography often enough a study of relayed influences? Does not climate, for instance, have an effect on diet and disease? And should not the work have been more closely coordinated in order to follow these indirect, reflected influences, rather than being, as I think, rather too sharply divided into the three successive inquiries we have indicated?

I have similar regrets about book 2. Here a few paragraphs about undomesticated plants and animals would have been welcome, as well as on the proliferation of wild animals in the deserts and other regions of the oecumene insufficiently inhabited by men, of which E.-F. Gautier delighted to speak. And what of the forests, those half-free, half-subject associations, which have also been incorporated into the "human order" of which Maximilien Sorre speaks, trees (even in tropical countries) being, far more than one might expect, dependent upon and in the control of man? As far as the chapters devoted to diet are concerned, the author tells us all that is necessary, but was there not material here for a properly autonomous book? One in which it would have been possible to increase the number of individual, closely observed case studies over and above the general remarks imposed by the world scale, and to produce as interesting a document as the map of the foundations of cooking[5] in France, for instance, given at the first congress on French folklore?

Finally, as far as the last book is concerned, have we not been denied one aspect of the subject? Is there not too much emphasis on parasitic diseases, and on vector diseases among them? Were the problems not seen too exclusively through the perspective of Brumpt's textbook? In short, has not the medical matter considered been too restricted? Nothing, or hardly anything is said of tuberculosis,[6] or of cancer, or syphilis. Mentioned only incidentally is the pale treponema (pp. 194 and 308), which has had such a brilliant career since it arrived in Europe from America[7] in the closing years of the fifteenth century. Nor do I think that enough place was set aside for all the useful remarks made by medical geography (and in particular by German *Geomedizin*). All diseases (or at least a good many diseases) vary according to location. Some, like goiter, occupy such a precisely defined area that the area itself can serve to explain them. Cancer, in the Indies, appears in particular forms; in French Equatorial Africa, in regions rich in magnesium salt, cancer does not occur (Delbet's theory).[8] There are in England, and doubtless in the United States, highly dangerous forms of scarlatina and influenza with which we in France are unfamiliar; they even have particular forms of pneumonia, so serious incidentally that much of the work done on pneumococci has been carried out by Anglo-Saxons. Maximilien Sorre takes care to distinguish his inquiry from a straightforward medical work. But I do not see how one could exclude the questions which I have just suggested from a book of geography.

If one considers the book on historical grounds there are also obvious complaints to be made. The historical illumination of problems would have gained from being less summary and more systematic. With our self-centered point of view, this is something we must particularly regret. Thus, in the first book, there is no treatment of the problem posed by the variations of climate in the historical era. This problem, which so many studies are raising afresh, even receives a rather hasty negative solution[9] in the last pages of the book.

Historical remarks are not lacking in the chapters relating to diet,[10] but we do not really find them sufficiently numerous here either, or at least not sufficiently detailed. So many historical examples in these areas seem so revealing of the dietary realities![11] The same criticism can be made for infectious diseases, the more so since, in one example (paludism and history, pp. 392–400), Maximilien Sorre has shown us the interest of these returns to the past. In this area, one could quote hundreds of historical examples which could have found a place without difficulty in the exposé contained in book 3, and which then would have lent themselves to useful cartographic interpretations: for example, the plague epidemics within and without the Mediterranean—I am thinking particularly of the plague in Palermo during the years 1590–1600, on which we have a good many medical observations. I am also thinking of that epidemic of "English" influenza during the fifteenth and six-teenth centuries, which curiously halted at the Baltic countries in its expansion east, or else of the waves of Asian cholera across eastern and central Europe, to which the high German regions regularly re-mained immune. Historians, particularly today, attribute the great di-saster of 1812 as much to the ravages of typhus, endemic in Russia, as to the winter. Do these and many other problems hold no geographical interest?

But this fine book does not pose only internal problems and questions of detail. Its value lies in the whole. After having read it and reread it, we are necessarily led to a reconsideration of the entire science of geogra-phy itself. These are its external problems.

Geographers know well that geography (like history) is a very un-finished science, much more unfinished than the other social sciences. Perhaps even as unfinished as history itself, that other ancient adventure of the intellect. It too is not entirely sure, is indeed even less sure of its methods, and still less is it in possession of a perfectly recognized sphere. Has not scientific geography built itself up, like Maximilien Sorre's book itself, by lateral conquest (by juxtaposition), by making forays, not into a sort of no-man's-land but into neighboring and already occupied territory? Maximilien Sorre's work is very like this great con-quest of the riches of nature and of the natural sciences, made and consolidated by geography only yesterday. But, in actual fact, how many lateral conquests remain to be made today, if one wishes to enrich geog-raphy as much as possible, that is, if one wishes to "finish it off," or at least to define its objective? Among the conquests to be made are those of history and prehistory—not yet achieved, despite all that has already been done in this direction (and it is a great deal) in certain theses and studies of regional geography. Conquests to be finished off too, in-disputably, are those which will reduce to geographical order the acqui-sitions made by economists,[12] folklorists, ethnographers, ethnologists and, in a general way, sociologists.

So long as these reductions are not made, I doubt whether a viable human geography, sure of its methods, can really be possible. Before that is done, it would be useless to resume Jean Brunhes's undertaking, which seems so questionable today though so useful in its own time. And these reductions would neither be possible nor fruitful—and this only complicates the problem still further—until the day when the main lines, the coordinating axes of geography itself are established, axes and lines in relation to which any reduction must be carried out. To draw your substance from others is all very well, but only if you transform it into new riches.

I draw the line between myself and Maximilien Sorre when he considers himself, as many others do, certain of the geographical nature of his enterprise as soon as he arrives at considerations of space—a map, let us say, or as he would call it, an area of extension. I certainly do not deny that geography is above all else a description of the Earth,[13] nor that it is, in its own way, a science of space. Who would deny it anyway? But is this task its only one? Geography may perhaps find in space an end and a means, that is, a system of analysis and control. But it does perhaps also have a second aim, a second coordinate—which is to arrive not at man, but at men, at society.

Geography seems to me, in its totality, to be the spatial study of society, or to take my thoughts to their conclusion, the study of society through space.

In Albert Demangeon's last book one can find this exhortation: "Let us give up considering men as individuals."[14] We are given the same advice, on even more substantial grounds, in *La Terre et l'évolution humaine*, by Lucien Febvre, but was this not a book which appeared before its time (it was published in 1922)? Man is bound quite as much by the nets of his social context as he is by spacial ties—and there can be no geography that is not prepared to seize this social reality with both hands, in all its known variety, being at once a subject for history, for political economy, and for sociology. There can be no geography that does not seek to discern the major themes "of men against things"[15] and the constraints and creations of collective life, which can often be seen in the very soil.

It follows that any reduction of human events to a geographical order must, it seems to me, be at least twofold: reduction to space, yes, of course, but also a reduction to the social—that social reality which Maximilien Sorre's book is careful to avoid and skirt round, and into which it plunges only when forced by the indivisible living unity of his subject. One might even go so far as to say that Maximilien Sorre was in fact preoccupied with stopping himself from proceeding down this path: thus he stops short when dealing with artificial microclimates, which pose the sizeable problems of the geography of clothing and shelter.[16] Or again, when dealing with certain infectious diseases, which are hardly mentioned in his text. His wish was to confine himself as much as possible to an ecology of man as a biological individual; but frequently this ecology of the individual can be nothing more than an abstraction, too narrow and impassible a path, or at least an extremely difficult one.

Yet, I must admit that Maximilien Sorre himself was perfectly well aware of the restrictions which he was laying down, and that he devotes a word or two in his preface and in his conclusion to explaining them. One will even have no difficulty in finding there the very terms which we have been using in our criticism of his aims. Is it not he himself who writes: "It is yet oversimplifying matters to speak of man. It is of men which we must speak—those of the present . . . those of the past" (p. 10). It is he too who writes, on this same page of the preface: "The interaction of the social environment and the natural environment will thus be *evoked*. . . . There are influences which cannot be separated." *Evoked*, the word we have italicized reveals a good deal, evoked and not carefully studied, far from it. Of course, it is always unfair not to content oneself with the riches which a work like this bears in such profusion. Let us say nonetheless that it is to be regretted that this fine book was not conceived on an even larger scale and that it did not explain its overall architecture more insistently and clearly—an architecture one might have wished more clear-cut, above all more unified, better organized on the inside, perhaps simply more ambitious.

But this book will have its full effects just as is—however ill chosen, alas, the time of its publication. A rich future awaits it. The geographical sciences—and all the social sciences—will be able to profit from it, and historians will not be slow in consulting it. In the quality of its writing, which is reminiscent of Jules Sion, in its ability to evoke landscapes scattered throughout the world in a few brief touches, or to make the climate of some vanished age apprehensible, in the richness of its direct experience and of its scientific acquisitions, in its skill in aligning facts in series and in linking developments together, in placing an example or a detail from history or legend, through its constant referral to the classic shores of the Mediterranean, this book, in its spirit and through its humanism, is well in the brilliant tradition of the French school of geography. Intellectual life is a combat: this book is an example of a fine, a magnificent enterprise. In this very difficult and highly exciting field of human geography, no book of such quality has been offered to us for a long time, not since the *Principes de la géographie humaine* by Vidal de la Blache, not since *La Terre et l'évolution humaine* by Lucien Febvre.

Notes

1. Paris, Armand Colin, 1943. The subtitle seems debatable to me: can there be, simply, an ecology of man, as a living machine, studied outside his social realities? Though Sorre writes, it is true, *Essai d'une écologie*, and not just *Écologie.*—As for the title, the word biological can be taken in two ways: it means the biology of man, certainly, but it has also become the custom to speak of a biological geography, meaning the geography of plants or of animals. In book 1, we find one of these two meanings, the biology of man; in books 2 and 3, we find both meanings, but especially the second. In actual fact, though, are not the words "human geography" open to discussion as well?

2. As far as *écologie* ("ecology") and *oekoumène* ("oecumene") are concerned, I

have preserved the spelling used in the book. It is, of course, open to discussion.

3. Sorre, p. 188.

4. Is there, in Nicolle's hypothesis, a suppression of the *vector* in certain diseases, and a subsequent direct transmission of the germ from man to man, as is the case in tuberculosis? Cf. Sorre, p. 293.

5. [Since Fernand Braudel has seen fit to recall this work which I conceived and which was carried out under my direction (though it should properly have been called "An attempt at mapping the use of cooking fats in France," the foundations of cooking being something else again), it would in fact be good if it could be taken up again by reliable researchers. There is an army of them among geographers. It would also be appropriate if their investigations were historically as well as geographically oriented. The history of the substitution of one fat for another would be intensely interesting. (Lucien Febvre)].

6. Is it in the way that these diseases entail a study of the action of man on man, and thus a *social* study? Tuberculosis, disease of cities?

7. Maximilien Sorre does in fact come down in favor of its American origin, though without offering any proof. See p. 342: "Syphilis seems certainly to be of American origin, whatever may have sometimes been said."

8. We have not been able to obtain Pierre Delbet's book, *Politique préventive du cancer* (Paris: Denoël, 1944).

9. P. 394, on the subject of the destruction of the first Mayan empire and E. Huntington's theories. Can the climate change before our very eyes? It is, after all, a question which should be of interest to climatologists and geographers. Such a variation of climate would surely, if it existed, have an effect on all questions, on all the order and balance of life. Many authors would say that this is so, though under cover of proofs and authorities whose doubtfulness I am ready to concede. The most categorical among them would maintain that stretched over several centuries at a time there had been slow modulations of climate, moving through a succession of extremely feeble variations and by the gentlest of gradients from dry periods to periods which were less hot and above all more humid. Can the question be disposed of by a simple negative or by simply not asking the question at all? All the same, there are the examples of the glaciers in the Alps (and indeed in the Caucasus) advancing and retreating, and the diminishing of the polar ice cap which has been fairly clear along the Russian and Siberian borders since the end of the nineteenth century. The whole Soviet policy in the Arctic North is presented to us as being based on this hypothesis of a current increase in Arctic temperatures. Is that wrong? Historically speaking, dubious but disturbing examples proliferate. Was it only because of man that surface springs dried up in Sicily in the ninth century? Should one go along with Gaston Roupnel in believing the European disasters of the fourteenth and fifteenth centuries to be attributable to climatic disturbances? There is, at the end of the sixteenth century, if I may make so bold as to remark, a noticeable worsening of climatic conditions in lower Tuscany, producer of cereals, or there were at any rate devastating floods and harsher winters, winters so hard they sometimes froze the olive trees. Similarly, was Huntington right, in spite of everything, in maintaining that the first Mayan empire fell victim to a cataclysm, to a change in climate? Maximilien Sorre does not think so. "E. Huntington," he writes, "has

sought to explain this peculiarity [the disappearance of flourishing urban communities in the countries of Péten and Usumacinta] by the hypothesis of changes in climate entailing an alteration in mortality rates due to infectious diseases. *Such a hypothesis is not necessary.*" I have italicized the phrase, but is the fact certain? In an analogous case, in order to explain the recrudescence of malaria in Italy in the sixteenth century (and generally all over the Mediterranean at that time), Philipp Hiltebrandt assumes the arrival of a new and virulent strain of germ, that of a *Malaria tropicalis,* making its way rapidly (perhaps too rapidly) from America. But could one not, following Huntington's example, imagine, particularly where the seventeenth century is concerned, a modest increase in rainfall and atmospheric humidity, and a consequent rise, in the low-lying countries of the Mediterranean, of any stagnant waters, and thus an increase in habitats suitable for the anopheles mosquito? All the while bearing other possible explanations in mind: notably the increase in population, and the growth of land "improvement" schemes, which led (especially in the beginning, but later too if they were not carried through properly) to a worsening of the malaria situation, like any other disturbance of the soil in these unhealthy regions? Many other small facts could be quoted, though they tend to be both obscure and questionable: they do nothing to solve the problem when facing the opinion of geographers committed to the immutability of climates during historical ages. It is not beyond question, but I nonetheless feel that such facts pose the problem more clearly. Cf. on this subject the careful notes made by d'E. de Martonne in *La France* (*Géographie universelle,* 1943), Part 1, p. 313: "The scholar's mind turns rather toward the notion of periodicity." And, p. 314: "A periodicity of around thirty years seems not unlikely."

10. Note the paragraph devoted to the vestiges of primitive diets, p. 239, and the note, p. 240, on the ancient primacy of boiled cereals and especially of millet: "One might even speak . . . of an age of millet."

11. It is a pity no mention was made of the consequences deriving from some of the great dietary revolutions which have taken place in modern Europe. There is a summary table of these revolutions in Kulischer's classic textbook on economic history. For certain social aspects (respecting coffee, tea, and beer) see Henri Brunschwig, *La Crise de l'état prussien à la fin du XVIIIᵉ siècle et la genèse de la mentalité romantique.* Contemporary French historians are in general neglectful of the history of diet, though it may prove, in the final analysis, quite as interesting as the system of law or any of the great classic questions. Is there a history of French cooking, or rather, of all the different kinds of French cooking? or is there, for instance, a history of oil or of butter—such as that enacted in the Mediterranean in the sixteenth century—a history of rancid butter which was then transported by ship from Bône to Algiers, from Djerba to Alexandria, and perhaps even as far as Constantinople? Are many historians familiar with the difficulties of biscuit manufacture, in the Mediterranean of round ships and galleys, as a condition of the most glorious armadas? No wheat, no fleet, one could almost say. Or indeed how many are familiar, as a random choice, with W. Sombart's revelatory note on the rise of the manufacture of preserves in the fifteenth and sixteenth centuries, or with the northern European and Atlantic history of salt beef which H. Hauser liked to expound during his lectures?

12. Cf. on this point François Perroux's note: "It [geography] defines the terms which it employs only rarely and to little effect" (*Cours d'économie politique,* 1st year, p. 137).

13. André Cholley, *Guide de l'étudiant en géographie* (Paris: Presses Universitaires, 1943), p. 9. But for a "homeocentric" description, see p. 121.

14. Albert Demangeon, *Problèmes,* p. 28.

15. In Maurice Halbwachs's phrase.

16. Pp. 37–38. It is highly characteristic of Maximilien Sorre that he should have reserved (cf. p. 10) for another book, a book yet to be published, a study of the urban climatic environment.

# On a Concept
# of Social History

I am late in discussing Otto Brunner's complicated, alert, and ambiguous book: *Neue Wege der Sozialgeschichte,*[1] which was published in 1956 but has only just reached *Annales* (after a series of rather fortuitous misadventures). Historians who are readers of general reviews will at any rate be familiar with two of the ten articles brought together in this volume, having read and appreciated them when they first appeared: one, on the very problem of any sort of European social history, was published in the *Historische Zeitschrift*[2] in 1954, and the other in the *Vierteljahrschrift für Sozial- und Wirtschaftgeschichte* in the same year (on the bourgeoisie in Europe and Russia).[3] By themselves, they already posed certain problems which this book takes up again, vast and fairly complex problems which finish by calling the entire methodology and even the very meaning of the historical sciences into question. One must say that it will not be easy to give an exact summary of this book which, despite its fundamental unity, is made up of different materials, of a series of separate studies, nine, or even ten of them, since chapter 6 is itself composed of two studies on the relationships between the bourgeoisie and the aristocracy in Vienna and Lower Austria (during the Middle Ages). Picture to yourself journeys offering successive points of view, the succession of which, by its very speed, does not appear to have any real logic until one has had time to think about it. Nor, unfortunately, is one's reading made any easier by the numerous references placed at the very back of the volume: you refer to the note, lose your place, and have to start all over again. It is true, however, that all this coming and going is accompanied by great delight.

Otto Brunner owes nothing to *Annales,* and the assumptions of his reasoning or his experience, his proofs, and his conclusion are not ours. This is what gives them their unique importance for us. But it entails a great effort on our part to understand and, here and there, to grasp fully and penetrate the subtleties of his language. Here in any case is a historian who speaks aloud of the present disruption of history, and strong in the power of his profession and in the help of neighboring sciences, attempts to dominate the disturbed times with which we are confronted. As he has need to rely on his peers, an almost complete

*Annales E.S.C.,* no. 2 (April–June 1959), Débats et combats, pp. 308–19.

procession of German historians forms around him almost from the start, historians both of yesterday and of today. Even if Otto Brunner does not have their complete assent—and that is more than likely—he presents himself in their company, and that is an added attraction of his book. We can find here some of our old reading companions: Werner Sombart, Max Weber, Georg von Bulow who only yesterday counted the young Marc Bloch among his listeners, Meinecke whose thought has remained unjustly foreign, or at least substantially so, to our own historiography, Heinrich Mitteis, author of some splendid works on medieval institutions, Otto Hintze who would be granted the major position he deserves among us had his complete works not been published during the most inauspicious years of 1941 and 1942, Thomas Mayer, and many others. Not less numerous in these notes and references are the names of the new specialists in the history of philosophy, of sociologists, of economists and, finally, of historians: Gerhard Ritter, Werner Conze, Wilhelm Abel, Herbert Hassinger.[4]

Otto Brunner thus lays open to us with liberality, I was going to say in addition, a journey through the old and new highways of German historiography. But that makes it only the more difficult, in the end, to distinguish the true aspect of this nimble, enthusiastic thinker who fears neither contradiction nor an unfinished argument. It is true that the reader gradually grows accustomed to his procedure, to his feints, his enormous abridgments, and his frequently excellent explanations. As a medievalist our author finds himself placed at just the right juncture, at that of the destiny of the West. But the opportunity is always too good for him to be able to resist going beyond the conventional limits of the European Middle Ages, be it toward antiquity, or toward full modernity. "From Plato," he writes, "to Joachim of Floris and Bossuet," or equally, "from Homer to Fénélon." But do we at *Annales* have any right to complain of these great strides and not to be indulgent with regard to a historian who speaks of Europe without lingering over events ("the skeleton of history," as one of our shortsighted pedagogues once said), without lingering over individuals, or at least presenting them in serried ranks, in groups, as delegates of social or cultural wholes? We follow him, of course. But, let us reiterate, nothing in all this ensures that once one emerges from the essays, which one has to read and reread one by one, one can really come to grips at the end of the day with Otto Brunner's true thought, confronting problems which are not precisely our own, the prey of memories and experiences which we have not shared. I am not, however, so indifferent a reader that I did not pause once or twice over some reflection or other which, if prolonged, would have led us straight to the present. But I think it is futile to dwell on this sort of interpretation, difficult as it is, and mistaken as it well may be. Futile too to refer, in order to make things out more clearly (except for such reference as I shall cite later on) to the dense, solid body of work of our author. I propose to examine only this single, intelligent, subtle book, which has come rather tardily to call upon us, and to see what it has to bring exclusively on the level of scientific speculation.

## Western Originality (11th to 18th Century) Reduced to a "Model"

If I am not mistaken his first aim is to suggest to us, and to have us accept, a structural and conservative social history as opposed to a liberal, flexible, evolutionist sort of history. In practical terms we are offered a certain *particularized model* of *European social history* in the waters of the *longue durée*, from the eleventh to the eighteenth century. This model brings out the continuities, the immobilities, the structures. It abandons the event, underestimates the conjuncture, prefers the qualitative to the quantitative, and unfortunately is not for a moment interested in Ernest Labrousse's mathematical approach. The undertaking (confined to the medieval context) fits nonetheless quite easily into a social history as I conceive it and which has all the characteristics and dimensions of a global history.

The substantives and adjectives by which I thus attempt to circumscribe Otto Brunner's thought clearly only half define it, and may even to some extent distort it. Only the words I have italicized in the preceding paragraph can be found in Brunner's argument in the sense in which we commonly use them. In actual fact it is clearly a question, if I may return to the phrase for a moment, of a social *model*. But other continuities get added to the argument as it proceeds. Otto Brunner is happy to point out obvious continuities of ideas. His book is interlaced with their lines, constantly cutting across time. He also takes great delight in seeking out whatever the most original aspect of the present could contain of the distant past. Thus he sees the very old medieval concept of soul and body (though not in the sense of living organism which biology was later to give it) as being at the heart of the thought and vocabulary of Oswald Spengler, or suspects the physiocrats or even Karl Marx himself of taking up on their own account some idea or other from old medieval "oeconomia."

But it is above all society which is the object here of serious "modeling," in the specific field of the West between the eleventh and the eighteenth century. Apart from some dead ends here, some stagnations there, or particular exceptions elsewhere which must necessarily prove anomalous, Western society presents the same sort of framework, the same ruling factors everywhere: specifically the town with its bourgeoisie, its craftsmen, and its charters; the countryside with its entrenched peasantry (there were obviously the other sort too, fired by adventure, but they do nothing to hinder the existence of the former, strong in their rights) and their lords, both groups more preoccupied with the household than with profit and loss and economics, in the sense with which our modern society invests it. For economics began as, and was for many centuries, economy, care and consideration of the house (the "Rustic House," as Charles Estienne and Jean Liébaut called it, even as late as the sixteenth century): taking care of the servants or slaves, educating the children, deciding what should be cultivated, and in general being little bothered by the urban market and its "chrematistic" concerns. The old books on *oeconomia* may not overlook the market completely, but it is not at the heart of the subsistence economy which they describe. Their horizon is the "house," the "whole house." So we need not be surprised that they should include moral homilies, a summary of practical medicine, and sometimes even a collection of recipes. German historians and economists have long noted the riches of this *Hausvaterliteratur*.[5]

Within the model, these ruling components have their own autonomy, their own color, their individual meaning. But they work harmoniously together. They are crystals with clear-cut facets, through which passes a common light.

The different compartments communicate with each other: the peasant goes to town (with their fragile populations, the cities, even the stable ones, have a constant need for men). Here is a newcomer; later his son may become a craftsman; then one day the craftsman may become a merchant, the merchant a lord. For anything can and does happen: it is only a question of patience, of the care of generations, of a lucky chance. Son of peasants and himself a country weaver, Hans Fugger, the founder of the great family, arrived in Augsburg in 1367. Sometimes, on the contrary, the lords wish to become bourgeois. One cannot claim that such links were common, but such as they were they served to relax and break down certain tensions, and to maintain a long-standing balance. Yet it is a balance which is constantly threatened. If the exchanges accelerate, the initial crystals may in the end become altered. This is what is suggested by the example of Vienna (chap. 6), to which Otto Brunner devotes what are in my opinion the best pages of his book. It is true that the case is in fact a marginal one, that the "model" does not float too easily on these particular waters, that here the prince intervenes early in the dynamic processes of exchange. He facilitates the passages of the bourgeoisie into a nobility which bit by bit loses its virtue, its roots, and its territorial reality. In Austria and elsewhere, the state could perhaps be said to turn its own wheel in the millrace of these social ascents. And while during the Middle Ages in the West, the political organization merged into the social organization and was indistinguishable from it (the lord being both lord and landowner), gradually, with the growth of the modern state, the distinction, the division is made: state on one side, economic society on the other. And the old model or, if you prefer, the *ancien régime*, breaks down. For whoever is determined to pinpoint this breakdown chronologically, the night of 4 August 1789 offers a pretty spectacular watershed. In one night feudal rights, village communities, urban charters, were all abolished. This of course is only a manner of speech; but all the same, suddenly the French Revolution appears as the culprit. And next to it in the dock, so to speak, shading into it but not to be substituted for it, stands that other gloomy figure, the Industrial Revolution.

That in any case was the end of one of the great phases of Western history, whose beginnings had their origins seven centuries earlier, between 1000 and 1100. During that far-off time, the West underwent an increase in strength and a long-drawn-out demographic increase (which soon set off colonization east of the Elbe and a sizeable emigration from France toward the Iberian peninsula). Henri Pirenne, and a good many historians after him, see the urban renewal which followed as a consequence of the general revival of trade. Yet there was also a general increase in Western farming; the land produced more abundant food and more men than previously—men and food without which the urban expansion, though doubtless stimulated by commerce, could never have taken place. It led to a relatively demographically dense European peasantry who, in the northern countries, thanks to the triennial rotation of crops, was able to achieve increased production from the fields. The peasant, from now on entirely taken up by intense rural labor, becomes a peasant full time. It was then up to the lord to assure his means of defense, and also confiscate it.

Rural prosperity and urban prosperity supported each other from the beginning. They formed the foundations of the European economic order, which was without a doubt a new economic order and one which was destined to last. During the previous centuries, the trade conducted by traveling merchants had brought rare and precious goods—rich cloths, spices, slaves—or basic necessities like salt and wheat. The only thing that counted then, or almost the only thing, was the custom of princes and rich men. But from the eleventh century onward, the proportion of manufactured goods being traded increased. Europe established itself as an exporter of textiles; the glory of Champagne fairs and of the Mediterranean trade grew and established itself. The merchant put down roots. The towns grew, forming archipelagos, pyramids, each coming to a head at a city, a mercantile center of greater importance. And all this in symbiosis with a peasant and seigneurial world which formed the permanent base, the nutritious soil for these successes.

This scheme obviously needs to be touched up and put in context. But this is something with which Otto Brunner is not overly concerned. His case is long and often repetitious, but his conclusions are always brief and always the same. They aim for the general. They take on a slight amount of coloring only when he is dealing with the second "pole" of his model, the peasants, lords, aristocracy, and in general that *Adelswelt* to which he is secretly drawn. He is only too ready to magnify the role and importance of this world, presenting it as a series of mutual responsibilities, with a peasantry at the base which at the very worst maintains a certain degree of freedom and autonomy. He places this *Adelswelt* at the heart of a civilization of *longue durée*, lasting right up to the physiocrats, an aristocratic civilization steeped in a spirit of true and effective freedom, a civilization which was not only coarse and violent in some aspects, but also delicate and full of obvious virtues—as the libraries of the aristocracy (in Austria and elsewhere) bear witness from the fifteenth century onward. The bourgeoisie of the towns have a share in this civilization. Who would not see in this a certain weighting of the evidence, even a reversal of the facts? But a thesis is a thesis.

## The West and Russia

The reader will see that my aim is to present rather than to discuss these authoritarian abridgments, and to try to ascertain the inspiration and the will of the man behind these theses rather than their justification. So let us for the moment just accept these sweeping explanations covering the eleventh to the eighteenth century.

These centuries certainly have something in common. For myself, I would rather have said the thirteenth to the eighteenth century, but what does it matter! I would concede fairly readily that there is a certain unity, a certain "horizontality" of time over a long period, from 1000 to 1800. Gino Luzzatto and Armando Sapori have both said so, each in his own way, by asserting the "modernity" of the thirteenth and fourteenth centuries. Armando Sapori, thirteenth century "man," refuses to let himself be dazzled by the Renaissance. Henri Hauser, sixteenth century "man," proclaimed its obvious modernity, particularly by comparison with the eighteenth century. But these gambits are neither familiar to Otto Brunner, nor indispensable to his thesis or even to his method of argument. His own approach is at once more complicated, more arbitrary, and a good deal wider, I was about to say a good deal more dangerous. It consists in a fairly particular dialectic: to see in succeeding historical landscapes what it is that unifies them, and then what it is that makes them different. Which means that, according to the whim of the demonstrator, the deck of cards is either open, showing every different suit and number, or else it is shut, the cards all gathered together into a single pack in the player's hand. Otto Brunner, in order to assert the global originality of the West, has had to shut a deck having quite a number of cards. For his model is valid above all for the lands and towns of Germany. Would it work equally well for the lands and towns of Italy or Spain? Here and there correspondences can be made to fit, not without a certain amount of deck-stacking. I can imagine in advance that Armando Sapori would be sure to react against this vision of a monotonous West, just as he reacted earlier against the overall view which Werner Sombart put forward of the medieval economy. Still more to the point, what historian would accept the existence of this long period of horizontality throughout a Middle Ages cleft by difficulties and by social and economic crises? The modern state has its beginnings in the fifteenth and even more in the sixteenth century, and the break, the bursting-forth of the "state-society" does not in fact wait until the French Revolution. The same with the market economy, which had penetrated deeply into Western society before the eighteenth century was over. It needs constant ingenuity to circumvent or disguise these difficulties.

The ingenuity of our colleague lies in making us accept from the outset that his initial simplification is in fact a sensitive recognition of the fundamental, unique originality of the West, and then immediately to transfer the discussion outside the West so as to demonstrate, with drums beating and flags flying, the originality of Europe with regard to whatever is not Europe. Who could believe in the unity of the great Weberian abstraction (Max Weber, of course)—the zone of the so-called oriental city which holds in its net all Islam, India, and China? Or that Max Weber really carried his famous urban sociology right to the heart of the problem?

But let us leave these half-formulated criticisms. Carried thus to the eastern frontiers of Europe, we readers are called upon to measure the differences between the Western system and the Russian (that is, the oriental) system. The demonstration immediately denies the possibility of what some historians have claimed, namely that Europe, or the West if you prefer, begins again, reorganizing its destiny according to the Russian setting with a certain distinctive coloring, some lagging behind, and some distortion due to the hostility of the forests and swamps and the thinness of the population. To which one could also add the enormous cataclysm of the Mongol invasion.

Otto Brunner, contrary to some Russian historians but supported by others, maintains that there was a lagging behind even before this cataclysm and that, even more significantly, there was an intrinsic difference between the social structures of the two worlds. Novgorod was not an enclosed city on the Western pattern, but an "ancient" city open to the surrounding countryside and integrated into its life. Russian cities were certainly of considerable size and population, but they were few and distant from each other: Kiev, for instance, or Moscow. They did not rely on a pyramid or reservoir of smaller towns, as was the case in Europe. Besides, they would not or could not keep a monopoly of crafts to themselves: side by side with an urban industry of wretched craftsmen thrived a lively, polyvalent peasant industry outside urban control. The Russian winter freed an abundance of manpower in the villages during several long months, and it was impossible to try and compete with this. As for the peasants, they had been poorly rooted for a long time. Their cultivations remained itinerant. They set themselves up to the detriment of the forests, but it was not a case, as in the West, of subjugating this virgin land once and for all, establishing lasting plowland and tearing out the stumps of the trees. Rather as in America opened up to the European peasant, waste of territory was the rule. In addition the artisan was no more entirely free in his movements than the peasant. Final characteristic: right up to the time of Peter the Great commerce in Russia was concerned with natural products, salt, furs, honey, and with luxury goods and slaves. It was itinerant and caravan-based. These archaic characteristics complete the picture. Europe, on the contrary, had a semifree peasantry, towns which were independent or nearly so, and an active, advanced mercantile capitalism with its merchants settled in one place. Western towns meant craft industry and trade outside state control, like so many free little islands ready for short or long distance capitalism. This is one of the urban innovations, in Max Weber's sense, of medieval Europe: neither the "ancient" city nor the "oriental" city knew anything of such a division, or rather such a distinction, between town and country, industry and agriculture—in a word, of this super-charge of the urban.

Is this demonstration sufficient to illuminate the "Russian enigma" of which Gerhard Ritter was speaking again only recently? [6] Or the be-wilderment of the German observer faced with this immense landscape? The reader must decide. For myself, I wonder what would be the out-come of a parallel drawn like Otto Brunner's, but this time between Europe and the colonial America of the Iberians (from the sixteenth to the eighteenth century). In the New World, at the end of the fifteenth century, a new Europe more or less successfully took root and began again. It began again with the cities. These cities either preceded the slow construction of the countryside (Rio de la Plata), or else relied on an Indian peasantry. Wherever they were, these towns were open to the countryside; they were "ancient" cities functioning according to ancient formulas and dominated by the great landowners—the *homens bons* of the municipal councils in Brazil, or the great *hacendados* of the Spanish *cabildos* (magistracies). Within the whole, two or three modern cities at the very most, large, extremely isolated "Russian-style" cities were established, in viceregal Mexico, Recife during and after the Dutch, Bahia with its sugar exporters, Potosi. Add to this picture trade conducted by mule train, and what have we got? Europe before the eleventh century? Or Russia before Peter the Great?

## What Is Social History?

These questions and half-criticisms do not really deal with more than a half or a third of this energetic book. Otto Brunner not only intends to enclose the whole irreducible originality of the Middle Ages in the West, to sing its praises, tell of its greatness, and indeed to almost assert its "miraculous" nature. Unless I am very much mistaken, he also intends to make use of the illumination shed by this great spectacle in order to turn (with more ingenuity than real forcefulness or clarity) toward the present—second encircling operation—and toward the very structures of the historian's profession, third and final operation including and transcending all preceding ones.

In actual fact, the Middle Ages in the West before the eighteenth century are separated from us by a variety of obstacles. Belonging to an age more or less cut off from the distant roots of Europe by all the mutations and discontinuities of the eighteenth and nineteenth centuries, how can we historians and men of the twentieth century easily rediscover the realities of a social history of Europe between the eleventh and the eighteenth centuries? The very words we use, especially economy, but society too, and even state, tend to mislead us. Behold us cut off in spirit from our object, from that distant landscape, by a smoke-screen in which everything merges: ideologies (which have their birth in the eighteenth century), those ideas charged both with truth and with illusion; old explanations; the very attempts being made by the new social sciences. In a chapter which I only partially understand despite having read and reread it, we are put on our guard against the anachronistic, against the obvious perils of a past-present dialogue, and are placed moreover face to face with the heavy responsibilities of history. But is this not in fact a hunt for ideologies in the manner of Karl Mannheim? Are we not being invited to a hunt for witches and will-o'-the-wisps? Are ideologies running out of steam, or not? Maybe. But on either side of their curtain, what judgments, what comparisons the author commits himself to—such as no foreign reader could hope to catch immediately. Who is being judged, who condemned or, if you prefer, whom are we being directed to love? For this obvious eulogy of the old social order, as lying outside the profit and tyrannies of the state or ideological distortions, must have a meaning. A *laudator temporis acti* is never without ulterior motives relating to the present.

These uncertainties constantly create difficulties in advance and undermine our ability to formulate an answer to the fundamental question which our colleague has asked, about the destiny and justification of history. But let us nonetheless carry on as if we were sure of the road ahead.

Right from the very beginning, just like Henri Berr in 1900 at the beginning of the *Revue de synthèse*, Otto Brunner attempts to elevate himself above the compartmentalization of particular histories. They are numerous, one knows: the history of law, of institutions, the history of philosophy, of ideas, of literature, of science, the history of art, religious history, the history of daily life, economic history. One knows equally well (cf. Heinrich Freyer) that they each have their own rhythm, their own rate of respiration, their own chronological dimensions. Now these individual sectors have to be mastered, to be dislocated. Thus the empire of *Kulturgeschichte* is heteroclite, exaggerated. In the same way, although it is never clearly stated, economic history, which is simply one sector, cannot inflate itself to the dimensions of an entire history without excess or scandal.

In short, history allows only of two general planes: on the one hand, the political plane, on the other, the social plane. As in descriptive geometry, the entire body must be projected onto one plane or the other. It is, of course, myself who suggests such a debatable image. Otto Brunner would say more precisely that social history for him is not a specialty *(Fach)*, a particular sector *(Sondergebiet)*, "but a way of considering one aspect of man and of groups of men in their communal life, in their social regimentation *(Vergesellschaftung)*." As for political history, he used to claim (in 1936) that everything came under that heading: "Any purely historical problematic," he wrote then, "derives from political history. . . . From this point of view, all history is, in the strict sense of the word, political history."[7] Today he is of a quite different opinion, not that I would reproach him for it—quite the contrary. In substance, what he says is that history always has man as its object, but that there are two ways of considering him: first of all in the mirror of social history, "and then the internal construction, the structure of social relationships, will be in the foreground"; or, the second possibility, as reflected in political history in the Aristotelian sense, and then the object to be seized would be political action, "men's self-determination." I repeat, two planes between which everything is, or can be, divided. It is impossible for the historian to confuse them or, which comes to the same thing, to present them both simultaneously.

It would be important to follow page by page the allusive sketch of a history brought back to the political arena, such as is presented in this book, which is so ready to assert and never to contradict, and is thus almost entirely free of the negatives which would serve as reference points: the history of man as a "political man" is, if I have understood properly, in some measure the history of his movements, his actions, his free choice, and even sometimes a *Machtpolitik,* and thus it tends often enough toward traditional history. On the other wing of the diptych, to the extent that social history profits by immobility and the *longue durée,* we find all the heavy thickness of social reality, resistant to all inclemency, to crises and sudden shocks; it is strong in its slowness and its powerful inertia. Economic history, thrusting forward, wears itself out trying to stir this great mass and to pierce its heavy armor.

Besides, for the Middle Ages, let us repeat, there is but one history, social history. It has devoured and assimilated everything; the state has broken down into the various bodies of which we have already spoken: cities, seigneuries, village communities. The market economy may well have its crises and even its convulsions, but the *oeconomia* simply turns in on itself. It is sheltered from small storms. The centuries belong to it. The state and the economy come later.

All I have sought to do throughout this article is to clarify for myself and for my French readers a way of thinking which is almost entirely unfamiliar to us. Contact has so long been lost between French and German historians that often all that is needed is for a word to be misunderstood, an assertion to be too hastily made, for the discussion to lose all meaning. Both parties would surely gain from an exchange of ideas which have become to such an extent foreign to each other. So I have as far as possible forbidden myself the mental attitude of a critic, leaving the initiative in the debate to Otto Brunner.

At the end of this confrontation, have I been convinced? That is another question. I am torn between a certain sympathy and some fairly lively misgivings. In truth, a social history of the *longue durée* could hardly avoid seducing me, even though it seems to me to be only *a* social history among many others, those which move slowly, those which are permanent, those which are inert, those concerned with structures, and over and above these relatively still waters we must also place the not inconsiderable figure of the conjuncture. Nor, of course, is there anything to be said against a political history which, whether "Aristotelian" or not, rejoins the traditional history of the last century. But it seems to me that there is everything to be said against Otto Brunner's authoritarian dichotomy, the duality in which he encloses history. Whatever the reasons or the ulterior motives which dictate his choice—and they remain unclear for the French reader—I cannot subscribe to it.

At the risk of being taxed with an unrepentant liberalism, I would claim on the contrary that all doors seem to me good when crossing the multiple threshold of history. Unfortunately, none of us can know them all. The historian first opens the door with which he is most familiar. But if he seeks to see as far as possible, he must necessarily find himself knocking at another door, and then another. Each time a new or slightly different landscape will be under examination, and there is no historian worthy of the name who has not been able to juxtapose some of them: social and cultural landscapes, cultural and political landscapes, economic and political landscapes, and so on. But history gathers them all together; it is the sum total of all these neighbors, of these joint ownerships, of this endless interaction.

So Otto Brunner's two-dimensional geometry could not satisfy me. For me, history can be conceived only in $n$ dimensions. This generosity is indispensable: it does not dismiss onto a lower plane, that is, outside the explanatory area, the cultural insight or the materialist dialectic, or any other analysis. Its fundamental definition is of a concrete, *pluridimensional* history, as Georges Gurvitch would say. Beyond this multiplicity, needless to say, each individual remains free—some even feel called upon to assert the unity of history, without which our job would be unthinkable or would at least lose some of its dearest ambitions. Life is multiple, but it is also one.

Notes

1. *Neue Wege der Sozialgeschichte: Vorträge und Aufsätze* (Göttingen: Vandenhoek und Ruprecht, 1956).
2. Vol. 177 (1954), p. 469 *et seq.*
3. Vol. 40 (1954), p. 1 *et seq.*
4. This quotation (working in the very same direction as Max Weber's thought) which, for two or three reasons I find so enchanting, is from Heinrich Freyer: "The age of enlightenment [*Aufklärung*] is not only the historical phenomenon of limited bearing which we commonly intend by this expression, but also a fundamental tendency, we might even go so far as to say, above all, a trend of European history."
5. Cf. Gertrud Schröder-Lembke, "Die Hausvaterliteratur als agrargeschichtliche Quell," *Zeitschrift für Agrargeschichte und Agrarsoziologie* (1953).
6. *Lebendige Vergangenheit* (Munich: Oldenbourg, 1958), "Das Rätsel Russland," p. 213 *et seq.*
7. Otto Brunner, "Zum Problem der Sozial- und Wirtschaftsgeschichte," in *Zeitschrift für Nationalökonomie* 7 (1936): 677.

# Demography and the Scope of the Human Sciences

The history which we would defend in this review is one which wishes to remain open to the different human sciences; and today it is the totality of these sciences which concerns us even more than history itself. I believe it is useful to state this again at the beginning of this account, which aims to examine the assumptions and the essential orientation of demographic studies by considering them from the point of view of the whole, and not of history alone.

But be assured: I do not intend, because of this bias, to undertake the facile condemnation of a certain *demographism*, an imperialistic, unilateral, often hasty explanation of social reality. Every science, especially if it is young, or rejuvenated which comes to the same thing, attempts to take up the whole of social organization and to explain it all by itself. There has been and there still is an *economism*, a *geographism*, a *sociologism*, a *historicism;* all fairly naïf imperialisms whose pretensions are nonetheless natural, and even necessary; at a certain time, at any rate, this aggressiveness has had its advantages. But perhaps today it might be time to call a halt to it.

Without a doubt, it is the term *auxiliary science* which most embarrasses or rankles with the young social sciences. But to my mind all the human sciences without exception are each auxiliary the one to the other in turn, and it is only right that each of them domesticate all the others to its own use (for each of them has and must have its own personal point of view, although this should not be its only point of view). So there is no question of a hierarchy established once and for all, and if I on my part, from my own particular egotistical point of view, have no hesitation in ranging demography among the sciences auxiliary to history, I also hope that demography considers history as one of its auxiliary sciences. The crucial thing is for all these explanations of the whole to harmonize and finish together. Or at least let them suggest a meeting place.

It is on this level that I would wish to pitch the present dialogue with our colleagues and neighbors the demographers, and not at the level of methodological discussions, *pace* Louis Henry and René Baehrel. I do not for an instant deny the intrinsic value of methods, and only partially share the anger which Lucien Febvre[1] feels at the interminable squab-

*Annales E.S.C.*, no. 3 (May–June 1960), Chronique des sciences sociales, pp. 493–523.

bles which they ordinarily promote. All the same, "at the top" it is not only the methods and the means which matter, but the results, and even more the interpretation, the application of the results. In a word, that by which one can correct, should the need arise, more than one error due to method.

It is thus the general orientation of the human sciences which will be in question in this present account. Such an aim obliges me to choose my interlocutors, and, on a practical level, to come more than half out of the narrow and insufficient current bibliography. I do not believe that the backward glances that this point of view imposes on me are entirely without their uses. It is never too late to speak of important works.

## Ernst Wagemann's Thresholds

Despite the fact that it is neither entirely fair nor entirely convenient (to my knowledge, none of our critical reviews has attempted it), let us first of all present the authoritarian and irritating works of Ernst Wagemann. As we confront them, there is an initial difficulty to give us pause: it is hard to make your way with any certainty among all these first editions, new editions, translations, enlargements, selected summaries, articles rehashed ten times in a row, wholesale transpositions and repetitions.[2] Nonetheless, it should be enough, and in our case it will be enough, simply to take a sounding among all these repetitions. So I shall discuss two works of which I learned a long time ago, in Santiago, Chile, where their publication in 1949 and 1952 caused a certain not unjustified stir. The first, translated from the German into Spanish, is entitled "Population in the destiny of peoples";[3] the second, "The world economy," [4] seems to be a first edition in Spanish but derives whole passages from the preceding book, as well as from other earlier publications. I will also be referring to a small volume which appeared in 1952, shortly before Wagemann's death (1956), published by Francke in Bern as part of their vast collection *Die Zahl als Detektiv*,[5] and which, though only a reedition itself as well, is a masterpiece of clarity at the same time. In this book Sherlock Holmes discusses figures and statistics and relative dimensions of economic growth with his good friend Doctor Watson as if all these were villains and suspects. This book better than any other bears witness to the mastery and the sometimes rather off-hand agility of a guide who thinks he has made out a path through the complications of social life, from which things can be seen from a great height and arranged according to the deductions formed by intelligence and by arithmetic.

To complete our initial presentation let us add that, as all economists will know, before the Second World War Ernst Wagemann was director of the celebrated *Konjunktur Institut* in Berlin. After the fall of Germany, he took the road to Chile, of which he like a good many other Germans was a native. There, for several years, up until 1953, he was given a chance to hold a chair at the University of Santiago, which explains, if explanation were necessary, why the books I cited above were published in Chile. But it is the works and not the man which are on trial.

Works which are, truth to tell, hasty, written anyhow, unfinished, fevered, amused, amusing, if not always entirely reasonable. Where history is concerned they are often fairly ordinary and even frankly mediocre, but never boring. In the first of the works referred to, "Population in the destiny of peoples," the first hundred and fifty pages have a certain bearing and style: this economist by training here wishes to be a demographer, and an enthusiastic, innovatory demographer.

His very first aim, moreover, is to get away, whatever the cost, from the economic studies and points of view which have long been his own, and even to get away from that economics closely tied to place which according to him is the most intelligent form of economics: the economics of von Thünen who he tells us is "with Karl Marx, perhaps the greatest of German economists." To gain his freedom swiftly and spectacularly, he piles denials and diatribes one on top of another and overthrows commonly held explanations. All this is more amusing than serious. When the curtain goes up, Malthus is one of his chosen targets. Should one not beware, he argues, of those pseudodemographers who are pessimists or optimists according to whether the conjuncture is one of economic upswing or downturn? "The strongly marked dependence on the economic situation which demographers betray is of itself proof that this discipline does not have sufficient methodological foundations."

Having said this, Wagemann successively rejects the notion of continuous development so dear to Gustav Schmoller; the theory of demographic capacity—the weight of men which a given economic system can support—deriving from the remarks made by that "empiricist in economics," Friedrich List; and this or that definition (nonetheless intelligent in its own way) of *overpopulation* or *underpopulation,* attributable to economists like Wilhelm Röpke or Gustav Rümelin. When all the old and new links between economics and demography have been severed, he then seeks to set this last up as a world apart, in an autonomous scientific region which in his mind, if I dare to say so, is to some extent that of first causes. "One of the preferred theses of the political economy of vulgarization is that the rapid growth of the modern population must be due to the success of capitalism, and its exuberant expansion. Without doubt, those who maintain the opposite seem even more justified: that is, the technological and economic progress of the nineteenth and twentieth centuries must be due to the rapid increase in the population." There we have it: demography is in control.

All these demolitions, all these daring gestures, some more to the point than others, are only a curtain-raiser. In order to give demography the status of a science, it must be given specific, clearly defined tasks to accomplish. According to Ernst Wagemann, demography must be above all a study of demographic variations and their consequences. By that token, it must be a science of the conjuncture, improbably modeled on conjunctural economics. But, in passing, do not let us smile at this apparent contradiction, at this seeming regression.

In any case, it is from the conjuncture that the great demographic fluctuations of the past arise, this long ebb and flow of the waves, these essential movements well known to historians which Ernst Wagemann considers the first object of study worthy of constituting demography's true field. *Grosso modo* he sees the following demographic rhythms in the West: tenth to thirteenth century, appreciable growth in population; fourteenth century, catastrophic fall owing to the Black Death; fifteenth century, stagnation; sixteenth century, sharp increase (in Central Europe, specifies Wagemann); seventeenth century, stagnation or slight fall; eighteenth century, considerable growth; nineteenth century, "untimely" increase; twentieth century, continued growth but at a slower rate. Thus there were three great upward surges of the population, according to the European clock: the first before and during the Crusades, the second just before the Thirty Years' War, the third from the eighteenth century until now. That these fluctuations are universal is certain of the last one (that of the eighteenth, nineteenth, and twentieth centuries), and likely for the second (that of the sixteenth century). As for the first (tenth to thirteenth century), Ernst Wagemann's reasoning is a bit hasty: according to him there can be no upward surge demographically without a major war. Now, the very name of Genghis Khan (1152 or 1164–1227) is an indication of how disturbed the global destiny of Asia was at that date. Can one then deduce that Asia too was undergoing a large growth in population just at the time more or less of the Crusades? No prudent historian will fall in with our guide to rally to such peremptory conclusions, even if he is justifiably struck by the number of analogies which can be drawn between the West and the Far East. All the same, Genghis Khan apart, all that we can glimpse of the demographic tensions of tropical and Central Asia do not invalidate Wagemann's assumptions, quite the reverse. Besides, if demographic oscillations can be seen taking place on a global scale from the sixteenth, and certainly from the eighteenth century, then he has at least the right to assert that the world population grows in more or less rapid waves which tend over a longer or shorter period of time eventually to affect all humanity. In saying which, incidentally, he will find himself in agreement with an opinion of some weight, that of Max Weber himself.

At the same time, all the customary explanations of historical demography and, beyond that, of demography itself are more or less excluded by him. One must no longer say that everything in the eighteenth and then in the nineteenth century was engendered by the developments in hygiene or in medicine, by overcoming the great epidemics, or in technology, or in industrialization. This, as we have seen earlier, is to reverse the order of events, for these explanations have been cut to fit Europe or rather the West. They rest uneasily on the distant bodies of China or of India, although demographically these countries seem to be progressing at the same rhythm as our own favored peninsula. Ernst Wagemann is well justified in giving historians and all those involved in the social sciences a valuable lesson: there can be no essential human truth except on a global scale.

So we must come away from our customary explanations, even if for the moment we cannot find any ones suitable to fit these movements as a whole. Roberto Lopez like myself thinks that climate might provide a key. Not so long ago the price specialists, also despairing of finding a reason, turned their thoughts to sun spot cycles. But Ernst Wagemann—once the independence of demography has been established—is not at all bothered to find an answer to this perfectly natural question. The problem for him is first to make out and then to try and grasp "universal phenomena which are subject to repetition," and I would add although he himself does not say it, which can if possible be measured. For lack of anything better, scientific speculation can simply stop there, unless like Ernst Wagemann it wishes to examine that "biological law (which would explain everything) but which we do not yet know, either in its roots, or in its linear development." It is better to say that he is contenting himself at this stage (as with his "alternations" which we shall come to in a moment) with what are simply working hypotheses; that is, with a theory whose only function is to take account of known data and to point the way to better research. The criterion is that they should work. By this token it is less the nature of these fluctuations than their consequences, or at least some of their consequences, which will be examined under the heading of alternations.

Wagemann's "alternations," which I would be happier to call "thresholds," form a dynamic or, as he says, *demodynamic* working hypothesis, and a seductive one though it is certainly much too simple. To give a brief summary of it would distort it even more, and moreover lead the reader into the trap set by a misleading vocabulary, for the terms *overpopulation* and *underpopulation,* which are crucial here, must evoke an image of increasing and decreasing numbers which it is extremely difficult to get rid of, despite all the author's warnings. I would have preferred for my part to replace these words by the neutral terms *phase A* and *phase B,* which I logically enough found myself recalling, for Ernst Wagemann's explanations accord perfectly with the language of François Simiand, with which all historians in our country are familiar.

It is a question, then, of the mass of living men and their ceaseless variations. To speak (for convenience's sake) on the level of the abstract and the general, let there be a country *P,* situated outside real time and in no specific geographical region. Its population, which we can vary according to our wishes, is assumed to be on the increase. Its density per kilometer—and it is this which will be under examination—will thus successively reach every value. Of this succession we will retain a few significant figures, true golden figures in Wagemann's demonstration: 10, 30, 45, 80, 130, 190, 260 inhabitants per square kilometer. Each time the population crosses one of these "thresholds," according to our author, it undergoes a profound mass transformation; and not only a material transformation either.

Before the threshold of 10 inhabitants per square kilometer is reached, our country *P* is in a phase of underpopulation, let us call it phase A; from 10 to 30, it is in phase B of overpopulation; over 30, it returns (and it is here that we must abandon our customary associations) to underpopulation; and so on, one after another in alternation. It is clear that this is to give to the words *underpopulation* and *overpopulation* an elastic meaning quite outside common speech. These concepts would certainly need to be defined. But if we wait for our guide to provide a definition, we wait in vain. He declares that he is rejecting all the usual definitions put forward by economists, and that at this stage he is ready to make do with extremely provisional definitions. But it only goes to show that in science too, unfortunately, the provisional can be fairly long-lasting!

In fact, these alternations can be clearly understood only if they are translated into economic language. Essentially, what is under examination is the relation between population and economic resources, the relation, to which we will return later, between two kinds of growth. Ernst Wagemann says it in his own way. There is overpopulation when men, having multiplied, have not increased their resources proportionally. At that stage, observation can regularly discern the following signs: unemployment, as in England before 1939; poor utilization of the labor force (according to an expert one could, in this same year 1939, subtract 750,000 workers from Bulgaria without lowering its agricultural production); monetary and credit crises, slumps. Then there is the second case, of underpopulation: if one did not point out forcefully and from the very beginning the chronic narrowness of the markets and the poor development of economic relations, the situation would seem altogether too rosy. Nonetheless, auspicious signs abound: the demand for manpower remains constantly unsatisfied; there is a superfluity of fertile land, which is empty or at least easy to take over; immigration is said to be necessary (whether spontaneous or controlled); the economy sets itself up and develops under the standard of freedom.

Are these transitions from A to B and from B to A, and the considerable changes which they entail, slow in coming about, having to go through some fairly long term pauses when things remain in equilibrium, or do they happen suddenly, in sharp catastrophes? The two explanations are offered to us one after the other, without our being able to know whether the author would have us add them together as is likely, or choose between them. But, here and elsewhere, let us leave the responsibility with him.

Beyond these "provisional" definitions which go only halfway toward clarifying the problem, we are granted a rapid series of particular "proofs." This time, the theoretical plane where everything should have been completed and crowned with an explanation is quietly abandoned. It is up to the figures alone to tell the tale, as though they could speak for themselves! Here we are, in any case, brought back in contact with tangible realities, in the midst of a variety of examples in which the historian will be happy to recognize his customary perspectives and contingencies. But the demonstration loses its power; it divides into separate rivers, and then into tiny streams.

The first example is a river, however, dealing with almost the whole world. But it is the only one of this exceptional category. Imagine that one should divide as many contemporary countries as possible according to their density of population, which means grouping them together above or below the "thresholds" (10, 30, 45, and so on), and that one should then calculate for each of them, on the basis of Colin Clark's figures, their national revenue per active member of the population; and that one should place opposite these figures those for infant mortality, taken with some justification as a touchstone. The result is the table and graph which we have in our turn reproduced here.[6] Similar graphic demonstration is offered in the case of external trade per member of population according to increasing density. These variations according to place—though not to time—proclaim concomitant fluctuations in well-being above the different chosen thresholds, sometimes in one direction and sometimes in the other. If the calculations are correct, and that I cannot say, then these golden figures seem to have some foundation, at least in contemporary reality.

We are then given analogous demonstrations, with the same simplified statistical apparatus, concerning the different states in the United States (classified according to their increasing population density); concerning Lower Saxony between 1925 and 1933, whose districts are classified in the same way; concerning the variations in national revenue in the United States between 1869 and 1938; and finally concerning the marriage rate in Prussia between 1830 and 1913, on one side and the other of the year 1882 in which Prussia crossed the significant threshold of 80 inhabitants per square kilometer. This amusing graph shows the difference between the two periods: before 1882, severe fluctuations in the marriage rate related to fluctuations in a strained economic situation; after it, a gentle curve. For Wagemann, this transition from disturbance to calm is the transition from an overpopulated country to "a country in equilibrium," soon to be underpopulated and thus comfortable.

Where should one stop in the enumeration of endless examples, some of them insubstantial and carrying little conviction, though never without interest? At the example of the regression of the black population in the British West Indies? More illuminating is the return of Ireland, after the massive emigration which followed the 1846 crisis, to a now supportable demographic tension. At the beginning of the nineteenth century, in 1821, Ireland represented half the population of England; England could ensure its own security only by dominating its overpowerful neighbor. In 1921, Ireland was ten times less populated than England; there was no longer any problem in conceding it its political independence. So reasoned the English demographer Harold Wright, in whose footsteps our present author follows.

But we cannot analyze them all, so let us stop at one highly symptomatic example. Around 1912, in the state of Espirito Santo (north of Rio de Janeiro) whose capital is the port of Victoria, there lived a colony of 17,500 Germans. They owned a territory of some 5,000 square kilometers (with a density of 3.5 in 1912 for 17,500 inhabitants; of 7.0–8.0 in 1949 when there were 35,000–40,000 souls living there). A backward and undoubtedly underpopulated country. The only means of transport in 1949 remained what it had been in the old days of colonial Brazil, the mule, or at most the wooden wagon. There was only one technology at the service of men: a hydraulic mortar for pulping the coffee, precious produce whose export ensured the few purchases which had to be made from the outside: dried meat *(charque)*, flour, tobacco, alcohol, ironmongery. All the same, as far as basic necessities went, all the food came from the colonials' own land. And there are a good many other signs of autarchy to be seen: the little house built with the neighbors' help, furniture (everybody having what they can make themselves). The earth is highly fertile, of course, and every time cultivation has worn out the soil and the crop becomes meager, then they attack some new portion of the forest. This means that men and cultivation are both nomadic. Santa Leopoldina, which had 300 families in 1885, lost more than half of them during the next thirty years. One has to live, but schools, civilization, not

to mention the quality of life—that goes without saying!—accord ill with
the nomadic life. And yet, they thrived. In the vast area open to him,
man multiplied: mortality 7.0 per thousand, birthrate 48.5 per
thousand, incredible figures which one must go back and read twice
before being able to credit. So there are primitive economies, and they
do thrive. This one is a good example of an ancient way of life, without
crafts, with a reduced trade in the hands of the *tropeiros,* mule caravan
owners who created the first Brazilian economy of continental dimensions beginning in the eighteenth century. What can one conclude
from this? That population dominates the economy, that it dominates
everything.

I hope that these few scraps and summaries give a proper sense of the
interesting nature of Wagemann's thinking. There can be no question
here of taking up his assertions and associations in order to subject them
to any kind of rigorous, useless verification. For a start, their author is no
longer here to defend himself—and he would have been able to do so,
vigorously. Besides the reader, as he went along, will have formulated
for himself the criticisms and reservations which are to be made. And
finally, and above all, this thinking demands to be appreciated as a
whole, not quibbled over in detail.

Like any economist, like any committed intellectual, Ernst Wagemann
has doubtless seen too much of the present time, the time on which, for
good or ill, he has had to work. The figures which he offers may indeed
mark out present thresholds, but their succession does not hold good *ipso
facto* for the past. Who in fact could believe in the validity of a series of
figures of population density, set out once and for all, existing "outside
the natural or technological conditions and all the particular conjunctures of history," and in which one can read all our destinies already
inscribed, as in the simplest horoscopes? France in 1600 had about 16
million inhabitants, population density 34. Let us refer to the unchanging scale: it is declared to be underpopulated, although all the known
signs of life then prove that it must belong to the other category—a
strong emigrant movement toward Spain alone proves it. It is true that
one could object that the figure of 16 million is not absolutely certain.
But let us proceed: is France in 1789 overpopulated? in 1939 is it underpopulated? Even the rapidest of studies will show that there are any
number of reasons why a country grappling with its history and with its
real territorial extension should have too few or too many men. It all
depends on its capacities on various levels, or even on the vitality that the
demographic changes crossing its destiny infuse it with. It is all a question of relationships, and these "total" values of which Ernst Wagemann
speaks, though I would prefer to call them dominant, never stop

changing according to the changing shape of a complex equation. The number of men is in turn a determined and a determining factor, sometimes crucial, sometimes relatively secondary, and so on. I do not believe in *one* explanation capable of serving as "total value" or first cause of the multiple density of man.

But let us not quit Ernst Wagemann at this point of too easy criticisms. It is no small merit to have killed certain myths and raised so many problems which we will find again, in a moment, under the nimble pen of Alfred Sauvy. And even if we retain only his theory of mutations under the weight of an increase in population, then we will not have entirely wasted our time. There are probably not any unchanging thresholds, but mutations there certainly are, at variable demographic levels, according to time and place. These mutations make deep rifts in the time of history. They give an added meaning, a new value to the old and always useful game of periodization.

Nor is it any small merit to have sought to define and make more specific, more scientific, a discipline which is still under construction, however much it has increased its rate of progress during recent years. Nonetheless is it wise to enclose it, as Ernst Wagemann does, solely within problems of conjuncture? To exclude it from the measurements and explanations which are able to grasp the *structure,* term which despite its relative imprecision is fairly clear in its meaning today? This would certainly be a pity for a science whose role and whose ambition is to go right down to the very foundations of human life. Even to have recourse to history[7] like Wagemann, one would need more care and, above all, less haste.

## Alfred Sauvy's Models

I have now come to the classic, crucial book by Alfred Sauvy, a double or even a triple book, for in all fairness one should add to the two volumes of his *Théorie générale de la population* I: *Économie et population* (1952); and II: *Biologie sociale* (1954),[8] the earlier book, *Richesse et population* (1943), which already sketches out the major themes.[9] I should apologize for speaking of books which have been published for so long already, but it is not too late to mention their worth: we have not exhausted all they have to teach us.

A vast work consecrated to the whole of demography, making over-flights throughout its territory, can be conceived in many ways. Alfred Sauvy rests his on the economic and then on the social; I do not go so far as to say on economics and sociology. In fact, the first volume is a designedly abstract, mathematically oriented attempt to sketch out as full a "model" as possible; the second volume confronts the model, or rather "models," thus constructed and then complicated at leisure with all the realities of experience. So there are two movements: first of all the problematic, and then its experimental verification. It is right and proper that it should be so.

At the outset, then, we are outside the complications of the real and all its tangled contingencies. The field is clear: calculations and reasoning can and do let themselves go lightheartedly, outside all the prudence and pusillanimity of concrete observation. We are not dealing with a real population, with a real country, with a real time, real resources, real revenues. Let us suppose, says Alfred Sauvy amusing himself, an island peopled with goats and wolves. Let us suppose, he suggests another time, that England numbers two hundred inhabitants. Just as with Wagemann, we come first to the ideal country of calculations, with a population which we can see increase or decrease not for biological or historical reasons or in accordance with some rule or other, but simply because we want it to, making it grow from 0 to infinity, or, if need be, the other way around.

The problem to be resolved is simple, or at least simply stated. The more reason to pay attention to its various elements. The question is to illuminate the relation constantly binding and opposing a given population to the various resources at its disposal. Imagine a rather particular set of scales which can accommodate populations in one of its pans, and the heterogeneous resources on which they live at each moment of their history (or of their "growth," if you prefer) in the other. The resources will go up now faster, now more slowly than the men. Phases will follow each other and witness successive reversals (it would hardly be a scientific way of speaking to say in a good, and then in a bad direction). But the image of the scales is not very scientific either. Let us leave it and go on to the curves which Alfred Sauvy offers us, and to the theorems and models which he derives from them and which will remain the firm foundation on which his observation, as complicated and subtly shaded as he desires, will subsequently rest.

These curves are essentially three, and in each case the population is mapped on the abscissa and assumed to be on the increase. The first curve comprises the *total productivity* of each of these successive populations, the two others being curves of *average productivity* and of *marginal productivity*.

This last is the best suited to our aims. To each value $x$ of the population, it establishes a corresponding value $y$ of marginal productivity, that is, the productivity of the last man intervening in the production chain. Let $x = 1,000$, then $y$ is the productivity of the 1,000th individual to be introduced into our growing population. The $x$-axis is assumed to begin at 1. The productivity of the first man, plotted on the $y$-axis, is assumed to be equal to the minimum subsistence level; otherwise the first man would not be able to await the arrival of the second. We have reproduced, with slight modifications, this important graph.[10] The first thing one sees is the rise in marginal productivity, that of the 1,000th individual being greater than that of his immediate predecessor, and so on down to no. 1. In fact, each new arrival profits, in his exertions, from the work and equipment of those who have gone before. So for a long time marginal productivity is on the increase, until the equipment seems to find its optimum personnel. At that point, productivity begins to decrease. Each new worker will place himself with difficulty, or at least less profitably than his predecessors within the ranks of the active population. Let us suppose this reversal point at $M$, for a population arbitrarily fixed at $x = 2,000$. Let us suppose that the point $M_p$, where the descending curve rejoins the minimum subsistence level again, corresponds, always arbitrarily, to a population of $x = 6,000$ persons. Above this figure of 6,000, marginal productivity will henceforth be lower than the minimum subsistence level. From then on, the contribution of the last come is no longer an advantage to the community. He will live to some extent at their charge.

This curve of *marginal productivity* also gives us—and this is the important part—the rise in total productivity. Let us suppose, in fact, that we wish to calculate this productivity for the population $x = 2,000$. It is immediately given to us by the surface whose four boundaries are this curve; the ordinate of $M$ corresponding to $x = 2,000$; and the two axes. Each of our 1,000 workers has inscribed his own personal productivity on this surface in the form of a straight line of variable length at the moment when he entered the proceedings. The sum of these lines is the surface to be considered (in actual fact, the so-called primitive function of the marginal productivity curve).

Under these conditions, the global productivity for the population $x = 6,000$ is represented on the graph by the hatched surfaces, surfaces which break down into two stages: below, a rectangular piece corresponding to the minimum subsistence level; above, the part which Alfred Sauvy calls "the hump," or the surplus. Let us suppose our population put on short commons; it would consume only the rectangle, the rest being at the disposal of its masters, lords or rulers.

I do not maintain that this language is of an obvious clarity for the reader, especially if he is confused by the elementary mathematics which this explanation assumes. But I have no doubt that on a second reading he will be able to decipher its simple message. He would then be in a position to concede that the *optimum power*, that is, the population giving over the most considerable "surplus" to its masters, corresponds to the population $x = 6,000$. The word *power* is doubtless rather vague, since power depends on the use to which one wants or is able to put the surplus. According to a variety of decisions and possibilities, it could be the luxury of the ruling classes, the prince's wastefulness, fruitful investments, or preparations for war. One could go on for even longer than Alfred Sauvy does, discussing this surplus, these "plus-values." Socially quite as much as materially, their importance is very great; Marcel Mauss has said as much in his rapid, half-enigmatic way: "It is not from productivity properly speaking that society has taken its impetus . . . luxury is the great promoter." [11] Yes, often enough it is luxury which has been the factor of progress, on condition of course that a theory of luxury lights up our lamp: Sombart's definition is only half satisfactory.[12]

But let us get back to the curves, and to Alfred Sauvy's preliminary discussions. What he is seeking as far as possible to do in this initial approach is to fix the terms of the problem in a clear mathematical language which will reduce them to an obvious and acceptable formulation. For my part, I can see no better way of fixing this essential relation between population and material life, in which one must constantly keep in mind the variable factors of both one and the other. There is no optimum for population as such, but different optimums, each of which answers different (and above all material) criteria. Thus, with the curves we have obtained, we have not a perfect but an acceptable definition of the *optimum power*. With another curve one can define the *economic optimum,* or any other optimum, provided that the criteria fixing it are clearly expressed. But let us say straightaway that these different formulas about this or that optimum are more a way of clearing the terrain than of organizing it. To rely entirely on fixed points would mean immobilizing the demographic movement. "The notion of optimum not lending itself to many practical applications, the thing to study is a population in movement," explains Alfred Sauvy himself, quite rightly, at the beginning of his second volume.

So all this initial schema is really an elementary model, a way, I repeat, of cutting the problems down to size by simplifying them. The ideal population, for example, cannot begin at either 0 or 1. One must have a small group at the beginning, the smallest group capable of living on its own: the *isolate.*[13] Nor is it true that average productivity exactly corresponds to the level of existence, or that all the population is active, or that productivity curves take such elementary forms. All productivity is dependent on the level of technology, and this changes slowly. But change it does, and since the end of the eighteenth century, its variations have from on high dominated the entire lives of men. It is not true either that the minimum subsistence level is the simple parallel that we have traced. Consumption, wages, real wages, components of diet, all these factors vary and complicate the problem. We have hardly drawn our curves before they come to seem too rigid. Alfred Sauvy, having once simplified everything, does not deny himself the pleasure of then proceeding to complicate it again, and of going from a schema which was too clear cut to an extremely detailed concrete situation. His first book, although theoretical in principle, is full of incidents, anecdotes, examples. In the constant coming-and-going between the real and the explanation interpreting it, a thousand particular cases come pressing forward: the Black Death in the fourteenth century, the categories of age in a population, the three sectors of activity (primary, secondary, tertiary), unemployment, prices, manpower costs . . . All this is presented with great verve, activity, and intelligence. By the end of the book, the reader has the feeling of having reached the open sea: but he is still within the misleadingly choppy waters of the harbor.

The second volume of the *Théorie générale de la population* is entitled *Biologie sociale* (a fine program). All the same, if I may say so, it did rather surprise me. The large-scale return to experience and observation, the proliferation of examples which speak even more of themselves than they do of any general topics, the living disorder of the book are all not without their inconveniences for a reader who is seeking to learn a technique. Is he ever so gently being teased? In the first instance, or first volume, Alfred Sauvy told us: "This is how things should happen." So when we left it we had a few "provisional conclusions." In the second instance, or second book, everything is set against experience, both contemporary and historical. And then, "what theory sought, history (he could just as well have said life) has denied. . . . Once man has been restored with the initiative which the earlier conventions removed, only some of these provisional conclusions can be retained." I am sure that all this precise, multiple demolition, carried out frankly in the name of man, "that embarrassment . . . the eternally overlooked," in the name of history and experience would have delighted Lucien Febvre. "History is man," he wrote, and he meant by this a succession of surprises, not all of them happy ones.

What are the "provisional conclusions . . . retained" by our colleague? I confess I nowhere found an exact list of them. But it hardly matters! Let us simply remark that Alfred Sauvy—as was his right—wished to be deliberately careful and relativist in this second wing of his diptych. Allusive too, sometimes, and questions raised occasionally go without an answer. "Is the increase in populations the cause of wealth, or vice versa?" he asks, leaving us the trouble of answering yes or no, or of not answering at all in our turn. Nor do I really have any clear idea of what he means by a particular collective psychology, which is often invoked but never defined.

If one follows the line of steepest incline of a text which is always intelligent and full of information and vivid insights, I think that perhaps the thing that stands out most clearly once the book is closed is a long-considered examination of the very body, the destiny of France, in the light of demographic pressures and considerations. It is careful, sincere, honest, and almost always convincing. Who among us could remain indifferent?

Thus the many examples which one might have supposed included for their own sake (modern Spain between the sixteenth and eighteenth centuries, overpopulation in Italy, Holland) do doubtless fall into the thread of a general explanation; but openly or insidiously, by their contrast they also illuminate the French case, that typical *Malthusian* case. The sociology thus sketched out, though never systematically developed, is precisely that of a population aging because of a fundamental slowing down in its birthrate; thus it constantly has a bearing on France, which was the first to give an example of a population in which a voluntary restriction on births, as early as the eighteenth century, affected first the higher classes, and then the whole of the nation. If a demographer should calculate the demographic evolution of our country afresh, disregarding what actually happened and imagining different coefficients—those of our neighbors—the results would be so disproportionate to what our fate has actually been that it would throw a glaring light on the case of this stationary country, the victim of false calculations and a mean and narrow carefulness. The exposé turns to special pleading. The author "commits" himself, and sits in judgment. I find his commitment too much like my own to have anything to say against Alfred Sauvy's incisive arguments, against what he has to say about the aging of populations, and still less against his prejudice in favor of the young and innovatory impulse, in the (alas!) only too conservative setting of a society such as ours.

But in giving himself up like this to his natural inclinations, has not Alfred Sauvy to a certain extent restricted the range of the second volume of his *Théorie générale*? Putting France and the West too much at the center of his argument, he does not speak enough of the case of the underdeveloped countries. He deals only briefly with the Far East and Latin America, with their high growth rates and ethnic mixtures, and he barely touches on the immense problems of the whole of the world population.[14] Finally, has he not seen both the aging of the population in the West and the slow alteration of the demographic balance in France too much in terms of a central case? Even more important, is this aging measured sufficiently on the world scale (for, like Wagemann's precious "demodynamic" waves, it too tends to generalize itself) and, a point to which I will return, on the scale of history?

What I have my doubts about in the end is whether a general theory of population can stand on these two feet: on the one side calculations based on economics, on the other observations based on experience. The construction of a model should involve every sphere of social organization and behavior, and not only one or two areas. Thus there is a whole body of nonclassical economics, geography, anthropology, sociology, history, human biology in Henri Laugier's compelling sense, probably even a body of microdemography: Alfred Sauvy's thinking seems to me to be singularly inactive in all these directions. I do not believe that the word *ecumene* is ever mentioned, or population density,[15] or that there is any evocation of an urban geography.[16] Can a general theory of population really be built thus more or less independent of considerations of space and certainly without the least map, without the least reference to Vidal de la Blache's *Principes de géographie humaine,* or Maximilien Sorre's weighty volume, or reference works like that of Hugo Hassinger, to cite an old one, or Kurt Witthauer, to mention an extremely recent publication, or Mme. Jacqueline Beaujeu-Garnier's book? These last two, I admit, were not available to Alfred Sauvy, but their existence substantiates my criticism. I have similar regrets over the fact that our colleague made use of no anthropological works, and that the key words *civilization* and *culture* are practically strangers to him,[17] and that notwithstanding its inclusion in Georges Gurvitch's series, the *Bibliothèque de sociologie contemporaine* his book should in fact have so little sociology about it.

Finally, despite the great variety of this research, history is regularly allotted a rather meager role. Alfred Sauvy's ruling passion for the history of ideas, and, in particular, for men like Malthus, Cantillon or Quételet, or Quesnay, is no alibi. Malthus does not interest me, he has been discussed too much; nor even does Marx, although this book does not make sufficient mention of him to my mind; what interests me is what the world was like in the age of Marx or Malthus.

In my opinion, Alfred Sauvy too often lets himself be seduced by a facile history, a politicizing history of events. And it is a pity. The present time, the time in which his quick mind places his arguments, his examples, his surprises, and our amazement, is only an instant in the life of the world. This instant can not be fully comprehensible without plunging it back into the time which dictates the direction and speed of the general movement which carries it along. This historical time is too much a stranger to Alfred Sauvy. If he does touch on history from time to time, it is as a target of ironic humor: "It is a facile, and terribly difficult undertaking to try and reconstruct historical developments in terms of the length of Cleopatra's nose." Of course it is, but why should anyone want to try? Or what about this stone cast into the sixteenth-century specialist's pond: "The fall in the French birthrate is, in short, the outcome of a 'repressed Reformation' "? Even at the cost of a little boredom, I would have preferred that a demographer of this quality should have taken up the thick file already put together by historical demography, which is not a new, "untamed science," but well-founded research and already of long standing. I would have liked to know what he thought of the historical works of Julius Beloch, A. P. Usher, Paul Mombert, the brothers Eugène and Alexandre Kulischer, and Eugène Cavaignac, not to mention the recent studies by Daniele Beltrami, Alfredo Rosenblatt, Marianne Rieger, or Van den Sprenkel.

But here I am, talking too much, or not enough, about history. For this sort of criticism by bibliographical enumeration is altogether too facile and tedious, if nothing tangible is evoked by the titles quoted. It would be better to plead the cause of a historical demography with Alfred Sauvy himself, attempting to meet him on his own ground, but with a historian's arguments. Let us thus consider the French senescence over the *longue durée* which is, not unreasonably, at the heart of our author's way of thinking and acting.

Does he really believe that all it needed to set this movement going was a few perverts and a little stealthy falling away from Rome in the sixteenth century, and the successful use of contraceptive methods among the aristocracy and the bourgeoisie which slowly permeated the whole of society in the eighteenth century? "And this at the very time (to quote a passage from one of his recent lectures) when world expansion was about to run riot. . . . The whole course of France has been influenced since by this crucial event which occurred at the end of the eighteenth century." So France then was a century ahead of everyone else in terms of an aging population. But is there any reason why this aging over the *longue durée* should not have been *long* prepared, in France's past? Alfred Sauvy says rather briefly that "there was a parallelism in the development of the Western nations in the eighteenth century." Yes and no. Yes, as far as cultural, economic, or political life is concerned; no, if one thinks of the demographic past.

In the eighteenth century France was emerging from a long period of overpopulation, which had been chronic since the thirteenth, or, better, the twelfth century. For four or five hundred years (except for the regression between 1350 and 1450), it had been living in a situation analogous to India's today, "suffocating" under its own birthrate, near that pole of "power" which often goes with lack of food and waves of emigration. Is it not possible that all these emigrations, all these conquests, these *Gesta Dei per Francos,* all this wear and tear should have profoundly determined a future which it might be easy, but pointless to attribute solely to immorality, dissipation, and a bad example? Can a phenomenon of the *longue durée* be derived from little causes? I doubt it. And in support of the thesis which I have sketched out, let us draw attention to the fact that England, which is so often invoked as an example by Alfred Sauvy, did not share in our biological exuberance from the twelfth to the eighteenth century. It was not an overpopulated country either in the thirteenth or yet in the sixteenth century. Perhaps it was in the seventeenth, but at that time the religious disputes dictated a certain exodus. In short, when the eighteenth century arrived, England did not have what A. P. Usher has called "biological maturity," or it had had it for only a short time, the opposite of France. Now, would not aging take place, here and there in the world, at the end of a period of exuberance over the *longue durée?* I will be told that in the past fifteen years France has undergone a sudden revival and that this is all due to a few extravagant politicians: but that is to rely too much on the specific "event" again.[18] A flow starts up because a previous ebb has so to speak prepared the way for it and made it necessary, and our political figures had the good sense—when they did have it—to fall in with this "wind of history." But if they alone were responsible for this auspicious rise, then all I can expect is that it will fall back soon. The great demographic waves of history cannot depend on mediocre reasons.

I would not like to conclude with these criticisms, which are themselves debatable, but rather with the sympathy inspired in me by a way of thinking which is always open and unprejudiced, always flexible because always honest, and always profoundly enriching, whatever minor disagreements there might be. This demographer is above all a man of his time, prodigiously interested in the world which surrounds him, from every angle. He never deliberately puts up any barriers. It is never not worth attempting a dialogue with Alfred Sauvy. Certainly, all dialogues tempt him, and he knows nothing of the intellectual limitations of disdain.

## Louis Chevalier: Toward a Biological History

Louis Chevalier, a historian who has turned to demography, has just published a compact and vehement book, *Classes laborieuses et classes dangereuses à Paris dans la première moitié du XIX$^e$ siècle,*[19] assuredly a fine subject, and equally assuredly a fine book. I have read it and reread it, less to weigh its documentary exactitude and correctness—others have had no hesitation in setting about that already—than to try to distinguish its intentions and its "doctrine." It is on this level, I think, that the true value of this book, at first sight so difficult and disconcerting, lies. Not that it is easy to make out the grain of such an abstruse work, which is often unclear simply because of its very richness and the multiplicity of its intentions. What is more, it was not written but dictated, and this explains the occasional tedious passages, the repetition, the redundancies, the flashes of bravura, and also the disdain for the clear phrase or formula, or for neatly aligned arguments. But, we must say immediately that the book is also full of passages which have a dark beauty. Besides, the whole book—whether the author wished it or not—is a black book on that "ill-known" Paris of the first half of the nineteenth century, a "dangerous, unhealthy, terrible" place. Its sores, its abominations, its savagery, its landscapes of the damned, and its unspeakable wretchedness are like dark Romantic engravings, like outbursts from Michelet: both to the honor of this book.

But what path does he follow? Rash question! Louis Chevalier gives ten different answers. All the same, in order to see how these successive answers accord with one another, one must go through the whole extensive work, two or three times. Then, when everything has been weighed and the key passages reread pen in hand, the declarations of the last two pages—those pages of truth—take on their *true* meaning. Then those assertions, that offensive offhandedness, those declared lacunae so bitterly justified and so little comprehensible at first sight finally fall into a coherent pattern. This book was conceived, above all, as a dare, a bet, a "manifesto," as a pioneering work. Never for a moment does the author forget its originality. Impatient, he would even wish that this originality, which personally I would certainly not deny, should be immediately recognized, that his revolt against the dreary rules of our profession should be taken seriously, and that the new rules which he has chosen should be accepted in all their abundance. Everything has been sacrificed to this; the aim of the book is essentially methodological, and the Paris of the Restoration and the July Monarchy is nothing but a splendid pretext. It is the "manifesto," at once a dare and a bet, which dominates everything. And of course it is this which I would like to analyze first as far as possible. An operation of no little awkwardness, but something which has to be done.

Not that this "manifesto" comes down simply to this freely asserted dare, but though occasionally misleading, this dare forms an initial first line of approach. It is a dare directed first at history (a certain kind of history, strictly the province of demographers), at an economics seen as shortsighted and facile, at a sociology hardly spoken of at all, at a sociology of work which is quite simply ignored, at the criminologists who "speak of crime in Paris during these years as they would for any other city, in any other age," even (oh, base ingratitude!) at "the statistician, meaning the man least likely to understand . . ., strong in his specialty, but impoverished by it."

As for the bet, there can be no doubt: especially in the case envisaged and in the period decided upon, demography alone, in the strict sense of the word, with its multipronged approach should be able to distinguish and explain the various problems of the laboring, and, yet more, the dangerous classes of the Parisian agglomeration. "The demographic measurement comes into its own there, it is in a privileged position, and can freely dispense with any other manner of measurement," he writes. And, even more clearly: "For reasons to do with documentation [sic], demography is in charge." The reasons are not exclusively to do with documentation, since traditional documentation and legal documents, which do exist, have been excluded in a dictatorial way as being useless. But with a rather winning but stringent obstinacy, our colleague has simply remained faithful to the program he mapped out in 1952, in his brilliant and arrogant inaugural address to the Collège de France. For him, history breaks down into two zones, one of light, of awareness, the other of darkness, "that area . . . in which man escapes from man and isolates himself in instinctive, elementary forms of existence, no longer those of the organized city, but those of the crowd, of space." These "depths" are accessible to demography, and not to history and economics which have to do with the "organized city." The demographers want to be alone, or at least Louis Chevalier wishes to make this descent alone.

I confess to finding this project extremely exciting, even though it is not in line with my usual preferences: on the contrary, I am in favor of associated projects, carefully bound and linked together. I believe that they alone can work. But then, given that, how could I not be full of curiosity about the risks and results of such a venture as this? Can demography alone take over the tasks of history and the other human sciences? Should one believe what Louis Chevalier has to say?

The moment that one looks for them, the author's dares, his bets, and his statements of position are easy to find in this sensitive, pugnacious book. They crop up of themselves, the more so since the descents into the depths are not made without respite, and every time the author surfaces, the difficulties which had been set aside for a moment begin surreptitiously to crowd around again. Thus each time that *normally* the price of bread, or crime statistics, or whatever, would require a place in the narrative, the author feels obliged to tell us exactly why he denies them to us or offers them only in the most meager helpings, and why our hunger for them should and will remain unsatisfied. In just this way the description of working-class Paris in the first half of the past century is oddly interrupted by constant professions of faith, justifications, and digressions on the need to separate a serious analysis, in depth, from all other social explanations.

History is often the target in this game, a history which the author finds mediocre when he abandons it, but acceptable when he returns to it and deems it transformed by what he himself has achieved. "These statistics not only give history an additional way of measuring . . . they extend it and transform its program." But, outside the hands of the demographer, how poor is historical research, with its "incomplete program and rigid concepts"! Is Louis Chevalier unaware (like so many sociologists and philosophers, who at least have the excuse of not having been historians by training) that, for a long while, the concepts of history have done nothing but change, and that its program, whether complete or not, is today certainly no longer one of traditional explanation, the "chronological narrative" with which he appears to confuse it? There is even, in France, a history wide open to demography. I am thinking of Pierre Goubert's fairly sensational thesis on the Beauvaisis of the seventeenth century, of René Baehrel's revolutionary thesis on modern Haute-Provence, both of which have a vigor quite comparable to that of the present work. Innovators think themselves, wish to be, alone; in fact they are never unaccompanied.

But it is not only history which the author wants to ignore. He imposes a whole number of restrictions on himself, imposes them and respects them, though not occasionally without a certain disquiet or regret. He writes thus (and it is political economy which is here being excluded): "Of economic inequality we will have little to say, the study having already been fairly frequently made." This is a mere evasion: the problem is never to know whether a particular observation has been made or not, but whether or not it is relevant to the demonstration or research in hand. "There is little significance," he goes on to say elsewhere, "in the correlation which can be established between economic crises and criminality and between parallel rises in the price of bread and the number of offences." Little significance, indeed! All the same, three or four times he does justify himself to better effect. Paris then is above all seen as the prey, the victim of a massive wave of immigration which overwhelmed and determined everything. This immigration is the decisive variable (of the highest algebraic degree); the others vanish before it. "Engendered by the economic phenomenon, the demographic phenomenon then develops under its own impetus, from that point forward separate from the economic phenomenon, and of such an importance that . . . it acts as a cause and deserves attention at least as much as the economic phenomenon, if not more." So let us eliminate the begetter, the economic fact, insofar as the flow of immigrants toward the great agglomerations occurs quite as much during the ascent as during the descent of the economic conjuncture. All right, thinks the reader, but the demographic flow did not install itself in Paris in a material void. If we must, let us forget the conjuncture which made the immigrants set off. There remains that of when they arrived. From the moment when "it acts as a cause," does the demographic phenomenon, the overcrowding of a population between too narrow walls, have the same consequences during a climate of economic euphoria as in a situation of acute poverty and unemployment? The answer is obvious, but it leads us back toward forbidden territory.

The author is doubtless aware of it, and being neither able nor even particularly willing to deny the interest of economic explanations, he at least attempts to limit their value. According to him, they are only short-term explanations, and more or less superficial. Only the demographic facts are valid in depth and over the long term. To employ current jargon for a minute, this is to relegate economics to the conjuncture, while demography keeps the structure to itself. Now, there can also be demographic conjunctures (this book, as I will show later, is itself an example of one) and there are certainly economic structures, and even structures which are both economic and social at the same time. Capitalism is one of them, though not of course the only one; but there will be discussion neither of it nor of the rich, in this book whose very title—laboring *classes*, dangerous *classes*—had nonetheless seemed to suggest such a discussion in advance. From prejudice, let us emphasize, Louis Chevalier dismisses such "facile" explanations, and knowingly constructs his book on a certain economic void: no mention of wages, prices, of the workers' budgets, of the total revenue of the city, of the volume of its provisioning and diet, apart from a few odd particulars, particles of dust blown by the wind stirred up by the author's pen, almost in spite of himself (thus, p. 316: "The price of twelve or thirteen sols for four pounds [of bread] is . . . a real *physiological* limit"). In short, he has consciously constructed a book which is economically weak, and it is a weakness which surprises the reader from the very beginning. He may write humorously: "We must recognize that political history and economic history have often enough made good bedfellows, being quite sufficient unto themselves, never seeing the need to make it a *ménage à trois* when demographic history appears." But from all the evidence, Louis Chevalier is all for bachelorhood.

These assertions, these retreats sketch out an attitude rather than any firmly declared policy. Besides, having once evaded all social explanations, Louis Chevalier is not content to confine himself solely to demographic exploration; and if I am not mistaken it is here that, despite so many declarations of position, his thinking is not sufficiently clear. Anyway, it is not clear to my eyes or, doubtless, to those of any reader of good faith. I would not go so far as to say that Louis Chevalier also intends to challenge demography, although that would be amusing. What in fact he intends to do is to transcend what I would call traditional classic demography. In its place he would doubtless put the measurements and grids familiar to all historians interested in their profession—readers and, by that token, students of Alfred Sauvy and of his outstanding review *Population:*[20] immigration control, birthrate, marriage rate, mortality, makeup by sex and by age ... But these initial measurements, like the accompanying commentaries, are only a preliminary, the clarification indispensable to other research, that of a more profound and secret biology. The words *biology* and *biological* take on an excessive prominence under the pen of Louis Chevalier: they are almost a linguistic tic. Nine times out of ten, biological could be replaced, according to the sentences introducing it, by "demographic," "human," "social," "sociological," "juridical," and even "geographical." But enough of this useless squabbling.

In all the sciences, if discovery does not mean "grasping the ungraspable, understanding the incomprehensible," as Louis Chevalier claims, at least it means arriving at a little-known area. Now, although the realities and the structures which Louis Chevalier calls biological are ill-defined in the vocabulary and thinking of our author, they nonetheless exist. They constitute, as Georges Gurvitch would say, a "deeper level" of social reality, a major link to be constructed between and to be recognized by all the human sciences. Insofar as Chevalier's thinking accepts and above all proposes this research into "biological facts which had been covered by an enormous sedimentation of economic and moral [*sic*] facts," it is clear and justified in my eyes. I would even be able to accept its exclusions if I could believe in "biological facts" that can be isolated. In truth, all demography, all history, indeed all social life, all economics, all anthropology (and I could go on) are biological, are biological *as well*. If it were a question of biological foundations, a wide discussion would be needed, a discussion denied us in this book. Did not Maximilien Sorre define the "biological foundations" of human geography ten years ago? Louis Chevalier seems to think that the example of Paris is so illuminating that it can stand alone as a demonstration. That, one can say, is the danger of mixing a book with a manifesto. In any case, I do not find the definition which is offered to us two or three times a particularly satisfactory one—the definition being that these foundations would consist in "all that which, in social facts, is closely related to the physical character of individuals," for "how people behave bears a strict relation to their body, its structure, its needs, its demands, its workings." That is undeniably true, but I would have preferred a more circumstantial, meticulous definition of this corporeal and (I would add on my own account) *material* history, a history of needs satisfied and unsatisfied. If he had attempted it, would our colleague have persisted in enclosing this deep-seated reality within the framework of a demographic history, *stricto sensu*? I doubt it, for he himself quite visibly goes beyond this framework. Though suicide clearly falls within its province (and not within that of a timeless sociology, as he says at one point), crime, concubinage, adultery, putting newborn babies out to nurse, the popular theater, popular and nonpopular literature, these tools with which to grasp biological history are not all strictly within the domain of demography in the same way as births and deaths must be. All this evidence goes beyond its empire, without, in doing so, transcending that of the biological, which extends a great deal further still. Louis Chevalier's "biology" [21] would doubtless take no interest in our earthly nourishment. But does this not have an influence on the "behavior" of men, in close relation to their bodies? An assertion of Feuerbach's, which looks as if it were merely a play on words, claims that "man is what he eats" (der Mensch ist was er ißt). Folk wisdom.

One can see the ambition of such a theoretical formulation, and the multiplicity of problems and debates to which it gives rise. These difficulties join with the difficulties intrinsic to the example which this work sets out to tackle: the whole body of the social and biological problems of Paris in the first half of the nineteenth century. The fact that a "manifesto" of such wide scope should be mixed with an astonishingly complex example is doubtless what militates most often against any easy understanding of this generously proportioned book. The book is both too prolix if one thinks of its theoretical argument, and too short if one considers the great mass of facts offered to the historian by this half-century of Parisian life, under the revolutionary aspect of an acceleration in population which was unprecedented and, except in 1856, not to be repeated in the future. In this complex situation, Louis Chevalier is constantly hampered by a variety of interests, which often enough conflict with each other: he is caught between the general and the particular, between tradition and innovation in research, between clearly illuminated history (the history of those flashes of consciousness) and a history of the shadows. This variety of interests and points of view is what makes the value of this book, but also creates its inherent difficulty. Fruitful digressions proliferate, and that is both a cause for congratulation and complaint.

The whole first book—*Le Thème criminel*—is devoted to literary evidence. A strange start! If he had left it out, the work would have gained one hundred sixty pages or more. Why did the author, who had himself had misgivings about it, finally concede this sizable portion of his book to these "qualitative facts," to "this invasive universe of images"? I thought for a moment that Louis Chevalier, not wanting to owe anything to anyone, had had no scruples in turning to literature, which is not a social science, or at least does not appear to be one. It also occurred to me that the author has behaved a little like a theatrical director: the well-known actors and plays are good actors and good plays. *Les Misérables* can well bear being retold; it will give great pleasure. The author says he has other motives, but in fact nothing will convince me that the characters of Balzac, Eugène Sue, Victor Hugo, and Zola (although he belongs to a later period) do not hold an excessive position in a book which sets itself up as being scientific and even revolutionary. I continue to think that these interesting analyses would have been better put together in a separate book.

But the arguments opposite to mine also carry weight. Thus Louis Chevalier would see it as the need to introduce into his book the "qualitative" element, without which there can be neither a complete history nor a complete study. I entirely agree, but there is other qualitative evidence, of which the novel as a rule is the least sure. Another advantage: he made room for those moments of self-awareness without which history appears misleadingly disincarnate. I agree with this equally. He thought that, by grasping this literary evidence with infinite care, in depth, on a level beneath that of the event, he would be especially able to illuminate the major themes of his observation and discovery. From Balzac to Victor Hugo, we pass from a vision of criminality as "exceptional and monstrous," to a portrayal of a generalized, "social" criminality. "Crime ceases to be strictly confined to the dangerous classes and, changing in significance, spreads to the great mass of the population, to the majority of the working classes." These are drawn, by the simple weight of their numbers, toward the lurid borders of crime; this frontier is, in brief, their destiny. "Crimes," as Parent-Duchâtelet wrote, "are diseases of society." All this analysis of literary evidence and this evocation of the shady quarters of Parisian topography, the whole preamble, indeed, are excellently and powerfully developed. But, I repeat, it is a book in itself, that would like nothing better than to achieve its autonomy and independence, for this powerful (and innovatory) mixture of literary evidence poses problems of its own too, a good many problems. It demands precautions much more than any other sort of operation conducted on any other source. It needs stringent criticism not only of the realities being examined, but also of the distance which, consciously or not, any work of art puts between itself and such realities. These difficulties have not escaped our guide. What he has to say on remote-control monitoring by statistics in these difficult areas is of great importance. And not less so is what he writes about this sort of literary evidence, "evidence eternally present which one must know how to listen to. Not for what it claims to say, but *for what it cannot avoid saying.*"

These are some, though I do not claim all, of the various lively problems raised by this long first volume, a book which is certainly interesting though it does not always compel belief, especially in its major thesis. For how, in fact, does Louis Chevalier explain the tardy nature of literary awareness of "social criminality"? *Les Misérables* occurs right at the end of its age.

The second volume, *Le Crime: Expression d'un état pathologique considéré dans ses causes,* offers a study of housing, of urban arrangements, of the physical and material structures of the agglomeration, as well as classic demographic measurements. Who were the masses of men crowded together in the city? What was their distribution? Their age? This second volume is dense and solid. My only regret is that the maps and graphs included at the end should be so few and so inconveniently placed for consultation.

The third volume is entitled *Le Crime: expression d'un état pathologique considéré dans ses effets.* Louis Chevalier has sacrificed everything or nearly everything in his work so that this last part should stand out. In it he studies how the demographic and biological conditions of the working population in Paris deteriorated, and once again how public opinion, more or less acutely and in different ways, depending on whether it was a bourgeois or a working-class point of view, became aware of this immense transformation. The deterioration is marked by suicide (among the workers), infanticide, prostitution, insanity, concubinage among the workers, fertility, and finally death, the greatest inequality of all, "death the universal accountant," as Chevalier powerfully puts it. The problem is to form an estimate, with the figures and the correlations and hypotheses which these allow, of the approximate mass of indigents, both official and clandestine (between a third and half the inhabitants); and then of that dangerous fringe whose extent can be calculated without being able to add up its effective members. There is certainly a link between illegitimate births and a criminal tendency in one sector of the population. Bastards form a substantial part of the "criminal army." And Louis Chevalier takes a great deal of trouble to calculate this population, which was even more disadvantaged than the normal working classes and among whose ranks the tensions of social life were naturally at their most severe.

The causes having been examined, the effects will surprise no one: the whole working mass slips from the bottom of the slope toward this lurid obsessive fringe of multifaceted crime. Louis Chevalier will not ask criminal statistics to define this fringe, for one reason which he gives and another he implies. The first is that administratively registered crime forms only one part of real and actual crime. Certainly, but do not the judicial archives register the whole extensive range of "offenses," as well as crime?

The second reason, though not explicitly stated it is true, is perhaps yet again the author's desire to remain within the chosen parameters of his demonstration. The more so since this time I would agree that his controls provide him with an ample crop of information. Disease, mortality, suicide, infant desertion, illegitimate births, concubinage, the hospitals, old peoples' homes, sending babies out to nurse, all these "biological" signs (even though they are not, I would add, exclusively biological) make possible a laboratory study of unprecedented scope. A whole social pathology is thus revealed which is richly instructive for us. A realization of this provides a valuable methodological lesson.

Louis Chevalier is obviously right about the general direction of his inquiry. There is a definite line running from crime, a narrow band, to social danger, a wide band; to the poverty which casts its net over such a large part of the Parisian population; and finally to the whole of the working class, as a biological and social category. There is no question of "judging" this last (the whole book besides favors it) but of binding into a whole the series of figures which govern its multiple behavior and show it to be imprisoned in an inexorable destiny. No social mobility creates any compensatory upward movement, and any examples of it one can cite are merely exceptions which prove the rule.

I have attempted to follow and summarize this difficult book. It is not my intention, I repeat, to pass judgment on its correctness where Paris is concerned. Any endeavor as passionate as this is risky, and will and does give rise to reservations and criticism. My problem was to trace its general trend. This I attempted to do, at my own risk. As far as the application of the doctrine or "manifesto" to the example in which it is embodied is concerned, there could doubtless be endless discussion. But would it serve any good purpose just now? I hope that Louis Chevalier will give me the opportunity of coming to grips again with his complicated and authoritarian thinking in some new book. I would be afraid of limiting the scope of the debate, if I entered into such a discussion at this stage. It hardly matters, in fact, where the human sciences are concerned, whether Louis Chevalier is right about the Parisian case (as I think he is) or not; whether he made a mistake about some particular figure or reference; whether he was wrong to keep clear of the judicial archives, which I fear do not necessarily accord with his thesis. Nor does it really matter if he was wrong to stake so much on the literary evidence.

All the same certain lacunae in his Parisian study seem to me to be fairly serious, insofar as they are omissions of things which might tend to contradict or rather to limit the view taken by this book. I am amazed that the Paris of the Restoration and the July Monarchy was not more minutely studied in relation to the Paris which came before and after it.

Analyses, a host of figures, demographic and biological measurement could all have cast light on the matter. For my own part, I have the impression that the Parisian adventure which Louis Chevalier relates is unfortunately not so exceptional as he seems to think, and that, for instance, compared with the Paris of the sixteenth century and of Louis XIII, the horrors of the first half of the nineteenth century were positively a bed of roses. If I am wrong, prove it! Last but by no means least, what was happening at the same time in other cities and even in the countryside of France? In other European capitals? I am troubled by the idea that if the population of Paris nearly doubled between 1800 and 1850, that of London, of which Louis Chevalier speaks hardly at all, tripled (from 900,000 to 2,500,000). These comparisons would seem to me to be indispensable to any true understanding of Paris and of the demographic experience which was taking place there. They were even more indispensable to this book which was seeking force and conviction as a lesson in methodology. I am quite convinced that to get to the biological foundations of a society, to borrow Louis Chevalier's language, is to reach the most deep-seated of its structures. But I am amazed that one should wish to prove this to me by means of a study which in the final analysis is entirely conjunctural, one could say even narrowly conjunctural, exclusively concerned with what is presented to us as an unknown accident, as an exception in Parisian life; and not the least concerned, on the other hand, with setting that accident in the context of the centuries-long movement which carries along the deepest life of Paris, and of the other capitals, and of the whole of Europe. It is almost natural that Louis Chevalier should dwell on short-term conjunctures, fine as needlepoints, like the cholera epidemics in 1832 and 1849.

But an end to debate and reservations! What matters is the breach which this book has opened or has tried to open in the human sciences. What matters is its movement toward the new horizon of biological structures and realities, incidentally taking the risk of demolishing the imperialism of demography (in order to enlarge it, of course). To recognize this essential merit is doubtless the best way to pay due homage to this provocative book.

The three authors whom I have been considering could hardly be less like each other. If I have brought them together here, it was so as better to analyze the different positions of demography with regard to the whole of the human sciences, positions which I find increasingly more interesting the higher I place demography itself within this whole. It is an odd thing that Ernst Wagemann, an erstwhile economist, and Louis Chevalier (can one say an erstwhile historian? coming from history at any rate) are among the most fiercely nationalistic, one might even say xenophobic, in the face of demography's rival sciences. By contrast, Alfred Sauvy's thought naturally tends to a universal curiosity which preserves him from parochialism.

Now, at a time when the human sciences are shedding their old skins and breaking down the barriers which separate them (and I am doing my own sort of special pleading here), it is not the moment, it is no longer the moment for conscious or unconscious petty nationalisms. Or else I am entirely mistaken. There is no one science, no one career which will dominate this vast unstructured field of human knowledge. There is no "leading" history, still less a "leading" historical concept, any more than a "leading" sociology, economy, or demography. The methods, the points of view, the knowledge which have been acquired belong to all, I mean to all who have proved themselves capable of making use of it. As I have said before, the difficulty of having a common market of the social sciences is assimilating foreign techniques. Do not let us add spurious frontier disputes and quarrels over precedence. Any unilateral explanation seems to me detestable, and given the magnitude of the task nowadays, rather hopeless.

Consider Karl Marx, who had the authoritarian desire proper to every scholar to aim for the essential and the simple, and who held to a double line (at least it was double!) of a social and an economic explanation in his theories on the appropriation of the means of production. Between ourselves, Karl Marx had every right to be intoxicated with his own originality. Nonetheless he wrote on 18 March 1872 to Maurice La Châtre: "There is no royal road for Science." Do not let us lose sight of that! Many and difficult are the paths which we must tread.

Notes

1. "Let each work out his own method," he wrote to me in a note which I have before me now. "We don't need experts for that. If somebody can't be bothered to work out a method for himself, then *lascia la storia.*"
2. Mme. Ilse Deike, an old student at the École des Hautes Études, has furnished me with the following list of Ernst Wagemann's publications. It seems a useful idea to include it here. She has managed to introduce a little order into their variety:
*Die Nahrungswirtschaft des Auslandes,* Berlin, 1917; *Allgemeine Geldlehre,* I, Berlin, 1923; *Einführung in die Konjonkturlehre,* Leipzig, 1929; *Struktur und Rhythmus der Weltwirtschaft: Grundlagen einer weltwirtschaftliche Konjonkturlehre,* Berlin, 1931; *Geld und Kreditreform,* Berlin, 1932; *Was ist Geld?* Oldenburg, 1932; *Narrenspiel der Statistik: Die Umrisse eines statistischen Weltbildes,* 1st ed., Hamburg, 1935, 2d ed.,

Hamburg, 1942; *Wirtschaftspolitische Strategie: Von den obersten Grundsätzen wirtschaftlicher Staatskunst*, 1st ed., 1937, 2d ed., Hamburg, 1943; *Die Zahl als Detektiv: Heitere Plauderei über gewichtige Dinge*, 1st ed., Hamburg, 1938, 2d ed., Hamburg, 1952; *Der neue Balkan*, 1939; *Wo kommt das viele Geld her? Geldschöpfung und Finanzlenkung in Krieg und Frieden*, Düsseldorf, 1940; *Menschenzahl und Völkerschicksal: Eine Lehre von den optimalen Dimensionen gesellschaftlicher Gebilde*, Hamburg, 1948; *Berühmte Denkfehler der Nationalökonomie*, 1951; *Ein Markt der Zukunft: Lateinamerika*, Düsseldorf, 1953; *Wirtschaft bewundert und kritisiert: Wie ich Deutschland sehe*, Hamburg, 1935; *Wagen wägen, Wirtschaften: Erprobte Faustregeln–neue Wege*, Hamburg, 1945.

3. *La población en el destino de los pueblos* (Santiago, 1949).

4. *Economia mundial* (Santiago, 1952).

5. *Sammlung Dalp*, no. 80 (Berne, 1952).

6. See the graph, *Annales E.S.C.*, no. 3 (1960): p. 501.

7. Where he is concerned, this recourse seems to me unreasonable, but what is the good of launching into long explanations! Ernst Wagemann is not a historian. In this area he is too naïf for there to be anything to gain by following or by criticizing him.

8. Presses Universitaires, 1959.

9. I hardly like to say that one should also add the debatable but lively *Nature sociale*, which appeared in 1956, or the alert and intelligent *Montée des jeunes*, which just came off the presses a few months ago.

10. Cf. *Annales E.S.C.*, no. 3 (1960): 505.

11. *Manuel d'ethnographie* (Paris, 1947).

12. *Luxus und Kapitalismus* (Munich, 1922).

13. For a simple definition, see Louis Chevalier, *Démographie générale* (Paris: Dalloz, 1951).

14. In other words, chapter 11 seems too short.

15. Which means I find chapter 14 disappointing.

16. Bar a few lines, vol. 2, p. 236.

17. There is, alas! no index.

18. If, as I hope, this revival proves lasting.

19. Collection "Civilisations d'hier et d'aujourd'hui" (Paris: Plon, 1958).

20. Edited by the I.N.E.D., 23, Avenue F.-D. Roosevelt, Paris, VIIIᵉ.

21. In the index to his treatise *Démographie générale* (1951) we may be forgiven for smiling a little at finding no entry relating to his present research into biological structures.

*Part 3*                    *History and the Present Age*

# In Bahia, Brazil

## The Present Explains the Past

It is with enormous pleasure that one reads and rereads this delicate, intelligent book by Marvin Harris, of Columbia University. Its title, *Town and Country in Brazil*,[1] makes one fear that it will be a general, theoretical book, but happily such fears are unfounded. It is exclusively concerned with a journey and then with a stay made in a small Brazilian town. In the very first pages we arrive in Minas Velhas, right in the heart of the state of Bahia, deep in the interior. We are still there when the book closes, without ever having known a moment's boredom along the way in the company of a guide who knows how to see and understand, and how to make others understand. Besides which the descriptions are so vivid, the text so riveting that the whole work reads "like a novel." This is to my mind an exceptional compliment, for it is rare enough that a work which has been scientifically carried out, according to the strictest objectivity, should like a spectacle be able to take you out of the present time and lead you to the sources—here still living—of a reality, an "urban" civilization long past. A historian might dream of such a landscape, but actually to be able to see it, obsolete and archaic, with one's own eyes, to be able to reach out and touch it is a pleasure of quite another degree. And what an education! Let us hasten to enjoy it! Even in Minas Velhas the new dawn has its attractions: one day it will overthrow the whole of this old, fragile order, which has somehow, by a miracle, managed to survive.

## I

In the midst of ungrateful, mountainous, half-desert country, Minas Velhas—the Old Mines—was set up by the demands of the mining industry in the eighteenth century. It was among the important gold towns of the great Brazilian interior, some of which grew up precociously as early as the end of the seventeenth century; others, the most numerous, originated in the first decades of the eighteenth. Mining at Minas Velhas dates back to 1722, perhaps a little earlier. In any case, the town's charter goes back to 1725 at least, and by 1726 it had a town hall where the gold was melted down and the fifth due to the king of Portugal was levied. In

*Annales E.S.C.*, no. 2 (April–June 1959), pp. 325–36.

1746–47 the fifth went up to thirteen pounds of pure gold, or sixty-five pounds crude ore. To which obviously one can add fraud and gold in transit. As long as the gold in the seams and the sand was abundant, there was not really any problem for this active little town: supplies flowed to it from all sides, and sometimes from very far away. But at the end of the eighteenth century, the wealth of gold dried up in Minas Velhas, just as it did in Brazil as a whole.

The town somehow survived this disaster, despite its abnormal situation, precarious by nature. It continued on its way, and then managed to acquire and maintain the mediocre position of low-level administrative center. And so (somehow) it has muddled along until now, after many a disappointment: its administrative primacy—its second source of wealth—was fairly quickly contested and its "district" then refashioned, broken up, and fragmented. In 1921 came the last, and almost mortal blow: Vila Nova, its fairly prosperous neighbor, broke away from it with a district constituted according to its own desires, and needless to say, yet again to the detriment of the old town and its region. Added to all these mishaps, Minas Velhas had no luck either when it came to drawing up routes for the highways and the railroads: its geography was against it. The railway stops far short of it, at Bromado, and motor traffic has reached it only recently and with difficulty: one truck a day, with its cluster of travelers and its jumble of goods.

Besides, who would want to go to such a lost city? The traveler, having come to the last mountain, hesitates at Vila Nova, a town full of life in touch not only with the highway but with progress (electricity, the telegraph, Coca-Cola). If he inquires, he will hardly be encouraged to make his way on muleback across the Rio das Pedras Pass (which is intersected by, among other things, a gigantic waterfall), to the high valley and the plateaus of the *gerais* of Minas Velhas, exposed to the winds and dotted with stunted trees and sparse grasses. "Stay with us," the author was advised. "We have got electricity and cocoa-beans, an abundance of fresh fruit and pork. . . . Minas Velhas is the deadest place in the whole world. Nothing has changed there for the last two hundred years. If you like cold beer, you'd be better off staying here. There's only one bar in Minas Velhas and it does so little trade that it's not worth their while having an icebox[2]. . . . They are dreadfully backward. Things are terrible there. It is a sad, cold, dreary place, where nothing happens."

So the surprise is all the greater for the traveler when, having left "civilization" behind him, he arrives in Minas and finds a typical little town—an impression hardly offered by the Brazilian cities which are growing up today. Minas, oh miracle, has paved streets, houses[3] lined up along the sidewalks and freshly painted in blue and white, general cleanliness, inhabitants respectably dressed, and children coming out of school in their white shirts and blue shorts. There is a stone bridge, gateways, turnpikes, pseudoramparts, a main square with high stone church, also freshly painted in gold and white and blue, a park with formal gardens, the pride of the town and the meetingplace for the evening stroll. Has the traveler come to the enchanted city?

## II

And then? The best thing is to interest oneself in the happenings, the realities of the city, letting chance take its course. Bit by bit the problems become clear. No, Minas Velhas does not live exclusively on the fairly poor and meager villages which surround it: Serra do Ouro, Baixa do Gamba, Gravatão, Gilão, Bananal, Brumadinho, villages of white peasants, like the first, or black peasants, like the second, and all equally wretched. The earth, overly subdivided into tiny fields, is only moderately fertile; in total these villages contain 1,250 peasants. In contrast, Minas Velhas, which really is very small, nonetheless numbers 1,500 residents. Can one peasant alone support on his back the full weight of one city-dweller? No, of course he cannot. It would be asking too much of him, the more so since the surplus of the harvest—vegetables, fruit, sugar, rice, beans, manioc, a little corn, yams, sweet potatoes, coffee— does not go exclusively to the market in the town: the sellers go as far afield as Vila Nova, Gruta, or Formiga. So there is competition, though the old town, better situated, still tends to come off best. It also defends its rights through the estates of its "bourgeois"; the largest of these being the *fazendas,* not very extensive it is true, but often bordering the Rio das Pedras, on the best soil. These estates, whether small or middling, form an additional link between town and country.

In any case, it is in relation to these peasants that the man of Minas Velhas feels himself to be a city-dweller, right to the marrow of his bones, with a feeling far stronger than that which binds the Londoner or the New Yorker to his great city. To be a city-dweller is to be superior, to be able to tell oneself so, to think so, compared with the more unfortunate, or at least less fortunate, than oneself. How different the countryside is! It means loneliness. In the town there is noise, movement, conversation, a whole range of pleasures and distractions. It is quite a different form of existence. Do not envy the man in Minas Velhas who lives in an isolated house apart; for the *real* house is one that touches its neighbors, clinging to them in order to line up with one movement along the street. If that street is quiet, if "in the morning, when you go out, there isn't a sound," then everything is spoiled. Town means the reassuring, brotherly sound of others. The occasion, too, as I have said, for feeling superior to those peasants, mere Saturday guests (Saturday is market day), to those customers so awkward in the shops, so instantly recognizable by their clothes, their accents, their manners, even their faces. How nice it is to laugh at them! They themselves, these country-men, know the town is highly superior to them. Just think, here every-body buys their food with money! The town for them is nothing but *el comercio*. As José, from Baixa do Gamba, explains, "The life of *comercio*, its only for those with plenty of money in their pockets."[4] His wife thinks that "*el comercio* is all right for a few hours. I enjoy the *movimento*, but after a little while, I am tired by it, and then I cannot wait until it's time to go home."[5] Poor peasant, or as they say in Minas, poor *tabareu*, poor *gente da roca*. "They're frightened of their own shadows," says Pericles, a true city-dweller though only a poor simple Minas brick maker. On several occasions he accompanied Marvin Harris on his trips out of town. If they were going to Vila Nova, Pericles would go barefoot, in his ragged everyday clothes. But if they were going to Baixa do Gamba, that was quite another matter. He would dress up, even to the extent of borrow-ing a pair of shoes. "At Vila Nova, nobody pays attention to such things, but after all, at Baixa do Gamba I cannot go around looking like one of those *tabareus*."[6]

These little glimpses—which abound throughout the book—say more than any long discussion can of the pride of the town, its self-esteem, its taste for dignity, its love of noise, and festivals as the quintessence of noise, its delight too in culture, Latin grammar for instance, to an extent that in 1802 was already an object of admiration for two German travel-ers, the naturalists von Spix and von Martius. They too were struck by the dignity of this little town (which then numbered 900 inhabitants) and . . . by the excellence of its Latin teacher.

## III

But you cannot live on noise alone, or on self-regard. Since the satellite villages provide only half the town's food—and that not free of charge—then it needs must work for its living in order to pay for what it consumes: what it buys from the peasants, and also flour and the in-dispensable kerosene fuel which come to it from Vila Nova. There are two solutions to this problem: on the one hand emigration, with what it can mean in terms of a flow of money back; and on the other, craft industry.

Let us leave the first of these solutions aside. Minas Velhas is one example among a thousand others of these great movements which af-fect the entire *Nordeste* of Brazil (town and country), and not only the state of Bahia. One would need to look at this gigantic problem, whose inexhaustible tragedy has been expressed in the novels of Jorge Amado, from the point of view of the whole. Minas Velhas is but a drop of water carried along in this tide. Equally obviously, though, everything there is transformed by it. Emigration draws off the young men, sometimes the most highly qualified, tempted by the higher wages in Bahia, and even more in São Paolo. Source of many a drama: the drama of waiting (the town has an excessive female population); the drama of returning. But can one really return? How can one readapt oneself to the intrinsically gloomy existence of the narrow town?

Besides these emigrants, Minas in order to live has only the labor of its craftsmen to rely on: workers in copper, smiths, saddlers, harness makers, makers of luggage. lace makers and makers of artificial flowers, brick makers, tinkers, dressmakers, tailors, carpenters. Imagine an extremely small medieval town, working for its home market, and when it could for distant markets as well. The home market is the peasants we were speaking about a moment ago, purchasers of saddles, harness, knives, whips. So, out of 95 craftsmen we can number 39 metallurgists (if one may call them that) and 28 leather workers. The forge with its rudimentary bellows is not much different from that which we knew in our young days, in the villages of France. In the shop, two or three workers help the owner, usually sons, or a young relation, or the owner's wife. The purchaser will thus buy products made virtually before his eyes. Behold us for a moment whisked at will back to the eighteenth or seventeenth century, or even further back in time, anywhere in the West.

Besides the home market there is the distant market (meaning the interior of Brazil), within the zone of the mule train, beyond that of the railroads, few as they are, or of motorized trucks, though they are rapidly moving in. This market extends westward as far as Chique Chique, to the shrine of Bom Jesus de Lapa on the São Francisco River, which is both a place of pilgrimage and a fair rolled into one. As well as the pilgrims, thither flock, in July, the traveling merchants of Minas Velhas, their mules loaded with a whole variety of merchandise. They sell, resell, barter, and sell again. The shopkeeper who has entrusted his knives or shoes to them has already agreed on a price, but the whole operation is conducted at his own risk: the retailer on his return will give back any remaining unsold merchandise when they settle up. This takes us right back in time, with a little exaggeration, to the beginning of the *commenda* and of mercantile capitalism. The one in control is not the manufacturer, but the one transporting and selling the product. As one might easily imagine, the area penetrated by this primitive form of trade is being threatened and constantly whittled away by the establishment of new means of transport and the arrival of new merchandise, the one bringing the other. Shoes made in the neighboring state of Pernambucco have already reached Vila Nova. Only twenty-five years ago, these internal trade routes connected Minas Velhas to Goyaz and even to São Paolo: not today. Nonetheless this curtailed area of supply still enables Minas Velhas to maintain all its traditional operations of exchange, barter, and purchase. Thus it procures its metals by some careful bartering: scrap iron, old railroad track, zinc from broken-up car engines, copper from old pots. Its merchants even bring it the metal necessary for its primitive, insecure nickel-plating. It would of course be far better to have sheets of nickel sent from Bahia. But how would one pay for them? What the merchants do is to get together the old nickel four-hundred-reis pieces, which are no longer made today but which, though removed from general circulation, continue to be found among these primitive routes and to accumulate among the offerings at Bom Jesus de Lapa. A bargain made, and behold them, after July, on their way to Minas.

The transporters are in a dominant position, and so too are the capitalists, the entrepreneurs. How have they come into being? It is not a question to which our guide finds a satisfying answer. He deals with it too briefly, but these capitalists do indeed exist, quite recognizably, though few in number. There are few where metals are concerned: here the world of the craftsman seems to have worked things out for itself by producing second-rate goods at speed. The smith João Celestino knows the score: "The smith has only his eyes to guide him," he said one day. But what is the point of being a fine craftsman with a good eye? "Life today doesn't give us the chance to produce a proper piece of work any more." What freedom, what deprivation!

It is quite different where leather work is concerned: encouraged by low wages, piecework comes into existence (the craftsmen, curiously enough, see in it a sign of their freedom and independence, and regard a regular wage as enslaving). At the same moment home working starts, and even specialization in new workshops, the timid beginnings of "manufacture." It could be the sixteenth or the seventeenth century. The boss is the entrepreneur, the man who "makes work," like Senhor Braulio, manufacturer of shoes, sandals, boots, and saddles, which he will then proceed to sell himself. He is in fact a merchant of the old school, such as existed all over the West, in the early stages of capitalism. He procures the raw materials, pays the wages, ensures sales. To the craftsmen of Minas Velhas he is a providence. I agree, but how long can he go on being one? Only as long as a system depending on the division of labor and the existence of extremely low wages can persist. Now this system is running up against factors a good deal more powerful than Senhor Braulio: there are machines elsewhere. There are none, or not really any, in Minas Velhas yet. But the day will dawn when not even the peasants, the *tabareus* from the surrounding countryside, will come in to buy their shoes, their whips, or their knives in the leather sheathes. For the struggle is on all over the country between the Brazil of yesterday, with its lack of any proper organization, and the imperious Brazil of today. The old town manages to withstand all these hostile conditions by means of an ascetic and fairly impoverished economy. It is a situation which offers a fairly low standard of living to its rich, or so-called rich, and an even worse one to its poor, who are truly poor. This general mediocrity can be measured by the position which all in the town regard as the one most to be envied, that of the shopkeeper of the *venta*. This retailer of foodstuffs, vegetables, fruit, crude sugar *(la rapadura)*, and brandy *(cachaça)*, this moneylender (for nearly everything is sold on credit), this grocer sitting all day long on his chair is the happy man to whom customers, gossip, the whole *movimento* of the town all come.

## IV

Will Marvin Harris forgive me for having insisted on regarding these images, these living documents which he has brought so carefully to light as evidence of inestimable value about the past? How better could one come to understand the "small" capitalism of the medieval shopkeepers or, if need be, their contemporaries' long-distance capitalism: they are both here before our eyes in the first chapters of the book, chapters crammed with a wealth of detail and information, as we have seen as we followed them step by step. Beyond these chapters, Marvin Harris continues according to the customary procedure of an ethnographic inquiry: having discussed the siting of the town and its economic life, he then goes on to speak about races, classes, municipal government, religion, popular beliefs, in chapters which are always vivid and precise, his constant desire being to show as far as possible the accord or discord existing between the town and the small villages in its neighborhood. He felt, not without some justification, that this was one of the major connections to be examined in any ethnographical inquiry.

May I say that I am nonetheless not entirely in agreement with this customary procedure, carried out once again in a most conventional way, according to rules decided upon *a priori*? Is a small town a good field for contemporary observation? Doubtless it is, as long as it is not studied exclusively in and for itself as ethnography too frequently does, and as long as it is treated as evidence which must be related to several different levels of comparison, both in time and space. As far as Minas Velhas is concerned, its whole past should have been examined, the past of its region, and the past of Brazil as a whole. Its present environment should have been examined, stopping at Vila Nova, just as the traveler did at the beginning of the book, but also going as far afield as Formiga, Gruta, and Sincora and staying there for a while, and even questioning the whole of Bahia State, its towns and villages. And then he should certainly have gone even further, and dealt with Brazil as a whole, and perhaps with other countries too.

But let us state our case even more clearly. From the very first pages of his book, the author does not hide from us the exceptional character of Minas Velhas, the surprise it is for the newcomer, particularly because of the citylike appearance it presents despite its size and poverty. From then on, the author's approach is simple: to study life in Minas Velhas in every aspect and in all its contemporary detail, and then thanks to a comparison with the criteria of urban life as defined by sociologists or ethnographers, to conclude that Minas is essentially a *town*. But the chief problem, for me, from the point of view of the human sciences, is posed in different terms: why is there this aberration? And how far is Minas aberrant? Is this a unique, extraordinary case? Or does it recur elsewhere, in visibly analogous conditions? Where, and how? The conclusion of the book hardly touches these questions, the only pages which are, in my opinion, evasive and imprecise.

It seems to me, that everything is not entirely original in the town of Minas Velhas. I would hold that according to the author's descriptions the aberration can essentially be reduced to the socioeconomic structures which I have just related. In a word, the salient fact to which I in the author's place would have dedicated all my care is that Minas Velhas should have survived after the failure of the gold mines, and survived, be it noted, as an old-time town, with poor revenues and a mediocre population. This survival, sufficiently amazing in itself, and the ancient mechanisms which it implies would have had my almost exclusive attention. I would have looked at them and looked at them again, analyzed them in themselves and also in the light of the medieval and semimodern mechanisms which we can see in European history. I would have measured this chronological falling out of step. I would have calculated and counted even more than our guide has done (global revenue by member of population), and precisely mapped and examined the area of trade.

Where the town's survival is concerned, since it has archives I would have looked at them closely. I would have tried to find out just what the town was really like at the time of the gold, with its miners, its craftsmen, its shopkeepers, its landowners, its black slaves, and its carriers, so as to fix its starting point properly. In the nineteenth century, Marvin Harris tells us, it survived as an administrative center, with the wages of these so-called clerks essentially taking the place of the gold dust. But the district had to make this new life possible, had to provide wealth and sufficient population, had to maintain a whole system of exchange—the same system that today lies under the constant threat of extinction—sufficient for Minas Velhas' urban existence. And a subsidiary question: where did the *nouveaux riches* who appeared in Minas in the nineteenth century suddenly spring from?

In 1947, in quite another region of the vast country of Brazil, I made a less poetic trip than Marvin Harris's, but one that was in its own way no less revelatory. Ubatuba, on the Atlantic coast, in São Paolo State not far from Santos, had its own era of splendor around 1840. It was at that time linked by an active mule-train route to Taubaté, over the mighty Serra do Mar, that green wall between the coast and the interior, in the same way as Santos was linked to São Paolo, which was then only a very small town. Taubaté-Ubatuba, like Santos-São Paolo, is the marriage of a central coffee exchange and a port exporting it the world over. In the competition which soon arose, São Paolo-Santos prevailed, to such an extent that the stations were all that was ever built of a projected railroad between Ubatuba and Taubaté. Even today, Ubatuba and Taubaté are linked by a bus which manages, God alone knows how, to follow the ancient mule track. It is a path which is all downhill—at one end Taubaté, to which industry has given a new lease of life, at the other Ubatuba, wretched and devoured by the tropical vegetation. Its old storied houses *(sobrados)*, abandoned, ruined by water and by the palm trees growing through cracks in the walls, but still impressive, and its cemetery with its stylish funeral plaques alone tell of the ancient fortune of this little port. The town of Ubatuba has not survived. It is a village of peasants, of *caboclos*. I met the daughter of a French engineer there, illiterate, not remembering a single word of her mother tongue, married to a *caboclo* and like him in every respect. And yet Ubatuba has its officials and its justice of the peace, a graduate of the faculty of law in São Paolo, a civilized man in exile in a country which has sunk well below the level of of Minas Velhas. For an entire evening I listened with him to a folk singer accompanied by a *violão* player (a *violão* is a sort of six-stringed guitar): folk songs had taken over again here, the only songs that seemed appropriate, and one song, improvised in the old way, related the epic of the *chegada da luz,* the coming of the electric light. Did they not have to cut a trench, a *picada,* for the poles and line, right through the forest which, descending from the mountain, surrounds the town? An impenetrable forest, but not virgin since, as the judge our guide remarked, it is possible to find remains of coffee plants in it here and there. The plantations have disappeared and so has the town, having had neither a surrounding district to keep it to some extent alive, nor the energy in itself which would have allowed it to adapt. Minas Velhas, in the slow-moving surroundings of the *Nordeste,* was luckier.

## V

Compared with this central problem, the rest, the second landscape which Marvin Harris offers us, seems to me of no great interest. In fact I doubt its originality. Despite all the subtle shades noted by the author, whether it is a question of beliefs, of municipal government, of political passions, Minas seems to me to share in the mainstream of Brazilian life. I am nonetheless troubled by the way in which Marvin Harris presents the color problem. Are things really as tense as he would have us believe? By and large, there are "rich whites" on the one side and "poor blacks" on the other according to the usual formula, and also of course whites who are by no means rich and blacks who are educated and well-off. This leads to a fairly bizarre social pyramid, stratified not horizontally but across the grain. A similar situation prevails elsewhere, does it not, in the neighborhood of Minas Velhas itself? Social and racial tension would be only the greater for it, I would willingly agree, particularly at the level of the poor white whose wife has to go out gathering wood herself, or down to the nearby river to do the washing or to fetch water, which is in itself a proof of poverty. The tension would be greater too at the level of the well-off black, invited into the houses of the whites but not as an equal and who stays in his corner, diffident, discontented, and on his dignity. Nonetheless, should one attribute to Minas Velhas, because of its tense and enclosed life, a particular racism quite outside the normal framework of Brazilian civilization? On the national scale, goodwill reigns between people of different colors, and Gilberto Freyre long ago noted their sexual fraternization. It is true that this fairly benign small-town racism, if it does exist, seems not to be connected to the historical line of the Brazilian past. I must say I would have liked more light on this point. I find the study of the rival clubs and bands and the auctions at the *fiesta,* and the portrait of Waldemar, the only black councillor in the town, only half-satisfying. What can one make of it, when there is nothing to compare it with! How do the same problems arise in the neighboring regions, in Gruta, Formiga, Vila Nova, the neighboring towns? Is the social and racial tension different in Minas Velhas, and particular to it? If so, if it can be distinguished from the mainstream of the country as a whole, who is to blame, the blacks or the whites or both? Think, though, of how the black in Minas Velhas has broken all his links with the African cults which elsewhere are the living source of his originality. This simple fact is of enormous significance. Similar remarks can be made against Harris's attitude where religion is concerned. The Catholicism of Minas Velhas seems to him to be a formal, external, and fairly empty affair. I am sure he is right. But I am equally sure that he is wrong to draw certain conclusions from this. I am afraid he has lacked contact with the various catholicisms of Europe, particularly with those of Italy, Spain, and Portugal which, to a Frenchman for example, seem just as formal and external. It is in relation to purer forms of Christianity, which have been, so to speak, more stripped down, that the Christianity of Minas Velhas can seem surprising. But then what about that of Brazil as a whole! The anticlericalism which our investigator seeks in texts of different dates and in "reliable histories" does not prove much: it is in the tradition of a young Christianity which does not mind free speech and slightly racy stories. I am amazed, in fact, that despite certain undeniable errors, ignorances, reservations, and deviations, Christianity should have set itself down securely in the old city, just as in the rest of Brazil, where it is an essential component of the civilization. I would say the same of the superstitions: they are not something of which modern Brazil is going to rid itself overnight. They are quite as alive in the hearts of the big cities as they are in a small urban center like Minas Velhas and its surrounding countryside.

But let us call a halt to our criticisms, which have after all been a way of prolonging the obvious pleasure we have had from reading the book. I would certainly have liked it if Marvin Harris had oriented it differently; if on two or three occasions he had been able to turn himself around, so that he could come face to face with the past of the small people he was studying; if he had distinguished the original evidence of these few men—the aberration of Minas Velhas—from the ordinary evidence of daily life in the interior of Brazil.

But if I have said all this rather forcefully, it is aimed less at an author whose subtlety, intelligence, and devotion are not to be questioned than at an anthropology which places too high a value on direct inquiry, which imposes a uniform treatment on any study of the present without troubling too much about the obvious individual variations which should be brought out. It is only in relation to extremely good books like this one that one can attempt to prove the necessary insufficiency of the method—since the author's own competence is not in question—and that one can warn once again against what Lucien Febvre called the rules of the "masterwork," confidently applied no matter what the subject and the particular approach it might have called for. What a pity![7]

Notes

1. Marvin Harris, *Town and Country in Brazil* (New York: Columbia University Press, 1956).
2. Besides, there is no electricity at Minas Velhas.
3. Built of sun-dried bricks, and a few stones, and roofed with tiles.
4. Harris, op. cit., p. 145.
5. Ibid.
6. Ibid., p. 143.
7. And what a pity that this book does not have the illustrations it deserves. Not a single photograph.

# The History
# of Civilizations

## The Past Explains
## the Present

The question under discussion in the present chapter is a fairly unusual one: can the history of civilization, as it has developed from the eighteenth century and Voltaire's *Essai sur les moeurs* (1756) to the present day, help us to understand the present time and thus, necessarily the future—for today can hardly be understood except in relation to tomorrow? The author of these lines is a historian for whom history means an understanding of both past and present, of what has been and is to be, of a distinction within each historical "time," whether today's or yesterday's, between what is lasting, what has and is vigorously perpetuating itself, and what is only provisional and ephemeral. He would answer readily that all history must be mobilized if one would understand the present. But, within this whole body of our profession, what precisely is represented by the history of civilization? Is it in fact an area on its own at all? Rafael Altamira did not hesitate to assert that "saying civilization comes to the same thing as saying history." And as early as 1828, Guizot was writing: "This history [of civilization] is the biggest of all, . . . it comprises all the others."

What is clearly in question here is a vast, immense part of our professional domain, but a part nonetheless, round which it has never been easy to draw a line, and which continues to change according to different interpretations from one century to another, from one country to another, from one historian and one essayist to another. Any definition must confess itself hard to arrive at and fraught with dangers.

And first of all, we get *civilization,* concept relating to humanity as a whole, and *civilizations,* scattered through time and space. Besides, the term civilization never travels alone: it is unfailingly accompanied by the term culture, a term which is not simply synonymous with it, however. Let us add that there are also *culture* and *cultures.* As for the adjective *cultural,* it has lavished its rather ambiguous services on us for some time, as much in the domain of culture (as is etymologically appropriate) as in that of civilization, which lacks a specific adjective of its own. A civilization, we say, is a collection of cultural characteristics and phenomena.

Chapter 5 of the *Encyclopédie française,* vol. 20, *Le Monde en devenir (Histoire, évolution, prospective)* (Paris: Larousse, 1959).

So here we are already with a certain number of shades of meaning and possible sources of confusion. But whatever the subject of this particular history may be called, civilization or culture, civilizations or cultures, it appears at first sight to be a procession, or rather an orchestra, of particular histories: history of language, of literature, history of science, history of art, history of law, of institutions, history of sensibility, of customs, of technology, of superstitions, beliefs, religions (and even religious feelings), history of daily life, not to mention the rarely attempted history of taste and of cooking (recipes) . . . Each of these subsections (and there are others I have not mentioned) is more or less developed, with its own rules, objectives, internal vocabulary, and individual movement which is not necessarily that of general history. The difficulty is to get them working together. During a year at the Collège de France, I vainly attempted to seek links, for the sixteenth century in Europe, between the history of sciences and technology and other areas of general history. All the same, whether these histories proceed at the same rhythm or not, this does not mean that they are indifferent to each other. Against the point of view of such as Léon Brunschwicg and Étienne Gilson, with their autonomous history of ideas, Lucien Febvre justly proclaimed the rights of a general history, conscious of the whole of life from which nothing can be separated, except in an arbitrary way. But reconstituting this unity is as endless a task as squaring the circle.

However, there can be no real hesitation where the history of civilization is concerned, particularly when it is a case not of just one of its sectors, but of that history taken as a whole. It is hard to see then how it could be separated from general or, as it is sometimes called, global history. For if the history of civilization claims generally to present a simplified point of view, it nonetheless remains an attempt to interpret and master History with a capital *H*. It may place particular truths and particular aspects of the real in the foreground, but these truths and these realities would like to be seen as explanations of the whole. Every time, there is thus an examination on different levels of the whole of history, taken necessarily, however briefly, over its full extent, and thus in all its aspects, traditional history quite as much as social or economic history. And if the history of civilization has long held a sort of primacy which is today being challenged, then that is because it offered what was then the only possibility of going beyond, or as Henri Berr said, of "enlarging" the scope of traditional history, enclosed as it was within the sterility of the political chronicle, and of "admitting events other than political ones, and actors other than official figures." New and more certain paths, in short, of reaching the horizons of a general history and explanation. This is what made yesterday's struggles in favor of *Kulturgeschichte* by Karl Lamprecht so lively. Since history has expanded

fairly recently toward the social and the economic, the history of civilizations no longer plays such an aggressive role, although it clearly remains
an exceptional field for consideration.

All the same, when all is said and done, to project a complex and still
uncertain history onto the present, to bring it into a position with which
it is totally unfamiliar, a "prospective" position as it is called these days,
cannot but entail the opening of a long and difficult debate. The present
chapter attempts neither to summarize that debate, nor to close it, but at
the very most to bring out its salient points.

Even so, some precautions must be taken. Two at least. First, following
the tradition of Henri Berr's Centre de Synthèse, we must have recourse
to some sort of linguistic research; those words which attract and divert
our attention must be tracked down to their origins, put back in their
contexts, so that we may know whether they are true friends or false.
Second precaution: we must ask ourselves what grouping, what constellation of *interrelated* forces, values, or elements should one in all good
faith assume beneath the term civilization or culture? Definitions here
must be clear-cut and imperative. If there is not a certain coherence
within the area to which we are committed, if preliminary and readily
accessible observation is not "scientifically" possible, if we do not keep
ourselves firmly out of the grip of a metaphysics of history, then of
course our attempt is doomed from the start.

## Civilization and Culture
### The Origins and Fortunes of these Words

*A priori,* let us express our amazement that there are but two words
(supple and dubious friends as we shall find them) to cover and grasp so
huge an area: *civilization* and *culture.* Their transposition into the plural
increases their significance but not their number, and *cultural,* which
came into our language and others from the German around 1900,
makes for an ease of speaking or of writing but nothing more. Two
words are very few, especially as only one of them is actually in use much
of the time.

Thus, up till 1800 culture had no importance. After that, the two
words were in competition. It still happens that they are or that one is
preferred to the other, and unless I am wrong, this tends to reestablish a
unitary concept of the idea of civilization or culture. But these tendencies toward unity are not the rule. Rather, the competition between the
two words is becoming increasingly fierce, and regularly results in divisions. So the unity of the great kingdom is broken up, and the integrity
of large problems fragmented: whence surreptitious wars between ideas,
and a good many resulting errors. In short, these quarrels between

words which can at first sight seem, and indeed often are, extremely boring, carry us right to the heart of the discussion, even though they cannot, of course, fully clarify it entirely by themselves.

Culture and civilization were born in France at just about the same time. Culture, which had had a long life already (Cicero speaks of *cultura mentis*), only really took on the specific meaning of intellectual culture toward the middle of the eighteenth century. As far as we know, civilization first appeared in a printed work in 1766, though doubtless it was current in speech earlier. In any case, it appeared long after the verb and the participle, *civilize* and *civilized,* which can be seen in action as early as the sixteenth and seventeenth centuries. The substantive *civilization* had to be frankly invented, and made up. From its inception, it referred to a worldly ideal of intellectual, technological, moral, and social progress. Civilization is "enlightenment." "The further civilization extends over the earth, the more one will witness the disappearance of war and conquest, slavery and want," prophesied Condorcet in 1787. Thus it can hardly be imagined without a well-bred, well-mannered, and "polite" society to sustain it. Opposed to it stands *barbarity:* it is over this that the former declares a difficult and necessary victory. Between the one and the other there is, in any case, a great gulf fixed. In 1776, Mably wrote to one of his friends, a Polish count: "In the last century, you were threatened with great danger when Sweden emerged from barbarity, under Gustavus Adolphus." Similarly: "Peter I [of Russia] withdrew his nation from the extreme barbarity into which it had sunk." But it is noticeable how the term civilization does not spring readily to the abbé's pen as a counterfoil. Its career as a word was only just beginning.

It was to be a brilliant career, more brilliant than useful, or at least that is the opinion which Joseph Chappey puts forward in his vigorous and persuasive book (1958). For half a century, "civilization" had certainly had a great success in language and literature, without being entirely successful in the field of science. "Man," wrote Chappey, "was not at that time able to appreciate the importance of the word." In order to satisfy him, all the budding human sciences would have had to put themselves at the service of this new word and the immense gains which it brought with it. But nothing of the kind actually happened. The human sciences were then in their infancy, and their concern was in finding their own feet. And the "polite," optimistic society which had given the word its initial stability was soon to disappear under the welter of transformations and revolutions with which the eighteenth century welded itself to the nineteenth. It may be that a great opportunity was missed.

In any case, toward 1850, after all sorts of vicissitudes, *civilization* (and *culture*) moved from the singular to the plural. This triumph of the particular over the general fits fairly well into the movement of the nineteenth century. But what a major step it was, a reflection of other steps and other transformations! Civilizations and cultures in the plural imply the renunciation of a civilization defined as an ideal, or rather as the ideal; they mean overlooking to some extent the universal social, moral, and intellectual qualities which had been implied at the beginning, and which still remained in the tendency to regard all human experience as being of equal interest, European and non-European alike.

This breaking up of the "immense empire of civilization into autonomous provinces" (Lucien Febvre) was due in no small part to the work of travelers, geographers, and ethnographers, even before 1850. Europe was in the process of discovering, of rediscovering the world, and had to adapt itself to it: a man is a man, a civilization is a civilization, whatever its level. So civilizations "of place" and "diabolical"[1] civilizations of a particular age proliferated. So civilization was segmented both in space and time, the ridiculously fragmented time of specialists. At the time of Voltaire and Condorcet, could one have spoken of the culture of the Eskimos, or (an even more striking example, which occurred in Alfred Métraux's thesis) of the civilization of the Tupi-Guarani, the Brazilian Indians? Yet it was Voltaire, in his *Siècle de Louis XIV* (1751), who without actually using the word first applied the notion of the "civilization of an age." The triumphant plural of the nineteenth century is undeniably a sign of new ideas, new ways of thinking—in short, new times.

This triumph, which became more or less clearly defined toward 1850, is visible not only in France but across the whole of Europe. We must not forget, in fact, that the crucial terms like this, and a good many other things too, are constantly on the move from one language to another, from one author to another. The word is tossed back and forth like a ball, but when it comes back the ball is never quite the same as when it left. Thus, on its way back from Germany—the admirable and much admired Germany of the first half of the nineteenth century—*culture* arrived in France with a whole new meaning and prestige. Immediately this modest secondary term became, or attempted to become, the dominant word in Western thought. By culture, the German language from Herder on intended scientific and intellectual progress freely removed from any social context. By civilization it simply intended the material aspect of man's existence. One word is devalued, the other exalted. Marx and Engels wrote in the *Communist Party Manifesto* (1848): "In today's society there is too much civilization, [meaning] too much means of subsistence, too much industry, too much commerce."

This position with regard to civilization and culture is one which persisted tenaciously in German thought. It corresponds, as has already been remarked,[2] to the dichotomy which that thought has customarily drawn between spirit and nature *(Geist* and *Natur)*. In direct line of descent, Ferdinand Tönnies (1922) or Alfred Weber (1935) continued to class the whole body of practical, and even intellectual knowledge—in short, all the impersonal means which allow man to act on nature—under the heading of civilization. Under culture, on the other hand, they recognized only values, ideals, normative principles. For Thomas Mann, "culture equals true spirituality, while civilization means mechanization."[3] Thus a German historian[4] wrote characteristically in 1951: "It is man's duty today to see that civilization does not destroy culture, nor technology the human being." Nothing could be more clear. Nonetheless, even in Germany this terminology did not have the floor to itself. From 1918 to 1922, Oswald Spengler slightly modified the usual relationship. He saw in culture the beginnings, the creative impulse, the fertilizing factor in all civilization. Civilization, on the other hand, he saw as autumnal, repetitious, an empty mechanism, a superficial splendor, a hardening of the arteries. For Spengler there was a "decline" in the West not because of particular difficulties, or tragic threats, though he does not deny these, but simply because the West had arrived at the stage of civilization, of living death. And it is thus that one can explain the recent phrase, so anodyne in itself, which flowed naturally from the pen of a German historian, G. Kuhn (1958), when speaking of the victory of the peasants from Germany over ancient Rome at the end of the great invasions. It was, he said, "the victory of peasants over warrior, of country over town, of culture over civilization."

But this long-standing German predilection for culture, which goes right back to 1848 and the Romantic movement, is by no means the last word in this continuing debate. In England, and in France too, incidentally, the word *civilization* has defended itself pretty well, and has managed to hold on to pride of place. In Spain too, Rafael Altamira's great history, written between 1900 and 1911, a revolutionary work in its time, was called *Historia de España y de la Civilización Española*. And in Italy one can remark the eminent part played by the extremely ancient word *civiltà*. In our own country, I doubt whether the authors[5] of a recent *Histoire de la civilisation française* (1958), the lively successor to Alfred Rambard's classic textbook, would see France as being either sunk in material existence, that enemy of the spirit, or in the grip of the monotony of repetition and old age, separated of necessity from the springs of youth without which no creation is possible. Henri Marrou suggested twenty years ago that the word culture in French should be reserved for the "personal aspect of the life of the mind" and civilization for sociological realities. Civilization would do pretty well in such a division. In fact, I believe Huizinga was on the right track to see an additional reason for Spengler's failure (a point I will return to later) in the way in which the German essayist underestimated the word civilization that he attacked so vigorously, that is, underestimated its "international" influence outside Germany.

But if there is danger for the word civilization, a word which I would neither defend nor attack, it is due much more to the arrival on the scene of anthropologists and ethnographers than to the perfectly defensible persistence of German thinkers. Since Edward Burnett Tylor's crucial book (1871), anthropologists and ethnographers are much less in the habit of talking of primitive civilizations than of primitive cultures. This would hardly trouble us historians were it not for the fact that they are almost alone today in attempting to speak scientifically, "objectively," of the problems of civilization.[6] As we read their works, their language becomes familiar to us. One fine morning it might just take over altogether.

What conclusion can one come to, but that culture and civilization have knocked about the world with its contradictory tastes and ways of thought even more than the lexicographers would have us believe, so that one should at least be on one's guard against their thousand in-carnations. All living words change and should change, these like any others. It must be so, if only because of the needs of a scientific vocabu-lary, because of the insidious progress of the adjective cultural (it is always the neutrals who get on), because of the crises of conscience and method to which all human sciences have been prey. In their recent work, A. L. Kroeber and Clyde Klukhohn, two of America's most emi-nent anthropologists, have made the position completely clear where culture in concerned. They have listed 161 definitions of the word, all of them different, of course, not to mention those that are yet to come! In his *Manuel de sociologie,* Armand Cuvillier has numbered at least twenty different meanings of civilization. That is a great many, perhaps too many. As for trying to arbitrate in these debates, it is best not even to entertain the idea. When the Centre de Synthèse was involved in the tempting project of trying to establish some sort of specific historical vocabulary, Henri Pirenne argued (1931) that the historian did best to make use of living words in current use to the exclusion of all others, and thus to separate himself resolutely from an immobilized, sclerotic vocab-ulary like that of the philosophers (which, incidentally, is constantly subject to change, like the mathematicians' language, whatever anyone may say). I would willingly agree with Pirenne. Let us use words as they fall to us, in their living, their provisionally living meaning. But let us also be aware of the other possibilities which they suggest and have suggested, and of the traps which they can lay for the unwary.

Because anyone can do much as he wishes with these living, un-disciplined words. A young American anthropologist, Philip Bagby, suggested in a charming and intelligent book (1958) that *civilization* should be reserved for towns, and *culture* for the nonurbanized countryside, civilization by this token always being high-grade culture, a higher level of culture. The solution might well be a good one, although not, incidentally, entirely original, but I do not really believe that it is possible to force words to settle down once and for all, however excellent the definition or convention suggested. Changes are still taking place before our eyes, if only because of the present tendency to harness our ambiguous substantives to adjectives which are less so, and to speak of a material, moral, scientific, technological, or even economic culture or civilization (a book by René Courtin is called *La Civilisation économique du Brésil*).

So the battle of the words is not at an end. And perhaps, in the simmering domain of the human sciences where so much that is unexpected is still going on, we have more need than we might think for words that can be molded, that are crammed with a variety of meanings, and that are able to adapt themselves to observation (and its surprises) rather than hampering it. Until the establishment of a new order, I must admit that I will go on using these two key words indiscriminately one for the other, making the meaning clear from the context. If such an alternation threatens to become dangerous, I will fall back on the adjective cultural, whose use does not seem to me to be "barbarous" (Joseph Chappey), but merely convenient. Besides, I could fill a whole page, going back only as far as Hegel, with the names of authors of greater or lesser stature who have used both words indiscriminately, without too great a regard for, or awareness of, preliminary definitions. There are, I think, more important areas of confusion and prejudice.

*Attempts at a Definition*

In any case, words being what they are, we will not have any difficulty in maintaining our freedom of judgment and of action where they are concerned: we have gained our first point. But we shall have more trouble dealing with the things signified. Unfortunately, we have to admit that just like other social specialists, historians who have concerned themselves with civilization have left us in great uncertainty as to what they actually mean by it. "Civilization" is to them a means, legitimate or not, of reducing history to great perspectives—*their* perspectives. Whence selectivity and authoritarian views, each justifiable in itself, but each breaking up the domain of civilization, and reducing it every time to only one of its sectors. That the sector should change from one author to another according to individual choice and intent does not make it any easier to decide the final usefulness of the history of civilization for an understanding of the world of today. None of our authors—not even

Arnold Toynbee—seems to have felt the need to give us a definition, an overall view of what civilization means to him. It is so obvious, isn't it? So obvious that we have to try to make out on our own, from book to book according to the context, just what each historian has seen as his task, and consequently just what ours might be.

*Guizot.* François Guizot's lovely books, which are always such a pleasure to read (*Histoire de la civilisation en Europe* and *Histoire de la civilisation en France* [1829–32, the former reissued with a new preface in 1855]) can be our starting point. Unfortunately, they do not of course actually specify their object. But for Guizot, civilization means above all progress, just as it did in the eighteenth century. A twofold progress, in fact, both social and intellectual. The ideal would be a harmony, an equilibrium between these two sides of the scales. But has not England tended toward the achievement of social progress, Germany toward the intellectual, France to both at once? But that is not really the point here. What is important is to see how, for Guizot, civilization with its double movement is embodied in a people—France—or in that other "people" (Lucien Febvre) which is Europe: in short, in a body of men. Unfortunately, he gains his point at the cost of limiting himself to the framework of political history, which greatly restricts its scope. The more so in that for Guizot, politics itself is in the final analysis subject to a Manichean division between the two principles of authority and freedom—a struggle which is abated only by means of useful and more or less sensible compromises, such as the July Monarchy perhaps. A great theory with a small result, one might say, although it is true that the spectacle of the present is rarely seen on the scale of history by a contemporary, even if he is both historian and man of action.

"Two great forces," wrote Guizot in his preface of 1855, "two great rights, authority and freedom, coexist and struggle together at the heart of all human societies. . . . I am one of those who, in moving from study to a more troubled scene, have sought within the political order for an active harmony between authority and freedom, a harmony in the midst of their struggles, their avowed and open struggles, contained and regulated within a legal arena. Was it but a dream?"

*Burckhardt. Die Kultur der Renaissance in Italien,* by Jacob Burckhardt, "the wisest spirit of the nineteenth century," as Huizinga not unjustifiably called him, appeared in a limited edition in 1860. Let us open it: it will take us to quite a different world from Guizot's. The West, this time, is examined neither in its full extent, nor with regard to the entirety of its past. One single highly luminous moment is retained from the whole vast album of Western civilization. The Renaissance, a term which

Burckhardt, following Michelet (1855), set on its career, is taken at its Italian source, with a wealth of researches and details which present learning might have superseded but not yet eclipsed. For so obvious and radiant is this book's intelligence that it constantly transcended the perspectives possible at its time. Nonetheless, was Jacob Burckhardt in the middle of his life fully in possession of his vision of history? Had he already reduced it to the "triad" to which he was to say later that all of man's past can be related: the state, religion, and culture? A large place, a splendid place, is given to the state, to the states of Italy in the fifteenth and sixteenth centuries; then the artistic values of the culture are studied with taste and discrimination (for him, artistic values dominate everything); religion, by contrast, gets only the leftovers. Worse still, beyond this "triad," nothing or almost nothing is said about the material and social bodies of the Italy of Lorenzo the Magnificent. The "superstructure" envisaged and attained by this never-less-than-dazzling book remains aerial, suspended, despite the taste for the concrete which informs it. Is this right? I mean, is it right for historians a century later to be content with this image of the whole which nobody since has ever really replaced?

It would be useful to see how far Jacob Burckhardt fits into the movement of German *Kulturgeschichte,* projected as early as Herder (1784–91) and popularized by the publication of Gustav Klemm's book (1843–52). German historiography of the mid–nineteenth century succumbed to a highly dangerous dichotomy, as is clearly shown in the single instance of Weber's great textbook, *Universal History* (1853), which, in translation, was to play such an important role in Spain. Weber's textbook draws a distinction between external history (politics) and internal history (culture, literature, religion). But can an "internal" history, on its own, constitute a reality in itself?

*Spengler.* Anyway, it is in such a world that Oswald Spengler doubly enfolds us in his vehement, still burning book, *The Decline of the West* (1918–22), over which we would do well to dwell awhile. I thought I should reread the book closely before writing these lines. It seems to me that it is possible today, in a way that it was not for Lucien Febvre yesterday, to form an opinion of the book outside the circumstances which surrounded its birth. It has certainly retained its impressive appearance, with its tone, the breadth of its views, its passion for understanding, and its taste for the heights.

For Spengler, every culture is a unique experience. Even if one culture derives from another, sooner or later it asserts itself in its full originality. Though it takes long enough, sometimes. Thus, as far as our own Western civilization is concerned, "it took a long time for us to find the courage to think our own thoughts," that is, to free ourselves of the lessons of antiquity. But in the end we did free ourselves. A culture always frees itself in the end, or it is not a culture.

And just what is a culture? It is at once an art, a philosophy, a system of mathematics, a manner of thinking, all of which are realities which can have no validity, which cannot be comprehensible, outside the spirit which gives them life. There are as many morals, declares Spengler, as there are cultures, as Nietzsche had already guessed or suggested. Equally, there are as many philosophies, and arts, and systems of mathematics (and histories and historiographies, should we add with a smile?). The West is distinguished by an undeniable mathematical originality: its discovery of numerical function. Thus it is the context surrounding the discovery of calculus which is presented in the opening pages of Spengler's work, pages which are besides of a beauty which nothing can tarnish.

As a culture defines itself by its few original lines, and even more by the particular bundle of these originalities, the method for the historian of civilizations is straightforward: it simply entails distinguishing and studying these originalities. It will then suffice to bring them together and compare them in order to compare civilizations. This immediately carries us off on a strange journey through time, through centuries and millennia. It is reminiscent of the descriptions and anticipations afforded us today by interplanetary travel: suddenly freed from the laws of gravity, all the baggage, all objects leave their places and float freely, in curious conjunctions. Thus in Spengler counterpoint music, the monarchy of Louis XIV, Leibnitz's infinitesimal calculus, painting and the magic of perspective, the Doric column, and the Greek city float side by side or bump into each other. All are baggage which has lost its historical weight.

This sort of ploy cannot deceive us. Spengler's thought, though particularly vulnerable to criticism, is like the most mundane or the most considered historical thought, constantly being brought up against the difficult and irksome problem of the relationship of cultural elements to one another, and even more (though here Spengler could hardly have been more discreet) the problem of their relationship to other noncultural elements. These last our author overlooks entirely, just as he overlooks anything that might for a minute get in the way of his reasoning. Money is thus nothing but "an inorganic magnitude," and that is pretty much that as far as economic history is concerned. As for sensational events, they are dispensed with no less lightly, in a decidedly curious phrase: "Think of the dey of Algiers and his fan and other similar chinoiseries [sic] filling the historical scene with plots from operettas." So no operettas, and at a blow one has got rid of all politics. Social life is disposed of no less briskly. What is one left with? "Cultures" and their bundle of relationships, which are all so obvious that there is no point in analyzing them: they exist, period. Is it not obvious, for instance, that music is at the heart of Western "development" in the eighteenth century? In this way Spengler writes without turning a hair: "Germany produced the great musicians, and as a result it also produced the great architects of this century: Pöppelmann, Schlüter, Bähr, Neumann, Fischer d'Erlach, Dienzenhofer."

In short, "each individual culture is a unified being of a superior order": the most important personage in history. But personage is not really a good term, nor would organism be any better. As has recently been remarked,[7] cultures in Spengler's thought are conceived of as beings, but not in any biological sense. Rather they are seen in the medieval sense of bodies which are inert unless invested with a soul *(Kulturseele)*. For what this enthusiastic book is hunting down is, in the final analysis, a mystical being, a soul. Whence the ritual pronouncements: "a culture is born at the moment when a great soul awakens," or, and it comes to the same thing, "a culture dies when the soul has fulfilled the sum total of its possibilities."

Here we are at the very heart of Oswald Spengler's thought, face to face with the explanation which so possessed and fired him. The history, or rather the "destiny," of a culture is a sequence, or as we would put it in our contemporary jargon, a dynamic structure of the *longue durée*. The slow development of a culture allows it to establish itself, then to assert itself over a long period, and eventually to die. For cultures are mortal. But each one develops, must first of all develop, the full range of ideal possibilities which has been contained in it from the beginning: the "Apollonian" spirit of antiquity, the "Faustian" spirit of the West. After a certain length of time, which is usually fairly slow to elapse, all creative power seems to become worn out, and the culture dies for lack of a program: "The culture suddenly congeals, it dies, its life-blood ebbing away, its forces breaking down: it becomes civilization." So civilization is thus defined as being the unavoidable end, and painted in pretty gloomy colors. A civilization always belongs to what "has been," not to what "will be." It has no destiny, for "destiny is always young." It is winter, old age, Sancho Panza! Culture, you can be sure, is cast as Don Quixote.

This somber destiny is unavoidable. It must come to all cultures sooner or later, like a life cycle whose phases recur, one like to another. So like, in fact, that Spengler has no hesitation in bringing them together across the great chronological or geographical expanses dividing them, expanses which we must remove in our thoughts if we are to see them and to show them as they are: "contemporary," and as Spengler would assure, really twin. With the coming of the French Revolution and of

Napoleon, events which for over a century shaped the destiny of Europe, the hour of Western *civilization* was come. The event is the same as that ushered in by the decisive conquests of Alexander and the zenith of Hellenism: Greece was a "culture"; Rome, which was soon to take over, would be a "civilization." Thus it is clear that Alexander and Napoleon are "contemporaries," that they are, the one and the other, "romantics on the threshold of a *civilization*." Or you could say in an analogous phrase: "Pergamum and Bayreuth make a pair," for Wagner is well deserving of Nietzsche's anger, being only a man of Western *civilization*.

It would serve no purpose to attack, as so many others have done, these sweeping and naïve simplifications. What would be the good? Comparing *The Decline of the West* with the *Déclin de l'Europe* (1920), Albert Demangeon's book, its more reasonable contemporary, is like comparing poetry with prose. That is something that can safely be left to others. But let us sum up: there are two stages distinguishable in Oswald Spengler's work. First of all, whatever the cost, he wanted to clear away all the lumber so to speak, all the false entanglements of history, so as to reveal the destiny of the spiritual values to which, for him, all civilizations and cultures can be reduced. Then, and this was the most difficult and most debatable operation, he wished to organize the flowering of these spiritual values into *one* destiny, one history, one coherent succession of phases; slow to emerge, these values are stronger than anything in the world, and yet one fine day they suddenly cease to live with their old dynamism. From the outset, this sort of double operation cannot seem justifiable to any reasonable historian, as I will show later on. But, happily, some historians are less reasonable than others. I believe that Arnold Toynbee, although without any of Oswald Spengler's imprudence, is one of these. His attitude with regard to these two specific points is no different from Spengler's.

*Toynbee.* I confess to having read and reread, sometimes with great enthusiasm, Arnold Toynbee's subtle arguments and intelligent descriptions. I love his changes of pace, the art he uses in constructing and defending, cost what it may, the system he has built up, however capricious that system might in fact be. I enjoy his examples even more (all historians base their reasoning on examples), his points whose weaknesses are often not apparent, or at least, apparent only on reflection. Can the revolution brought about by the great discoveries around 1500 really be said to be a victory for the European vessel over the caravan routes of the Old World, that terrestrial navigation over the "sea without water"? After all, there was highly successful Arab shipping, Chinese shipping . . . Even inadvertently or with subsequent reservations, can one really write that "the Albigensians were crushed only to reappear as the Huguenots"? But what does it matter? All that matters in a book are its achievements, and here they are manifold. In traveling with such an experienced guide, the reader of Arnold Toynbee benefits from an incredible wealth of information and ideas. In his company, the contemplation of vast historical horizons comes to seem a useful and even a delightful exercise.

One must admit, however, that Arnold Toynbee does not squander his ability to light up his path and ours. What does he mean by civilization, since that is the word he uses most readily instead of culture? (The word culture, as the anthropologists complain, never appears in his book in the sense in which they use it.) So what does he mean by civilization? Lucien Febvre put the question to him bluntly, in an article twenty years ago. But for all that he has written so much since, our author replied only in dribs and drabs: "Civilization as we know it is a movement, not a condition; it is a voyage, not a port"; "One cannot describe [its] aim because it has never been attained"; "Each culture is a whole, in which all the parts are suddenly interdependent." An atom, with its elementary particles and its nucleus . . . that gets us a long way! Another time he suggests that civilizations can be grasped in their actions, in their movement, "their births, their developments, their dislocations, their declines, their falls." They *are* because they *act*. Yes, of course, they could hardly die if they did not exist first, could they?

On at least one occasion, though, he seems to confront the problem head on. "Before having done with it [*sic*]," he wrote pleasantly, "I would like to say a word about a question which up until now (1947) I had thought already resolved, and that is: what do we mean by civilization?" But let us not rejoice too soon. These tardy good intentions do not go beyond the meager explanations offered in volume 1 of his huge book *A Study of History* (1934), explanations which he simply proceeds to repeat imperturbably: "We surely must understand something definite by it," argues Toynbee, "for even before having attempted to define its significance, this human classification [that of civilizations]—Western, Islamic, Far-Eastern, Hindu, &c.—seems to us to be effectively endowed with meaning. These words conjure up clear pictures in our minds, relating to religion, architecture, painting, traditions, and customs." But here is the declaration: "I mean by civilization, the smallest unit of historical study to which one is brought when trying to *comprehend* the history of one's own country." A hasty analysis of the past of England and the United States follows. If this analysis is not to lead one into an examination of the whole past of humanity, that vague and inaccessible unit, then where is one to stop? Moving from deduction to deduction, and always pushing the decisive chronological limit further and further back, Toynbee finally comes to place it at the end of the eight century, around the 770s, that is, at the birth of our Western civilization, which from all the evidence was then emerging or about to emerge from the legacy of classical antiquity. This Western civilization then sets a definite, short (or relatively short) limit to the scope of our inquiries. It allows us, as I am perfectly willing to concede, to transcend the usual framework of national histories, in which every historian worthy of the name has long ceased to believe. It offers a chronological framework, a field of operations, a means of explanation, a classification, but that is all. In any case, I do not see how the ploy of referring English civilization to Western civilization is supposed to provide any sort of answer to the question. "Civilization" and what it means to Toynbee are not, by that token, defined. But for want of anything better, let us judge the workman by his product, and follow him along the path he has chosen to take.

In the event, this path proves to be a series of interrelated explanations, but I will come to that in a minute. For just as important as the paths which he takes are the paths which he refuses to take, and it is these which I would deal with first. Toynbee's silences, more than his clearly declared standpoints, indicate the true movement of his work. It takes him only a word or a frivolous remark to rid himself of any troublesome contradictions or dangerous temptations.

Never mind about events! Toynbee retains only "salient" events. It is a way, and not necessarily one I disagree with, of drowning almost everything which is an event. But which in fact are the "salient" events which have this right to rise to the surface?

Geography, when examined at all, is referred to only in second or third instance. Could one really presume to explain civilizations in terms of their environment? Nothing so crassly material could determine them. It is precisely when this material environment says yes, and is lavish with its favors—a point I will return to in a moment—that civilization does not respond. But when nature reveals itself as savage and hostile, when it says no, then and only then, thanks to the *psychological* reactions which this arouses, does civilization make an entrance.

Put aside for different, but no less peremptory, reasons is the whole question of cultural transfers, of "diffusion," that "method" [*sic*]—so he writes—"by which much technology, many skills, institutions, and ideas, from the alphabet to the Singer sewing-machine, have been communicated from one civilization to another." Are the alphabet and sewing machines important? Let us think no more about them! All that matters are the great religious waves passing from one civilization to another. The rest of their exchanges, their collisions, their dialogues are all secondary. Instead of interesting ourselves in details like that, let us study "Greek and Roman History as one continuous history, following a single

indivisible thread." What does that mean? Given such a clear and decided bias, what would in actual fact become of all the ruptures, mutations, discontinuities, or shocks, as Claude Lévi-Strauss likes to call them,
those challenges to prediction, to calculations, and to the norm? Toynbee would have us deal only with the continuous.

In the same way, in this huge, prolix book, there is not a word, or
hardly a word, about primitive civilizations (or cultures), about the whole
vast domain of prehistory. The transition from culture to civilization is
made, we are told, by *mutation*. It is then left up to us to apply that idea in
order to reach the explanation which has been denied us.

Nor is there any serious treatment of states and societies, by which I
mean the social structures (except for a few dogmatic statements on the
active minorities which create civilizations, and on the proletariats, either
within or without these same civilizations). Nor is there any treatment of
technologies, or economies. They are just so many ephemeral, over-
ephemeral, realities. States, for example, have a derisory life span compared with the long existence of civilizations. "Western civilization,"
wrote Toynbee in 1947, "has got roughly speaking thirteen hundred
years behind it, whilst England has only a thousand, the United Kingdom of England and Scotland less than two hundred and fifty, and the
United States not more than one hundred and fifty." What is more,
states are apt to have "a short life and a sudden death." So let us not
waste our time with states, those little folk with their puny existence, and
still less let us waste our time with economics or technology. Just one or
two phrases, knowingly repeated: "Man cannot live by bread alone," or
"Man cannot live by technology alone," and that is that.

So Toynbee, having quietly whisked away the whole social and economic base, abandons it to the mediocrity of its fate. If two civilizations
collide, "these encounters are important, not because of their *immediate*
political and economic consequences, but because of their *long-term* religious consequences." I have italicized the two key words, which make the
idea so much more palatable. There are, of course, short-term religious
consequences and long-term political or economic consequences. But to
admit that would be to risk upsetting the order which has been laid down
once and for all. If one studies "history as a whole, then political and
economic history must be [put] in a subordinate position, in order to
accord primacy to religious history. After all, it is religion which is the
most serious concern of the human race." "The central core," one can
read elsewhere, "that is to say, religion." But are we even in agreement as
to what constitutes religion?

Thus, right from the beginning, there are a whole series of deliberate
silences, of premeditated exclusions, of executions so urbanely carried
out as to disguise their fundamental bias. In a few pages, which seem to

me to be barely comprehensible, Arnold Toynbee thus tells us that civilization to him is not one, and that progress is utopia. There are only civilizations, each in the grip of a destiny whose main lines are recurrent, however, and have been in one way or another predetermined. In consequence, if anyone can possibly understand this, there are several *civilizations,* but there is only one "spiritual nature of man," and above all, only one destiny, which is inexplicably the same and which embraces all civilizations, both those which have died and, in advance, those which are yet living. Such a way of seeing things necessarily excludes such an attitude as Marcel Mauss's, that "civilization is all of man's acquisitions"; and Alfred Weber's assertion even more, that all civilizations are caught "in the unified movement of a general and gradual progress"; or Henri Berr's wise remark that "each people has its own civilization: thus there are always a great number of different civilizations."

Arnold Toynbee, for his part, counts only a limited number. There are only twenty-one or twenty-two civilizations worthy of the name, all long-lasting, and all of which have had an influence over fairly vast expanses of the world. Of these, five are still with us today: the Far Eastern, the Indian, the Eastern Orthodox, the Islamic, and the Western. In order to keep to such a meager band, quite a few possible candidates have had to be rejected, some because they did not last long enough, some because they were not sufficiently original, some because of their obvious failure.

But let us accept this reduced list. If it is correct, it is of outstanding importance. That the complex history of mankind could thus be reduced to a score of dominant experiences, what a delightful simplification, if it could be justified! In any case, from this very first contact with Arnold Toynbee's way of thinking, from this initial problem of enumeration, it is possible to begin to discern his method of procedure, which is very like that of a scientist looking for a world system, a system whose clear order and exclusive relationships must be imposed authoritatively, for better or worse, onto the teeming mass of reality. The first thing is to simplify history. The next thing is to make out rules, laws, concordances, to build a series of related models, so to speak, in the meaning in which sociologists and economists use the word. Civilizations like people have a single, ineluctable destiny: they are born, develop, and die, although each stage, fortunately for them, is of very long duration. They never cease to spring up, to bloom, and to vanish.

So Arnold Toynbee has naturally enough constructed three groups of models: those for birth, those for growth, and those for deterioration, decline, and death. He has devoted a good deal of time, patience, and skill to this great endeavor. For at every moment each of these systems, like a series of engines, has a tendency to misfire. The law, the ruling tendency are constantly being threatened with exceptions: there are always new elements, disorganized and importunate. Just look at the difficulty Aristotle had, accommodating the aberrant motion of a thrown stone into the universe he had constructed. His system had not taken account of it. There are a good many stones like that in Arnold Toynbee's garden.

Of these three groups of models—birth, flowering, and death—the first two do not seem to me to be particularly original. The last is the most interesting, even though in the final analysis it is not convincing, even though it proves to be the most vulnerable of them all.

A civilization will come to life, maintains our author, only if it is faced with a difficulty—whether natural or historical—which has to be overcome. A historical difficulty is short term, but it is occasionally extremely violent. Geographically, the environment imposes difficulties and long-term challenges. If the challenge is taken up and stuck to, then the difficulty which has been overcome launches a victorious civilization and maintains it in its orbit. Attica is naturally poor, so it is condemned to struggle, and led on to transcend itself. In the same way Brandenburg owes its rude health to its sand dunes and its marshes. The heights of the Andes are harsh to man, happily for him: this hostility once overcome, the Inca civilization is the result.

Such is the "model" of "challenge and response." It reduces the role of environment to that attributed to the cane in some English public schools: a severe but effective moral tutor. But geographers like Pierre Gourou would reply that there are a good many magnificent challenges which man has not taken up. And Gerhard Masur has only recently maintained that the so-called harshness of the Andean uplands is gentleness and ease compared with the Amazonian jungle. So the Incas chose the easy way. I would also add that if Heine Geldern is right, as seems possible, then the Amerindian civilizations benefited more than anything else from repeated and *late* contacts between Asia and America. From this point of view, as in Pierre Gourou's explanation of northern China as a "typical crossroads," the *diffusion* which Arnold Toynbee so mistreated would have its own innocent and entirely justifiable revenge. For my own part, I do not think that civilizations catch fire only along the direct line of their descent, say Western or Moslem kindling from the flames of antiquity. Between strangers, small sparks can set alight huge, long-lasting blazes. But Arnold Toynbee has considered his challenge-and-response theory enough himself to know that, in actual application, it needs considerable arranging and rearranging. The only challenges which count, he is careful to say, are those which do not exceed man's power to respond. So there are challenges and challenges and, given that precaution, the model has been saved. But what he ends up by saying is hardly more than common sense.

Next stage: each civilization progresses only insofar as it is animated by a creative minority or creative individuals. This brings us back almost exactly to Nietzsche or Pareto ... But if the masses no longer allow themselves to be subjugated by this active minority, or if that minority loses its élan, its creative force, which is to say, more or less, Oswald Spengler's *Kulturseele*, then deterioration sets in. Everything, as usual, collapses from within.

Thus we are brought not only to the last models—those of decline—but also to the very heart of the system, for as Sorokin once lightheartedly remarked, Arnold Toynbee is a great slaughterer of civilizations. Their death seems to him the moment of truth, of revelation.

A civilization, for Arnold Toynbee, does not die until it has already existed for centuries, but its death has been heralded long in advance by insistent internal and external difficulties, from which the narrator, if narrator there is, cannot free himself. A whole chain of difficulties, one could say. These difficulties are quelled, one fine day, by the rise to power of the policeman, I mean the establishment of a vast empire. But this "universal" empire is only a provisional solution, lasting two, three, or four centuries, which is only an instant, the mere "blink of an eye," measured on the temporal scale of civilizations. So, soon enough, the empire breaks down in the midst of disasters and barbarian invasions (the arrival, as our author says, of an "external proletariat"). But at the same time, the universal Church has established itself, and that will save what can be saved. This, or approximately this, was the end of the Greco-Roman civilization which Toynbee authoritatively calls Hellenic. In the Roman example, we have a plan, the supreme plan, the "model" of the death of a civilization with its four ages—troubles, empire or rather universal state, universal Church, and barbarians. German strategists at the beginning of this century reduced everything, so we are told, to the model of the battle of Cannae. Arnold Toynbee seems to have reduced everything to the end, to what André Piganiol called the "assassination," of the Roman Empire.

So for each past civilization, he has sought and found all the "ages" of his model (thus for the Achmenid Empire, for the Incas, the Abassids, the Guptas, the Mongols, twenty-one empires in all), though not without some forcing or fudging here and there. Among historians accustomed to short but precise measurements of time, who would have thought the millennium between the Achmenid Empire and the caliphate of Baghdad, which sprang up almost in a day, had not ruptured an important link forever? Or is it acceptable that one should cross the Carolingian Empire, the empire of Charles V, the conquests of Louis XIV, or the empire of Napoleon I off the list of universal states, doubtless because they did not last long enough? Besides, all those who figure on Toynbee's list, a new list of twenty-one, which are thus recognized as being essential elements in the life of civilizations, of "real" civilizations, are not to be shown any favor, whoever they might be. The author's bias is against them. It is a short step from there to blackening their character, as the fate reserved for the Roman Empire serves to demonstrate. "The Roman peace," he writes, "was the peace of exhaustion." That is, to say the least, a bad beginning.

Such, in a brief summary, is the plan of this vast work, a plan capable of a variety of applications, according to the recurrent validity which its author attributes to it. It is valid for the past, and for the present too. Western civilization, though still living, is "giving at the knees" (Clough), and has been wearing out for over a century in a clearly visible succession of difficulties. Will it gain a new lease of life, thanks to some universal empire? Naturally an empire on the world scale this time, be it Russian or American, imposed in friendship or by force. A young historian and anthropologist, Philip Bagby, following a line of prognostication similar to that of Spengler and Toynbee, asks not only if we are on the threshold of a "Roman sequence," but if we are not really on the threshold of an American empire. Are we likely to have an American emperor?

Instead of trying to answer questions such as these, let us in our turn pose a fairly big question of our own. Suppose that between 1519 and 1555 there was a clear-sighted observer who held the beliefs which inform Arnold Toynbee's writings and had long considered in their light his own age and the long experience of the reign of Charles V. How often would he not have seen in the Europe around him a return to the Roman order, to universal empire, and even the establishment of a universal Church? For the Church which finally reformed itself at Trent was by all evidence triumphant, and new quite as much as renewed. Are our prophets any more clear-sighted today, and would the American emperor stand any greater chance than did Charles V?

But let us not take our leave of Toynbee with a smile. Historians have not been particularly kind to him, for various reasons to do with their profession, but occasionally without being entirely fair. If I am no exception to the rule, I can at least understand why Ernst Curtius greeted his work with such enthusiasm. It does indeed bring us some fairly important insights. There are explanations which are valuable, even for those who would contradict them.

In a past which he has simplified, as any system-builder must, without unfortunately always escaping the absurdities of simplification, Arnold Toynbee has instinctively taken the crucial, but hazardous paths of the *longue durée*. He has committed himself to "societies," to social realities, or at least to those social realities which persist forever. He has committed himself to events which continue to have violent repercussions whole centuries after they occurred, or to men well above the general run of mankind, whether Jesus or Buddha or Mahomet, men who are equally of the *longue durée*. I would quarrel less with the millennium between the Achmenids and the caliphs of Baghdad than would Lucien Febvre or Gerhard Masur. Émile-Félix Gautier claimed that the Arab conquest of the Maghreb and of Spain (from the middle of the seventh century to 711) reestablished the old extent of the Carthaginian dominions after almost a thousand years. Arnold Toynbee's great merit is to have handled these great tracts of time even at the risk of losing himself, to have dared to compare things which happened centuries apart, to have sought out these vast, somewhat unreal, but nonetheless important routes. What I find hard to take, what indeed I cannot take at all, is the way these comparisons insistently shed light only on resemblances, and obstinately reduce the diversity of civilizations to a single model, in short to one civilization, ideal at the least, the necessary structure for any human effort capable of achieving civilization of whatever form. It is one way—but not one I relish—of reconciling the singular and the plural which alter the meaning of the term civilization so vastly. "Over and above all the variety of cultures," Toynbee has written, "there exists a uniformity of the spiritual nature of man."

*Alfred Weber.* It is an assertion which would not be contradicted by Alfred Weber's profound, compact work, a work nonetheless little known in our country: *Kulturgeschichte als Kultursoziologie.* Published in 1935, in Leyden, translated into Spanish under the title *Historia de la Cultura,* the book ran into four editions between 1941 and 1948. It is a solid and powerful book. Alfred Weber (1868–1958), sociologist brother of the great Max Weber (1864–1920), became on this occasion, a historian, and an extremely discriminating one. He forces himself on us a good deal less than Spengler or Toynbee, for example. He does not have their brilliance, but nor does he have their rashness and capriciousness. All the same, the difficulties which they hurled themselves at resist him too, the more so since he treats them so gently. He opens his explanations widely to prehistory, anthropology, geography, sociology, economics, and Marxist thinking. And that is all to the good. It gives his book a solidity which the others lacked. But if at the outset of his analysis he admirably demonstrates the establishment of the first crop of civilizations, the Egyptian, the Babylonian, the Indian, the Chinese, he is less convincing when dealing with the complicated West (by which he means the Eurasian block, the West to the west of the peaks and valleys of the Hindu Kush). He shows the development of second and third generation civilizations as if the synthesizing explanation, valid at very great distances over time and space, becomes increasingly less effective the closer we come to our own time and our own civilization.

Above all, I doubt whether Alfred Weber has formulated, for himself and for us, a satisfactory definition (in my sense of the word) of a civilization, or, as he would say, a high-ranking culture. He sees it as nothing more than a "historical body," which would thus define itself within the context of the flow of history. But what precisely is that flow which so affects the destinies of the whole of humanity? And why should civilizations take the form of so many "bodies" ? Alfred Weber may not want a transcendent "objective" spirit (like Werner Sombart's spirit which can provide an explanation of capitalism all by itself and *verbi gratia* readily explain *civilization* or *civilizations*), but there is nonetheless a "spirit of the age" implicit in his thinking and his explanations, a spirit of man (his own awareness, his desire for freedom, his capacity for detaching himself, his aptitude for invention, for being *homo faber*). Is this the spirit which animates the historical body of civilization?

*Philip Bagby.* But we must cut short this review, which though so incomplete is already excessively long. A book has just been published (1958) on which appears the name of a young historian and anthropologist, a student of Kroeber's, Philip Bagby. He has the not inconsiderable advantage of being able to put us in touch with the most recent anthropological discussions which, as we have already said, appear to be crucial. Philip Bagby proposes to unite history and anthropology, thus giving himself an original position, close to though distinct from that of our own historical school at *Annales*. At *Annales*, following in the footsteps of Lucien Febvre and Marc Bloch, a science of history is slowly being built up which attempts to base itself on all the human sciences, and not just one of them, even if that one is anthropology. Now it is solely this union between history and anthropology which is considered by Philip Bagby.

In his view, there can be no science of history unless the too vast and too diverse domain of history is in some way simplified, unless one removes a particular scientific sector from it authoritatively, which is then artificially isolated so as to be easier to control. That is what physicists in their "objective" world have done with the principles of mass, and moment, and inertia, isolating and then exploiting a transformed reality which then proves fertile in application. So let historians turn toward the privileged operational field of civilizations—privileged because it allows of comparisons. Since there is only one history within the world of living beings, the history of man, then man must be compared with man, and our investigation must move from one experience to another, from one civilization to another. On condition, though, that this term be applied only to series of destinies which are mutually comparable.

So a choice of civilizations must be made from the beginning. At the top, the greatest, the major civilizations. Then the less great, the under-civilizations or secondary civilizations. Finally the smallest which have only the right, with certain variations, to be termed cultures. The question within each category is to weigh them one against the other, in order to discover whether they follow a common destiny, whether they allow the drawing of analogous curves, or the creation of regular dynamic structures which can usefully bring them closer together. Before attempting these great confrontations, one would need to get rid of any fanciful points of view, of any preliminary metaphysical explanations. For instance, a few fairly lively criticisms are fired off, not unpleasantly but firmly, in the direction of Arnold Toynbee, who stands accused—but what a thing to be accused of!—of being a historian in the humanist tradition and so of having no anthropological culture.

But let us get back to the major civilizations. How is it, though, that we can hope to understand them from the inside? Unfortunately Philip Bagby does not attempt a serious definition of them any more than any of our other authors. From among the heavyweight civilizations, he retains only nine as against Arnold Toynbee's twenty-one or twenty-two elect. I do not know whether that can be considered progress. I am afraid that they are really singing much the same song, that they are proposing much the same idealistic approach to the destinies of mankind. In finishing this book, which decidedly promised better, what can one in fact retain of the comparative study which he barely broaches? That civilizations in their slow development pass regularly from a religious period to a period which yields increasingly to rationality? Max Weber has already said as much about Europe, and many another before him, Auguste Comte for one. Heinrich Freyer[8] asserted recently that "rationality was the trend of Western thought": is it the trend of world thought? I am prepared to believe it, the more so since the historian must find this dualism, even more rigorously applied than Guizot's (religiosity, rationality), somewhat disturbing. Reason, religion, must they always be in opposition, like night and day? In an effort to be more just, let us call to mind Heinrich Freyer's remark: "The kingdom of reason has its beginnings in the kingdom of God."[9] The one feeds the other during interminable secularizations.

But the reader will be able to see once again just how high we should be aspiring, if we are to believe a young and intelligent anthropologist. So many repeated ascents would be enough to give us a taste for lower altitudes, if we did not already have it. Man cannot live by prayer and thought alone, he is also in actual fact "what he eats" (der Mensch ist was er ißt). In a similar witticism, Charles Seignobos once said, "Civilization is roads, harbors, quays ... " We do not have to take him absolutely literally. But this down-to-earth remark invites us to go down again, to look at things at or close to ground level, and risk noticing what it is that divides and individualizes them, not what makes them merge.

History at the Crossroads

The reader will already have got some idea of where I am heading. I believe, in fact, that the history of civilizations, like history itself, is at a crossroads. Whether it wants to or not, it must assimilate all the discoveries made by the different social sciences, of more or less recent birth, in the inexhaustible field of man's existence. A difficult task, but an urgent one, for only if history decisively commits itself to this path can it be of any substantial use in understanding the world of today.

In this direction, might I put forward some idea of the kind of plan which I would feel was necessary if I ever found myself, by the greatest of chances, called upon to write my own *Study of History,* or some such vast and endless work on civilization and civilizations?

The first task is a negative but necessary one, and that is to make an immediate break with certain habits of mind which, whether they are good or bad, it seems to me indispensable to leave behind at the start, even if only to come back to them later. The second task is then to seek a definition of civilization, the least unsatisfactory, meaning the most convenient one, the easiest to manage for the pursuit of our work. The third task would be to verify the extent of the domain of civilizations by summoning to this end not only historians, but all the specialists in the human sciences. And finally, instead of a conclusion, to suggest specific tasks.

*Necessary Sacrifices*

Let us renounce from the start certain ways of speaking. Thus let us no longer speak of a civilization as a being, or an organism, or a figure, or a body, even a historical body. Let us no longer say that it is born, develops, and dies, which comes to the same thing as lending it a simple, linear, human destiny. I would rather return to Georges Gurvitch's meditations on the global society of the Middle Ages in the West, for example, or on our contemporary society, despite all their obvious imperfections in a historian's eyes. He sees the future of both as hesitating between several possible destinies, all radically different, and this seems to me to be a reasonable assessment of the variety of life itself: the future is not a single path. So we must renounce the linear. We must not believe that a civilization, because it is original, is a closed and independent world, as if each one was an island in the midst of the ocean, whereas in fact it is their dialogues, the points where they meet, which are essential, especially as they are all increasingly coming to share a rich common basis. "Civilization," wrote Margaret Mead (using the word in the same way as Mauss, whom I have already quoted), "is all that man, henceforward, will not be able to forget"—language, an alphabet, number, the rule of three, fire, even numerical function, steam, and so forth. All the bases which today are impersonal, common to all cultures of every particular kind and level.

I would similarly give up the use of any cyclical explanation of the destiny of civilizations or cultures, and in fact any variation on that customary and insistent phrase *they are born, they live, they die.* This means rejecting equally the three ages of Vico (the age of gods, the age of heroes, the age of men) and Auguste Comte's three ages (theological, metaphysical, and positivist), Spencer's two phases (constraint, then liberty), Durkheim's two successive solidarities (the organic and the mechanical), Waxweiller's stages of growing cooperation, Hildebrant's economic stages, and Frédéric List's or Bücher's, the growing densities of Levasseur and Ratzel, and finally Karl Marx's sequence (primitive societies, slavery, feudalism, capitalism, socialism). They must all be left behind, though not without the occasional regret, and always with the possibility of returning later, for I would not claim to condemn all these explanations in a body, or even to condemn the principle of explanation which they apply—the model or the cycle. To the contrary, I think it a most useful principle, but it is nonetheless an exclusion which must be made at the start, as a precautionary measure.

To close this chapter of exclusions, in which of course can be found Spengler and Toynbee's rigid schemes, I would also reject the restricted lists of civilizations which have been suggested to us. I believe, in fact, that research in order to be fruitful must take hold of everything, from the most modest cultures to the major civilizations, and above all that these major civilizations must be divided into subcivilizations, and that these must be divided into yet more tiny elements. Let us set out under one heading the possibilities of a microhistory and of a history more traditionally oriented. It would be extremely interesting to know how far down one can go at the base of the ladder. Halfway up anyway, especially today, I think that states, peoples, nations all tend to have their own civilizations, whatever the uniformity of their technology might be in other spheres. Whatever the label, there is a distinct French civilization, a German one, an Italian, an English one, each with its own characteristics and internal contradictions. To study them all together under the heading of Western civilization seems to me to be too simple an approach. Nietzsche claimed that as far as one could see, since the Greek civilization there had been only one other—the French. "This does not admit of contradiction." It is a highly debatable assertion, of course, but one which it is amusing to compare with the fact that the French civilization finds no place in Toynbee's classification.

Marc Bloch's idea, if I have understood it properly, was on the one hand to resituate the French civilization within its European framework, and then on the other to break down that France into individual Frances, since our country like any other is a constellation of lively civilizations, however weak their individual rays. In the final analysis, the great thing would be to be able to see the link between these elements, from the smallest to the greatest, to understand how they overlap, how they affect each other and are affected by each other, how they suffer together or at each others' expense, how they grow, or not (on condition that there are secure criteria for similar growth).

### Criteria to Be Retained

Once the ground has been cleared, we can proceed to ask the question: what is a civilization?

I know of only one good definition, good in the sense of being easily used for purposes of observation and sufficiently removed from any kind of value judgment. It can be found, according to one's particular whim, either in the teachings of this or that anthropologist, or in some article by Marcel Mauss, from whom I borrowed it without ever having to regret it.

*Cultural Areas.* A civilization is first of all a space, a "cultural area," as the anthropologists would say, a locus. Within the locus, which may be more or less extensive but is never too confined, you must picture a great variety of "goods," of cultural characteristics, ranging from the form of its houses, the material of which they are built, their roofing, to skills like feathering arrows, to a dialect or a group of dialects, to tastes in cooking, to a particular technology, a structure of beliefs, a way of making love, and even to the compass, paper, the printing press. It is the regular grouping, the frequency with which particular characteristics recur, their ubiquity within a precise area, which constitute the first signs of cultural coherence. If to this spatial coherence can be added some sort of temporal permanence, then I would call civilization or culture the "totality" of the range of attributes. It is this "totality" which is the "form" of the civilization thus recognized.

Of course, the cultural area owes much more to geography than the anthropologists would generally allow. It is an area, moreover, which has a center, a "kernel," and frontiers, borders. And it is most often on the border that the most characteristic aspects, phenomena, or tensions can be found. Sometimes these borders and the area they enclose are immense. "Thus, for our own part," wrote Marcel Mauss, "we have long maintained that it is possible to believe in an extremely ancient civilization existing all along the coasts and in all the islands of the Pacific. . . . Indeed, there are a great number of coincidences . . ." There are numerous variations, too, which is what makes it necessary to go on to divide that enormous region, to analyze the contrasts, the differences, and to mark the axes, the "crests" of development. But the example of the Pacific could not easily be analyzed here, nor even a less extensive example. The important thing is that an area always comprises several societies or social groups. Which is what makes it necessary, I repeat, to pay as close attention as possible to the smallest cultural unit. How much, here or there, does it demand from its location, from men, from different social groups; what is its minimum subsistence level?

*Borrowings*. All these cultural goods, the microelements of civilization, are constantly on the move (this is what distinguishes them from ordinary social phenomena). Civilizations are simultaneously exporting or borrowing them in turn. This vast traffic never stops. Some cultural elements are even contagious, such as modern science and modern technology, although not all civilizations are equally open to this sort of exchange. It remains to be seen if, as Sorokin suggests, the borrowing of spiritual goods is carried on even more swiftly than that of technology. For myself, I doubt it.

*Refusals*. But not every exchange proceeds straightforwardly. There are, in fact, refusals to borrow, whether a way of thinking, of believing, or living, or just simply a tool. Some of these refusals are carried on deliberately and with great clarity, while others are performed blindly, as if determined by thresholds or locks impossible to pass through. And of course, every refusal, especially if it is consciously and repeatedly asserted, is of singular importance. It is thus, and in these situations, that each civilization makes its decisive choice through which it asserts and reveals itself. The phenomena of "diffusion," so little prized by Toynbee, seem to me one of the best touchstones by which to judge the vitality and originality of a civilization.

In short, in the definition which we have borrowed, there are three factors at play: the cultural area with its frontiers, borrowings, and refusals. Each one opens up its own possibilities.

*The Possibilities Opened Up to Research by These Three Factors*. The study of cultural areas and their frontiers is demonstrated clearly by a particular concrete example, the double frontier of the Rhine and the Danube. It was there that Rome once halted its conquest. A thousand years later, it was more or less along the line of the old border that the unity of the Church broke up: on the one side the hostility of the Reformation; on the other, faithfulness to Rome, over and above the powerful reactions of the Counter-Reformation. Besides, who is not aware of the remarkable spiritual frontier marked by these two rivers? Goethe was aware of it, when he reached and crossed the Danube at Ratisbon on his way to Italy. Mme. de Stael was aware of it when she crossed the Rhine.

Second factor: the borrowings. Whole volumes could not exhaust their interest or the fat file which they make up. Western civilization has come to dominate this planet, it has become a civilization "without frontiers," lavishing its gifts, both good and ill, its constraints, its collisions. Nonetheless, earlier it borrowed without stint from far and near, from Islam, from China, even from India. In the rather extravagant society of France under Charles VI, pronged and steeple headdresses and dé-colleté bodices arrived from the far-off China of the T'angs—fashions long vanished in the country of their origin. But these fragile goods had made their way, for half a thousand years, along the trade routes of the Old World, arriving, in the fourteenth century, in Cyprus and the brilliant court of the Lusignans. From there, the highly active trade routes of the Mediterranean took charge of these strange travelers in no time at all.

But there are other examples closer to home. In this way the Brazilian sociological historian Gilberte Freyre has enumerated all the borrowings which his country made from its European cradle in the eighteenth and nineteenth centuries. It makes an odd list: English or Hamburg beer, white linen clothing, false teeth, gaslight, the English bungalow, steam (a steamboat was working the waters of San Salvador bay as early as 1819), positivism later, secret societies earlier (coming from France, through Spain and Portugal, and then by the usual route through the Atlantic islands). It is not a story which has come to a close, of course. From 1945 onward, and this time over Latin America as a whole, Sartre's and Merleau-Ponty's existentialist message came from France. It was actually a German concept, but given new impetus from being filtered through our own country. For France still enjoys its privilege: in the complicated interplay of cultural transfers and exchanges, it remains as a crossroads of choice, seemingly a necessity to the world. The openness of this French crossroads (the geographers call it an "isthmus") is undoubtedly the dominant feature of our civilization. It is to this that we continue to owe our importance and our glory. Marie Curie was born in Warsaw, in that little house in the old town which Polish faithfulness has since reconstructed; Modigliani was born at Leghorn; Van Gogh in Holland; Picasso came to us from Spain; Paul Valéry has Genoese ancestors ...

The third factor, and the most revealing for placing us at particular points in history: the refusal. Thus there was the Reformation, that deep division so critical to Europe. Italy, Spain, France (this last only after dreadful hesitations) all said no to the Reformation, to reforms. An act with the most far-reaching, the most immensely profound repercussions, reaching right down to the cultural foundations of Europe. Another example: in 1453 Constantinople did not want to be saved by the Latins, their hated half-brothers: they preferred the Turks. This was another act that could bear being reconsidered, if only in the light of the intuitive, "heretic" and debatable, but nonetheless luminous writings of the Turkish historian Raschid Saffet Atabinen. If I had to choose an event for the spiritual battle demanded by a new explanation of civilizations, it would not be the assassination of Rome, but the abandoning of Constantinople.

Without wishing to make the refusal the center of everything, who would not be prepared to see that it is central to the dramatic case of today's militant Marxism? The Anglo-Saxon world profoundly rejects Marxism. Italy, Spain, France are not hostile to it, but they reject it too, and by a good many more than half their votes. It is not only economic levels, social structures, the recent past and its contingencies which can explain this. Cultures too play their role here.

You can see how far my faith in "diffusion" has carried me. Even as far, yet again, as being brought to stand shoulder to shoulder with Claude Lévi-Strauss. Did he not explain, in the midst of an argument he was propounding, that civilizations seemed to him like players around a gigantic card table, so that they all bear a certain relation to the general theory of games? Suppose the players help each other, telling each other what their cards and their intentions are: the more they connive, the greater the chance of one of them winning. Among other things, the West has benefited from its position at the meeting point of innumerable cultural currents. It absorbed all sorts of different things for centuries and from all directions, even from dead civilizations, before being able in its turn to give out and radiate.

*Toward a Dialogue between History and the Human Sciences*

The recognition of the whole extent of the "cultural," that would be our third stage. It is not something that any one historian can manage alone. There would have to be "consultations," bringing together all the human sciences, the traditional and the new alike, from the philosopher to the demographer and the statistician. It is in fact delusory to wish in the German way to separate *culture* from its foundation *civilization*. And if it is absurd to neglect the superstructure, it is no less so to neglect, as so often happens, the infrastructure. Civilizations have their feet on the ground. To put it perhaps too briefly, we would need, cost what it might, to go hand in hand with a Toynbee or a Lucien Febvre on the one side, and on the other with sociologists, anthropologists, economists, and even Marxists. The disdain with which Marx is regarded in the welter of idealism quite regularly offered up by the study of civilizations is so utterly childish! In fact, we as historians must undertake a whole series of dialogues with each of the great sectors of the human sciences.

With geography first of all. The location of civilizations is much more than an accident: if it consists in a challenge, then it is a repeated challenge, one of *longue durée*. One evening, at *Annales,* in 1950, during a friendly discussion of the vast theme of civilization between Federico Chabod, Pierre Renouvin, John U. Nef, and Lucien Febvre, geography came under consideration. Lucien Febvre insisted that at the basis of every civilization are its vital, endlessly repeated links with the environment, links which it creates or rather has to recreate throughout its long destiny, all those elementary and seemingly primitive relationships with the soil, the vegetation, the animal population, endemic diseases . . .

A similar dialogue must be engaged with the demographers: civilization is the child of number. How can it be that Toynbee concerns himself with this only incidentally? A demographic growth can and does entail ruptures and changes. A civilization may be under or over its normal load of men. Any excess tends to produce those huge, insistent migrations which, as the Kulischer brothers have explained, flow endlessly beneath the skin of history.

There must also be a dialogue with sociology, with economics, with statistics. May Lucien Febvre forgive me if, rather than siding with him, I side here with Alfredo Niceforo, even though it may be that his indices are poor gauges of civilization: there are no perfect gauges. I am equally in favor of Georges Gurvitch's "approaches" with regard to "global societies," that *body* (if I may make so bold as to employ the word in my turn) of civilizations. Even if these approaches remain too timid for my taste, how close they seem to come to comprehending the real, compared with Sorokin's eager idealism! There is, moreover, a whole debate to be taken up again in order to decide the relations between civilizations and social structures or classes. I would maintain in the end that there can be no civilization without a strong political, social, and economic armature, which also shapes its moral and intellectual life, in a good or a bad sense, and even shapes its religious life. After 1945, the French maintained that despite our lost vigor we still retained our intellectual influence. I am not alone in thinking otherwise. Strength is not enough to ensure influence. But everything works together. A civilization demands equally strength, health, and power. That is why, despite the admiration which I still feel for Jacob Burckhardt's book, I still think that it has to be rewritten, at least where its essential direction is concerned: the Italian Renaissance must reassume its voice, its *material* bodies. A culture cannot live on pure ideas alone. Shepard Bancroft Clough was right: every culture has to have an excess, an economic surplus. Culture means consumption, even waste.

## Breaking Down the Specialist Frontiers

But what practical procedures can be envisaged that could somehow put to the test this whole debatable assembly of precautions, exclusions, and commitments? What will give us the widest and, above all, the most reliable viewpoints?

It goes without saying that my first concern would be with sensible projects, with short phases in cultural life, with cultural "conjunctures," if one may extend to this domain, as I would like to be able to, an expression which heretofore has been exclusively applicable to economic life. I would see a great advantage in choosing, for these initial contacts, periods which provide the most minute illumination, with a precisely defined chronology. Let us not, please, spread out the whole expanse of the centuries and the millennia straightaway, even if such an operation does have its uses! The chronological location once chosen, our next task would be to see, without prejudice, just what are the relationships between those sectors which can be termed cultural in the strict sense of the word (art, literature, the sciences, religious feelings, and so on) and the others, whether or not they are accorded the dignity of being called "culture": by which I mean economics, geography, the history of labor, technology, customs, and so forth. All these sectors of human life are studied by specialists, which is a good thing, but almost exclusively by specialists, as if they were so many individual nations barricaded behind firm frontiers, which is a bad thing. But as for actually breaking down those frontiers, that is something more easily hoped for than achieved.

Henri Brunschwig has given a good example of it in his thesis on the social origins of German romanticism. He shows how the German civilization turned itself upside down between the eighteenth and the nineteenth centuries, just as if it had been an enormous hourglass. At the outset it is all "sweet reason," dominated by *Aufklärung,* by a French sort of intelligence. And then behold it preferring to what had up until then been the rule, instinct, imagination, romanticism. The crucial thing is to try and discern, through all the social structures and economic relations, just what it is that is fundamentally associated with this reversal of values. This is not precisely what was done, in a famous and assuredly fine book, by Huizinga in his study of the "autumn" of the Western Middle Ages, an "agony" of civilization, as he was to call it later. But in fact the agony, if agony it was, was not mortal: it seems to me to have been much more like a stage, a particular moment in Western civilization. But what I would most reproach Huizinga with is having kept his gaze fixed so obstinately high that he considered only the very last stage of the spectacle, the very top of the pyre. What a pity it is that he did not have at his disposal those demographic and economic studies, classics today, on the major decline in the West in the fifteenth century: it would have given his book the solid foundation it needed. For there is hardly need to repeat that great sentiments, either the highest or indeed the lowest, do not live their lives entirely independently.

Which is why I greet so enthusiastically the third part of Lucien Febvre's recent major work: *La Religion de Rabelais,* in which he attempts to distinguish just what the "mental equipment" would have been in Rabelais's time, what range of words, concepts, reasoning, and sensibilities would have lain within his reach. It is a question of making a horizontal section. But the lesson was one which came to us only at the close of a long life's work (1942), and Lucien Febvre always thought to complete it one day, and accord it its "full dignity." In fact, it still remained for him to separate this section, this example, from the fascinating but necessarily restricted case of Rabelais himself, and to see whether, fundamentally, early or late, the same level was or was not the rule throughout, to find out in fact when, why, where, and to what extent changes took place. The intellectual level of the first half of the sixteenth century does seem, if one can put it like that, boxed in in some way. Why? Intelligence doubtless carries within it its own causes, and its own effects. I am sure this is so. But perhaps it can also be illuminated, as Lucien Febvre's entire work suggests, by the inertia of social and economic life, or by the particular inertia of the *longue durée* which is so much a characteristic of civilizations themselves, weighed down with the enormous and *a priori* inconceivable weight of so many ancient elements.

*The Systematic Search for Structures.* That is how, with the greatest care, I would proceed. And then? Then there would be crucial risks to be run, risks integral to any systematic research into structures, into whatever endures through the storms of the short time span, through, if you will, Toynbee's "withdrawal-and-return." Logically, where this necessary quest for structures is involved, my concern would be to build models, that is, systems of explanations linked one to another first for one civilization, then for another. There is nothing to assure us beforehand that all civilizations are amenable to similar structuring, or that, and this comes to almost the same thing, they follow identical sequences of cause and effect throughout history. The reverse would be the more logical expectation. Georges Gurvitch speaks of "the illusion of the continuity and comparability between types of global structures (that is, in a word, civilizations), which remain, in actuality, irreducible." But unlike myself, the majority of historians would not agree that Gurvitch is right or very nearly so in this regard.

## History Face to Face with the Present

At the end of all these necessary analyses, of all this care and, why not admit it, of all these hesitations, I do not feel in a position to come to any particularly bold conclusion. The more so since it is not a question of going over what has already been more or less successfully expressed. Our task in these last pages is frankly to attempt, even at the risk of going against reasoning which has already proved arduous enough, some sort of answer to the question which is at the back not only of this chapter, but of this whole volume. History is called upon to demonstrate its virtues, its usefulness with regard to the present, and so finds itself a little outside its accustomed domain. I say history, for civilization is history, more or less. It is also more or less that "global society," the summit of Georges Gurvitch's highly workable sociology.

Which does not make a difficult answer, and one which I have not patiently prepared, any easier to arrive at. A historian, in fact, has an odd way of concerning himself with the present. As a general rule, his concern is only to get away from it. But it is undeniably valuable, inestimably so, in fact, to turn around occasionally and retrace one's steps. In any case, it is a venture worth attempting. So here we are face to face with the present.

### The Longevity of Civilizations

What we are perhaps more familiar with than any other observer of the social is the fundamental diversity of the world. Each of us knows that any society, any social group, whether closely or distantly, is deeply involved in a civilization, or more precisely, in a series of superimposed civilizations, all linked together and sometimes markedly different from each other. Each society individually, and all of them taken together, lead us into a huge historical movement, of very *longue durée*, the source, for each society, of its own internal logic and of innumerable contradictions. Thus to make use of the French language as a precise tool, to attempt to master its vocabulary, is, as we have all individually discovered, to know the words right down to their roots, their origins hundreds and thousands of years ago. But this example of language is one of a hundred others equally valid. Equally what the historian can assert better than anyone, is that civilizations are realities of the extreme *longue durée*. They are not "mortal," particularly not on the scale of our own individual lives, despite Paul Valéry's celebrated phrase. What I mean to say is that mortal accidents, if they exist—and they do exist, of course, and can dislocate the fundamental organization of a civilization—occur a good deal less often than is thought. In a good many cases, it is more a question of sinking into sleep. Ordinarily all that perishes are the most exquisite blooms, the rarest achievements, while the far-reaching roots survive many a rupture and many a hard winter.

As realities of the inexhaustibly *longue durée*, civilizations, endlessly readapting themselves to their destiny, exceed in longevity any other collective reality; they outlive them all. Just as, in space, they go beyond the frontiers of specific societies (which are constantly afloat in a world larger than themselves from which they receive, without always being aware of it, particular impulses, a variety of particular impulses), in the same way there exists in time, equally to their benefit, a similar transcendence, as Toynbee well knew, bringing them a strange inheritance, incomprehensible to anyone content to observe and know only "the present" in the strictest sense of the word. In other words, civilizations survive political, social, economic, even ideological upheavals, and indeed they insidiously, but occasionally very forcefully, promote such upheavals themselves. The French Revolution is not a total break in the destiny of French civilization, nor the Revolution of 1917 in the Russian, which some call, in order to broaden it still further, the Eastern Orthodox civilization.

Nor do I believe, as far as civilizations are concerned, that is, in irremediable social breaks and catastrophes. So let us not be too swift to assert too categorically, as Charles Seignobos once did (1938) in a friendly discussion with the present author, that there can be no French civilization without a bourgeoisie, a sentiment which Cocteau[10] voiced in his own way: "The bourgeoisie is France's firmest foundation. . . . There is a house, a lamp, soup, a fire, wine, and a pipe to smoke behind any work of any importance in our country." And yet, the French civilization can, like the others, change its social support if the need arises, or create itself a new one. Should it lose a particular bourgeoisie, another one might even spring up to replace it. At the very most, such an experience might alter its internal coloring, but it would still conserve almost all of its difference and points of originality where other civilizations are concerned. It would persist, fundamentally, in the majority of its "qualities" and "faults." At least, so I imagine.

Equally, as far as anyone interested in understanding the contemporary world is concerned, and even more so with regard to anyone wishing to act within it, it "pays" to know how to make out, on a map of the world, which civilizations exist today, to be able to define their borders, their centers and peripheries, their provinces and the air one breathes there, the general and particular "forms" existing and associating within them. Otherwise, what catastrophic blunders of perspective could ensue! In fifty or a hundred years, even in two or three centuries, these civilizations will more than likely occupy pretty well the same positions on the map of the world, whether or not the chances of history have been kind to them, that is, all else being equal, as the economists wisely say, and obviously only so long as humanity has not in the meantime committed suicide, as it now has, unfortunately, the means to do.

So our first act is to believe in the heterogeneity, in the diversity of the civilizations of the world, and in the permanence, the survival of their personalities, which comes to the same thing as giving pride of place in the present to the study of acquired reflexes, of fairly rigid attitudes, of set habits, deep-seated tastes explicable only in terms of a slow-moving, long-standing history, a history which is barely conscious (like the foundations of adult behavior according to psychoanalysis). We should be concerned with this even at school, but each nation takes too much pleasure in looking at itself before its own mirror, to the exclusion of all others. In fact, this precious knowledge is still fairly rare. It would entail considering—outside the terms of propaganda, which is valid only, if at all, in the short term—all the serious problems of cultural relations, and the need to find, from civilization to civilization, acceptable languages which respect and favor those different positions which are almost impossible to reduce one to another.

*The Place of France.* Yesterday, France provided just such an acceptable language, and it does so still today. It was, yesterday, "modern Hellenism" (Jacques Berque) to the Moslem world. It was tutor to the whole of Latin America—the other America, with its own attractions. In Africa, whatever anyone says, it has been and still is a useful source of illumination. In Europe it provides the only common illumination: a trip to Poland or Rumania provides more than enough proof of this; a trip to Moscow or Leningrad would indeed be sufficient. We can still be of use to the world, if the world wishes to live without destroying itself, in mutual understanding rather than provocation. In the very long term, this future is our chance, perhaps our very reason for being. Even if shortsighted politicians maintain the opposite.

*The Permanence of Unity and Diversity throughout the World*

And yet all observers, all travelers tell us, whether enthusiastically or gloomily, of the increasing uniformity of the world. We should hurry up and travel before the world looks the same all over! It seems as though there is no answer to these arguments. Yesterday the world was full of the picturesque and of variety, today all the cities, all the peoples seem almost alike. Rio de Janeiro has had skyscrapers for twenty years, Moscow reminds one of Chicago, everywhere there are planes, trucks, railroads, factories, and everywhere national dress is disappearing. All the same, are we not in danger of making, beyond some fairly obvious observations, a series of rather serious mistakes? Yesterday's world already had its own uniformity. Technology—and it is technology's features and effects which we remark everywhere—is certainly not the only element in man's existence. Above all, are we not running the risk, once more, of confusing *civilization* and *civilizations*?

The earth is constantly shrinking, and men find themselves more than ever "under the same roof" (Toynbee), having somehow to manage to live together. Because of this, there is a certain sharing of goods, of tools, perhaps even of certain common prejudices. Technical progress has multiplied the means available to man. Everywhere *civilization* offers its services, its stock, its different merchandise without always actually giving them away. If we had before us a map of the distribution of the major factories, blast furnaces, electricity generating stations, and, tomorrow, atomic power stations, or even just a map of world consumption of essential modern products, it would quickly become clear that this wealth and these tools are very unequally distributed throughout the different regions of the world. Here there are the industrialized countries, and there the underdeveloped nations trying with greater or lesser success to change their state. *Civilization* is not equally distributed. It has held out possibilities and promises, and excited covetousness and ambition. In fact, a course has begun which will have its A students, its average students, its failing students. By opening up the fan of human possibilities, progress has also widened the range of differences. The whole band would regroup if progress came to a halt: but it does not look as if that is going to happen. Truth to tell, only truly competitive civilizations and economies are even in the race.

In short, though there might well be an inflation of *civilization*, we would be childish to see it, once it has triumphed, as eliminating the different civilizations, the real figures, which always stay in place and last for ages long. It is they who join in the race where progress is concerned, bearing on their shoulders the effort of carrying it through, and giving it, or not giving it a meaning. No civilization says no to all the new goods, but each one gives them a particular individual significance. Skyscrapers in Moscow are not the same buildings as in Chicago. The temporary furnaces and blast furnaces of the People's Republic of China are not, despite certain similarities, the same as our blast furnaces in Lorraine, or as those in the Brazil of Minas Gerais or Volta Redonda. There is a whole human, social, political, and even mystical context to be taken into account. The tool makes up a great part of what occurs, but the tool-user makes a great contribution too, and the work performed, and the dedication with which or without which it is performed. We would have to be blind not to feel the weight of this massive transformation of the world, but it is not a transformation which is taking place everywhere, and where it is taking place, it is in forms and with a human dimension and resonance which are rarely ever the same. Which is as much as to say that technology is not everything, a fact which an old country like France knows only too well, I dare say. The triumph of *civilization* in the singular does not spell disaster for *civilizations* in the plural. Plural and singular hold a dialogue, add to one another, and are separate from each other, sometimes obviously so, in a way clearly visible to the naked eye, almost without having to be particularly observant. I have retained the memory of an Arab driver on the endless empty roads of the Algerian south between Laghouat and Ghardaïa, who at the ordained times stopped his bus, abandoned his passengers to their own devices, and went a few yards off to perform his ritual prayers.

These images and others do not constitute a demonstration. But life is full of contradictions: the world is being violently propelled toward unity, while at the same time it remains fundamentally diverse. It was the same earlier: unity and heterogeneity cohabited as best they could. To turn the problem around a moment, let us note the unity of earlier times which so many observers deny quite as categorically as they assert the unity of today. They think that yesterday the world was divided against itself by immense distances and the difficulty of crossing them: mountains, deserts, expanses of ocean, bands of forests made up so many extremely real obstacles. In this segregated universe, civilization was necessarily diverse. Doubtless. But should the historian turn toward those past ages, and let his gaze wander over the whole world, he will perceive as many astonishing resemblances and analogous rhythms working independently thousands of miles apart. Ming China, so cruelly vulnerable to the wars of Asia, was assuredly closer to the France of the Valois than the China of Mao Tse-tung is to the France of the Fifth Republic. Nor should we forget that even at that time technology could travel. There are innumerable examples that this is so. But it is not that which is the great creator of uniformity. Man is in truth the prisoner of limitations from which he can never escape. These limitations, though they vary in time, are sensibly the same from one end of the earth to the other, and it is they which place their uniform seal on all human experience, whatever the age being considered. During the Middle Ages, and even into the sixteenth century, the poverty of techniques, of tools, of machinery, the rarity of domestic animals brought all activity back to man himself, to his strength and his labor. Man everywhere was the same rare, fragile creature, with a life that was nasty, brutish, and short. So all activities, all civilizations were thus deployed within a very narrow range of possibilities. These constraints enclosed every endeavor, checking it in advance, and lending them all a profound similarity through time and space, for time only slowly managed to push these limits back.

And the revolution, the fundamental upheaval of the present age, is precisely the bursting of these old "envelopes" and multiple constraints. Nothing can escape this upheaval. It is the new *civilization,* and it puts all civilizations to the test.

## The Revolutions Which Define the Present Age

But let us agree on what we mean by the expression, the present age. Let us not judge this present on the scale of our own individual lives, in the daily slices, thin, insignificant and translucent, represented by our own personal existence. On the scale of civilizations and of all other collective constructs, quite other measurements must be used, in order to comprehend and grasp them. The present of civilization today is that vast tract of time which dawned at the beginning of the eighteenth century, and whose dusk is still far off. Toward 1750, the world with all its many civilizations underwent a series of upheavals, a chain of catastrophes (nor were they the prerogative of the West alone). We are still suffering from them today.

This revolution and these repeated troubles do not consist only in the industrial revolution, but entail also the scientific revolution (affecting as yet only the objective sciences, which has meant a lopsided world in which the human sciences are still trying to find their proper path), and, finally, a biological revolution, with many and various causes, but with one obvious result, which is always the same: an unprecedented flood of human beings such as this planet has never seen before. Soon there will be three billion people: in 1400 there were barely three hundred million.

If ever one were to dare to speak of the movement of history, it would have to be in terms of these combined, omnipresent tides. The material power of man uplifts the world, uplifts man, tears him from himself and thrusts him toward an unshaped future. A historian accustomed to dealing with a fairly recent period—say, for example, the sixteenth century—would still have the feeling, from the beginning of the eighteenth century onward, of having been transported to a new planet. And it is precisely present-day air travel which has accustomed us to the notion of unbreakable barriers that one day are broken: the sound barrier, the barrier of terrestrial magnetism enveloping the world up to 8,000 kilometers away. These were the sorts of barriers which, peopled with monsters, hedged off the unconquered expanses of the Atlantic at the end of the fifteenth century. Now everything goes on as if between the eighteenth century and our own time humanity, without always being aware of it, had come through one of these difficult zones, one of these barriers which still stand in its way, even today, in some parts of the world. Ceylon has only just become familiar, thanks to the miracles of modern medicine, with the biological revolution which has transformed the world, that is, the amazing prolongation of life. But the fall in the birthrate which usually accompanies this revolution has not yet affected this island, where that rate remains at its natural maximum. This is a phenomenon which can be found in various other countries, like Algeria. Only today has China entered fully, massively, into industrial life. Our own country is in it up to the hilt.

Is there any need to say that this new age breaks the old cycles and the traditional customs of man? If I stand so strongly against the ideas of Toynbee or Spengler, it is because these ideas persist in bringing humanity back to the old times, to the worn out, to the *deja-vu*. In order to accept that today's civilizations repeat the cycle of that of the Incas, or whomever, we would first have to concede that neither technology, nor economics, nor demography has any very great bearing on civilizations.

In actual fact, man is changing his appearance. Civilization, civilizations, all our activities, material, spiritual, and intellectual, are affected by it. Who can foresee what man's work will be like tomorrow, or what its strange companion, man's leisure, will be? What will his religion be, caught between tradition, ideology, and reason? Who can foresee what, beyond present formulas, the explanations of tomorrow's physical sciences will tend toward, or the aspect which the human sciences, which today are in their infancy, will then have taken on?

*Beyond Civilizations*

In the vast present which is still in the process of taking shape, there is thus a huge "diffusion" at work. It is disturbing not only the calm and ancient relationships which existed between civilizations, but also the internal relationships of each one. In our Western pride, we call this diffusion the radiation of our civilization throughout the world. If one is to believe the experts, the indigenous tribes of central New Guinea, or the peoples of the eastern Himalayas, are about the only ones excepted from this radiation. But even if the West was the instigator of this chain of diffusion, clearly these revolutions are proceeding independently of us now. They are the wave which is giving disproportionate size to the fundamental civilization of the world. The present time consists above all in this inflation of civilization and, it seems, the revenge, whose end is not yet in sight, of the singular upon the plural.

It seems. For—as I have already said—this new constraint or this new liberation, in any case this new source of conflicts and this need to adapt, if they affect the whole world, do so with radically different results. It is easy to imagine the upheavals which the sudden introduction of technology and of all the accelerations it entails must create within each civilization, within its own material and spiritual frontiers. But these upheavals are not a straightforward affair. They vary with each civilization, and each one, without wishing it, finds itself placed in a unique position, because of realities which have existed for a long time and which are highly resistant, being part of its very structure. It is from the conflict—or the harmony—between ancient attitudes and new necessities, that each people daily forges its destiny, its "actuality."

Which civilizations will tame, and domesticate, and humanize the machine and also that social technology which Karl Mannheim spoke of in the clear, intelligent, and rather sad prognostications which he dared to make in 1943, that social technology made necessary and instigated by the government of the masses, but which also dangerously increases the power of man over man? Will this technology be at the service of a minority of technocrats, or of everyone, and thus of liberty? There is a fierce, blind struggle going on, under various names, along various fronts, between civilizations and civilization. It is a question of subduing the latter, of channeling it and imposing on it a new humanism. It is not a question of toppling and replacing an aristocracy by a bourgeoisie, or an old bourgeoisie by a nearly new one, or even intransigent peoples by a grim and careful empire, or a religion which always defends itself by some sort of universal ideology, but of an unprecedented struggle. A good many cultural structures may give way, and perhaps all in a rush. The disturbance has permeated right down to the depths and has touched all civilizations, the oldest, or rather the most splendid, with their own establishments set out along the grand avenues of history, and the most modest alike.

From this point of view, there can be no doubt that the most exciting modern spectacle is that of the cultures "in transit" of the vast continent of Black Africa, between the new Atlantic Ocean, the old Indian Ocean, the very old Sahara, and, toward the south, the primitive masses of the equatorial jungle. The fact that these civilizations are "cultures," in Bagby's sense, explains incidentally why neither Spengler nor Toynbee, nor Alfred Weber, nor Félix Sartiaux, nor Philip Bagby himself ever discussed them. The world of "true" civilizations tends to make exclusions like this. This Black Africa, to relate everything once more to diffusion, certainly bungled its ancient relations with Egypt and the Mediterranean. Toward the Indian Ocean stand high mountains. As for the Atlantic, for a long while it stood empty, and then, from the fifteenth century onward, the great bulk of Africa had to tip toward it in order to receive both its benefits and its misdeeds. But today something has changed in Black Africa: it is, all at once, the intrusion of machines, the setting up of education, the growth of real cities, the harvest of past and present efforts, a Westernization which has made a large breach there, even though it has not yet sunk right in: as ethnographers like Marcel Griaule, devoted to Black Africa, know very well. But Black Africa has become conscious of itself, of its conduct, of its potential. The conditions in which this transition is taking place, at the cost of what suffering, and with what pleasure too, one can learn by going there. In fact, if I had to seek a better understanding of these difficult cultural evolutions, instead of choosing the last days of Byzantium as my battlefield, I would set off for Black Africa. Gladly.

*Toward a Modern Humanism.* Do we in fact today have need of a new, third word, besides *culture* and *civilization,* both of which have come to appear invalid to one or another of us? In the midst of the twentieth century, we have an insidious need, just as they did in the mid–eighteenth century, of a new word to conjure up possible dangers and catastrophes, and all our obstinate hopes. Georges Friedmann, and he is not alone in this, has suggested the term modern humanism. Man, civilization, must overcome the demands of the machine, even of machinery—of automation—if he is not to be condemned to enforced leisure. Humanism is a way of hoping, of wishing men to be brothers one with another, and of wishing that civilizations, each on its own account and all together, should save themselves and save us. It means accepting and hoping that the doors of the present should be wide open on to the future, beyond all the failures, declines, and catastrophes predicted by strange prophets (prophets all deriving from black literature). The present can not be the boundary, which all centuries, heavy with eternal tragedy, see before them as an obstacle, but which the hope of man, ever since man has been, has succeeded in overcoming.

Notes

1. Joseph Chappey, *Histoire de la civilisation en Occident 1: La Crise de l'histoire et la mort des civilisations* (Paris, 1958), p. 370.
2. Philip Bagby, *Culture and History* (London, 1958), p. 160.
3. Quotation taken from Armand Cuvillier, *Manuel de sociologie* (Paris, 1954), 2:670.
4. Wilhelm Mommsen, cited by Chappey, p. 444.
5. Georges Duby and Robert Mandrou.
6. On the basis of the culture: this, within a given group, is what is transmitted, not by biological but by social heredity—the "model" of social behavior, the "complex" of characteristic ways of life. See, on this subject, the point of view put

forward by the philosopher Pietro Rossi, in "Cultura e civiltà come modeli descrittivi," in *Rivista di Filosofia,* July 1957.

7. Otto Brunner, *Neue Wege der Sozialgeschichte* (Göttingen, 1956), p. 186.

8. Brunner, p. 17.

9. Hans Freyer, *Weltgeschichte Europas* (Stuttgart, 1954), 2:723.

10. "Le Coq et l'Arlequin," in *Le Rappel à l'ordre,* 7th ed. (Paris, 1926), p. 17.

# Index

Abel, Wilhelm, 121
Africa, Black, 97, 113, 211, 216–17
Aix-en-Provence, 99
Alexandria, 118n
Algeria, 213, 215
Algiers, 118n
Alicante, 96
Alps, 117n
Altamira, Rafael, 177; *Historia de España y de la Civilización Española*, 182
America. *See* United States of America
America, Latin, 26, 61, 146, 204, 211. *See also* New Spain
Americas: development of, 127; disease in, 113; Seville trade with, 91–103. *See also* America, Latin; United States of America
Andalusia, 102
Andes, 194
*Annales d'histoire économique et sociale:* article on Brunner in, 120–31; Castillo in, 102; and direction of historical studies, 68–69; discussion at, 206; Febvre in, 71; founded, 18; as historical school, 198; nature of, 34
Anthropology, 25, 147, 198–99
Antilles, Greater, 103
Antwerp, 13
*Archivo de Protocolos*, Seville, 95–96
Area studies, 26, 61, 202–3
Ariès, Philippe, 36, 66–67
Aristotle, 194
Armada, 15, 99
Aron, Raymond, *Introduction à la philosophie de l'histoire*, 66
Asia, Central, 135
Asti, 88
Atabinen, Raschid Saffet, 205
Atlantic Ocean: and Africa, 216; as barrier, 214; and French economy, 87; Seville and, 91–103; trade routes in, 14
Attica, 194

Augsburg, 123
Austria, 120, 123
Auxerre, 37
Azores, 94

Bachelard, Gaston, 48, 78
Baehrel, René, 132, 152
Bagby, Philip, 183–84, 196, 198–99, 216
Bahia: Braudel in, 10; study of, 165–75; and sugar trade, 128
Baixa do Gamba, 167–68
Baltic region, 13, 96, 114
Balzac, Honoré de, 156
Bananal, 167
Barthes, Roland, 59
Bataillon, Marcel, 20–21
Beaujeu-Garnier, Jacqueline, 147
Beauvaisis, 152
Beloch, Julius, 148
Beltrami, Daniele, 148
Bermudas, 94
Bern, 133
Berque, Jacques, 211
Berr, Henri: and Centre de Synthèse, 179; and *l'histoire historisante*, 64; and *Revue de Synthèse historique*, 68, 129; and *Semaines de synthèse*, 61; quoted, 178
Bilbao, 101
Biology: and history, 149–59; and human geography, 105–16, 154; Laugier and, 147
Black Death, 135, 145
Bloch, Marc: and *Annales*, 18, 68–69, 198; and discontinuity, 73; nature of his work, 20, 34, 58, 202; and von Bulow, 121; *Métier d'historien*, 66, 68
Blondel, Charles, 68
Bom Jesus de Lapa, shrine of, 169–70
Bône, 118n
Bossuet, 121
Brandenburg, 194
Brandi, Karl, 4

Braulio, Senhor (shoe manufacturer), 170
Brazil: blast furnaces in, 212; and development of Minas Velhas, 165–75; German community in, 139–40; Indians in, 181; landowners in, 127
Bréhier, Émile, 67
Bremond, Abbé, 58, 71
Brenner Pass, 14
Bromado, 166
Bruges, 96
Brumadinho, 167
Brunhes, Jean, 114
Brunner, Otto, *Neue Wege der Sozialgeschichte*, 120–31
Brunschwicg, Léon, 178
Brunschwig, Henri, vii, 207; *La Crise de l'état prussien à la fin du XVIII<sup>e</sup> siècle et la genèse de la mentalité romantique*, 118n
Bücher, Karl, 201
Bulgaria, 137
Bulow, Georg von, 121
Burckhardt, Jacob, 6–8, 29, 185–86; *Die Kultur der Renaissance in Italien*, 185, 206

Cadiz, 15
Canary Islands, 94, 101
Cannae, Battle of, 89, 195
Cantillon, Richard, 147
Caravaggio, Michelangelo, 21
Caravans, mule, 140, 169–70; and shipping, 189
Carioles *(carretoni)*, 14
Castillo, Alvaro, 102
Caucasus, 117n
Cavaignac, Eugène, 148
Cavendish, Thomas, 15
Celestino, João, 170
Center for Business Studies, Harvard, 60
Centre de Synthèse, 179, 183
Centre National de la Recherche scientifique, 62
Ceylon, 215
Chabod, Federico, 206
Champagne, 33, 124
Channel, English, 15
Chappey, Joseph, 180, 184
Charles V (of Spain), 100, 195–96
Charles VI (of France), 204
Chaunu, Huguette. *See* Chaunu, Pierre
Chaunu, Pierre, and Huguette Chaunu, *Séville et l'Atlantique, 1550–1650*, 91–103
Chevalier, Louis, 149–59; *Classes laborieuses*

*et classes dangereuses à Paris dans la première moitié du XIX<sup>e</sup> siècle*, 149
Chicago, 212
Chile, 133–34
China: in area studies, 26, 61–62; blast furnaces in, 212; and circulation of precious metals, 13, 99; as "crossroads," 194; demographic changes in, 136; and France, 213; and industrialization, 215; influence of, 204; in interwar years, 85–86; Moslem trade in, 97; and urban sociology, 126
Chique Chique, 169
Cicero, 180
Cipolla, Carlo M., 99
Cities. *See* Towns
Civilizations: concept of, 147; history of, 11–12, 177–217. See also *Longue durée*
Clark, Colin, 84, 138
Climatology, 107–8
Clough, Shepard Bancroft, 196, 207
Cocteau, Jean, 210
Cole, Arthur, 60
Collège de France, 151, 178
Columbus, Christopher, 95
Communications, 38, 43–47
Comte, Auguste, 6, 199, 201
Condorcet, 181
Conjuncture: Chaunu and, 93, 97; and demography, 135; as historical concept, 29–30, 48, 74–75, 77; and structural history, 87
*Conquista*, 95
Constantinople, 118n, 205
Conze, Werner, 121
Cordoba, 101
Counter-Reformation, 204
Cournot, Antoine Augustin, 8
Courtin, René, *La Civilisation économique du Brésil*, 184
Criminality, 156–58
Croce, Benedetto, 28
Crusades, 135
Cuenca, 101
Culture: and civilization, 177–217; as concept, 147
Curie, Marie, 204
Curtius, Ernst Robert, 31
Cuvillier, Armand, *Manuel de sociologie*, 183
Cycle, as historical concept, 29–30, 74
Cyprus, 204

Danube, 203–4
Dardel, Éric, 66
Death, 16
*Débats et Combats,* 52
Deike, Ilse, 160n
Delbet, Pierre, 113; *Politique préventive du cancer,* 117n
Demangeon, Albert, 68, 115; *Déclin de l'Europe,* 189
Demography: and concept of civilization, 206; as a discipline, 55; and the human sciences, 132–60
Desaunay, François, 90n
Descartes, René, 32
Diachrony, 35, 38–39, 48, 78
Diamond, Sigmund, 41
Dien Bien Phu, Battle of, 39
Discontinuity. *See* Sociology
Disease, 109–14. *See also* Black Death; Phylloxera
Djerba, 118n
Drake, Sir Francis, 15
Duby, Georges, and Robert Mandrou, *Histoire de la civilisation française,* 182
Dupront, Alphonse, 32; *Le Mythe de croisade: Essai de sociologie religieuse,* 57–58
Durkheim, Emile, 64, 73, 201

École des Hautes Études, 21
Ecology, 51. *See also* Geography
Economics: as a discipline, 55, 58; history and, 32–33, 35, 83–90, 206; origins of, 122–23; sociology and, 36; theories of, 147; and time, 78; Wagemann and, 134
Elbe (river), 124
Engels, Friedrich. *See* Marx, Karl
England: and concept of civilization, 182, 185, 190–92; and demographic changes, 139, 142, 149; diseases in, 113; rivalry with Iberians, 15; Seville and, 96
Epigraphy, 62
Erasmus, 21
Eskimos, 181
Espirito Santo, 139
Estienne, Charles, 123
Ethnography, 35–36, 56. *See also* Anthropology
Europe: in area studies, 61; bourgeoisie in, 120; and concept of civilization, 185, 192; demographic changes in, 139, 159; fluctuation of prices in, 13; French influence in, 211; Moslem trade in, 97;

and textile trade, 124
Event: in history, 48, 77; in sociology, 80. *See also Histoire événementielle*

Faral, Edmond, 5
Far East, 13, 135, 146. *See also* China; India
Febvre, Lucien: and *Annales,* 18–19, 68, 198; on civilization, 181, 206; on Europe, 185; on geography, 206; on history, 38, 69, 90, 178; influence of, 76, 94; on methodological discussions, 132–33; nature of his work, 20–22, 31–32, 58, 73; sociology and, 57; and Spengler, 186; on structures, 71; and Toynbee, 190, 197; quoted, 117n, 175; *Combats pour l'histoire,* 66; *Luther,* 19–20; *Marguerite de Navarre,* 19; *Philippe II et la Franche-Comté,* 19; *Le Problème de l'incroyance au XVIe siècle: La Religion de Rabelais,* 19, 32, 85, 208; *Le Rhin,* 19; *La Terre et l'évolution humaine,* 19, 115–16
Fénelon, 121
Ferrara, 13
Feuerbach, Ludwig, 155
First World War, 11
Flanders, 96
Flaubert, Gustave, 50
Fleets, 98; *See also* Ships and shipping
Florence, 13, 21
Formiga, 167, 172, 174
Francastel, Pierre, *Peinture et société,* 32
France: and China, 213; and concept of civilization, 181–82, 185, 201–2, 206, 211; and demographic changes, 124, 140, 146, 148–49; economy of, 87–88; influence on Brazil, 204; and phylloxera crisis, 109; and Reformation, 205; repatriation of merchants to, 13; in sixteenth century, 85–86, 100
Francke (publishers), 133
François I, 100
Franco-Prussian War, 6–7
Freyer, Heinrich, 129, 131n, 199
Freyre, Gilberto, 174, 204
Friedmann, Georges, 217
Fugger, Hans, 123
Fustel de Coulanges, 8, 29, 73

Galileo, 32
Gautier, Émile-Félix, 112, 197
Genghis Khan, 135. *See also* Mongols

Genoa, 88, 96
Geography: Chaunu and, 94–96; as discipline, 56; and history, 17–18, 58, 206; human, 105–16; isolation of, 51–52; theories of, 147; Toynbee and, 191
George I (of England), 11
Germany: Brunner's theories on, 126; and concept of civilization, 181–83, 185, 188, 205, 207; disease in, 114; repatriation of merchants to, 13; and Second World War, 20
Gibraltar, 15, 96
Gieysztor, Aleksander, 61
Gilão, 167
Gilson, Étienne, 178
Gironde, 14, 50
Goethe, 9, 204
Gold. See Metals, precious
Goubert, Pierre, 152
Gourou, Pierre, 194
Gravatão, 167
Great War. See First World War
Greece, 201
Griaule, Marcel, 217
Griziotti-Kretschmann, J., 99
Gruta, 167, 172, 174
Guilbaud, Th., 42
Guizot, François, 177; Histoire de la civilisation en Europe, 185; Histoire de la civilisation en France, 185
Gurvitch, Georges: and "global society," 200, 206; on historico-sociological debate, 65, 69; influence of, 18; and "levels," 71, 154; on nature of history, 131; nature of his work, 49, 59, 73; and structures, 208–9; and time, 78–79; Bibliothèque de sociologie contemporaine, 147
Gustavus Adolphus, 180

Halbwachs, Maurice, 68, 73
Halphen, Louis, 28–29, 66
Hamilton, Earl J., 92, 99, 101
Häpke, Richard, 38
Harris, Marvin, Town and Country in Brazil, 165–75
Hassinger, Herbert, 121
Hassinger, Hugo, 147
Hauser, Henri, 64, 76, 118n, 125
Haute-Provence, 152
Hegel, 184
Henri II, 100
Henry, Louis, 132

Herder, 181, 186
Hiltebrandt, Philipp, 118n, 201
Himalayas, 215
Hintze, Otto, 121
Histoire événementielle, 3–4, 27–29, 71, 87. See also History
Historische Zeitschrift, 120
History: biological, 149–59; changing nature, 8, 12–17; and definitions of time, 3–4, 17, 26–52; as discipline, 56; and economics, 32–33, 35, 83–90; and geography, 17–18, 206; narrative, 11–12; relation to contemporary setting, 6; as a science, 9; serial, 91–103; social, 120–31; and the social sciences, 4–5, 7–8, 17, 25–52, 64–80; structural, 74, 87, 93; of technology, 14–15; "unconscious," 39. See also Histoire événementielle; Longue durée
Holland, 146
Homer, 121
Hondschoote, 101
Hugo, Victor, Les Misérables, 156–57
Huizinga, Jan, 182–83, 207–8
Huntington, Ellsworth, 117n–118n

Iberian Empire, 15, 99. See also Portugal; Spain; Spanish Empire
Imbert, Gaston, 101
Incas, 194
India: in area studies, 26, 61–62; and circulation of precious metals, 13; and demographic changes, 136, 148; influence of, 204; Moslem trade in, 97; and urban sociology, 126
Indian Ocean, 13, 216
Industrial Revolution, 124
Inquisitori contra Bestiemme, 16
Intercycle: in Chaunu, 98–99; as historical concept, 29–30, 74. See also Cycle
International Historical Congress (1948), 30
Ireland, 139
Islam, 126, 204, 211
Italy, 21, 126, 146, 175, 186, 205

Jamaica, 94
Jardé, Alfred, 85
Joachim of Floris, 121

Kellenbenz, Hermann, 60
Kiev, 127

Klemm, Gustav, 186
Klukhohn, Clyde, 183
Kondratiev, 29
Konjonktur Institut, 133
Kroeber, Alfred Louis, 183, 198
Kuhn, G., 182
Kula, Witold, 58
Kulischer, Alexandre, 118n, 148, 206
Kulischer, Eugène, 148, 206

Labrousse, Ernest: and conjunctures, 48,
    77; on effects of American trade, 95, 99;
    nature of his work, 18, 20, 70; on origins
    of French Revolution, 74, 100; and so-
    cial history, 30; *Comment naissent les révo-
    lutions*, 30
La Châtre, Maurice, 160
Lacombe, Paul, 8, 27, 47, 64–65, 67, 71, 77
Lamprecht, Karl, 178
Langlois, Charles-Victor, 34; and Charles
    Seignobos, *Introduction aux études his-
    toriques*, 8
Language. *See* Communications
Lapeyre, Henri, 98
Las Palmas, 102
Latin America. *See* America, Latin
Laugier, Henri, 62, 147
Lavisse, Ernest, 17
Lazarsfeld, Paul F., 62
Leather, 95
Le Bras, Gabriel, 71
Lefebvre, Georges, 20
Leghorn, 96
Leibnitz, 187
Leipzig, 33
Leningrad, 211
Leontiev, Alexandre, 59
Levant, 33
Levasseur, Émile, 201
Lévi-Strauss, Claude: on civilization, 205;
    and communications theory, 43–44, 75;
    and discontinuity, 192; and history, 36,
    68; and models, 40, 45–47; nature of his
    work, 73; and social mathematics, 59,
    75; and structural anthropology, 25;
    *Structural Anthropology*, 71
Leyden, 101
Liébaut, Jean, 123
Lisbon, 13
List, Friedrich, 134, 201
London, 96, 159
*Longue durée:* Brunner and, 122, 125, 130;

Chaunu and, 93; and civilizations, 206,
    208–9; Gurvitch on, 79; and mathemat-
    ical models, 41, 45–46; nature of, 3,
    27–34, 38, 48; political economy and, 58;
    Sauvy and, 148–49; Spengler and, 188;
    and structures, 75–76; study of, 11–12,
    50–52; Toynbee and, 196–97
Lopez, Roberto, 136
Lorenzo the Magnificent, 21, 186
Lorraine, 212
Louis XIV, 187, 195
Luther, Martin, 20
Luzzatto, Gino, 125
Lyons, 13

Mably, Abbé, 180
Madeira, 94
Maison des Sciences de l'Homme, 62
Maize, 103
Malinowski, Bronislaw, 35–36
Malthus, Robert, 134, 147
Mandrou, Robert. *See* Duby, Georges
Manioc, 103
Mann, Thomas, 182
Mannheim, Karl, 128, 216
Mantoux, Paul, 66
Mao Tse-tung, 213
Marrou, Henri, 65–66, 182
Marseilles, 14
Martín, Felipe Ruiz, 101
Martius, C. F. P. von, 168
Martonne, Emmanuel de, 118n
Marx, Karl: attitude to, 206; context of his
    work, 147; and French Revolution, 6;
    and models, 40, 51; nature of his work,
    122, 134, 201; and study of class, 70;
    quoted, 39, 160; and Friedrich Engels,
    *Communist Party Manifesto*, 181. *See also*
    Marxism
Marxism, 50–51, 76–77, 205
Masur, Gerhard, 197
Mathematics, history and, 38–47
Mauss, Marcel: on civilization, 193, 201–3;
    influence of, 76; nature of his work, 18,
    73; on productivity, 144
Mayan Empire, 117n–118n
Mayer, Thomas, 121
Mead, Margaret, 201
Medicine, 113. *See also* Disease
*Mediterranean and the Mediterranean World
    in the Age of Philip II, The* (Braudel), 3–5,
    92–93

Mediterranean Sea: and biscuit manufacture, 118n; diet around, 110; economic rhythms of, 13–14; and French economy, 87; nosology of, 112–13; Seville and, 96; and ship design, 14–15; trade in, 124
Meinecke, Friedrich, 121
*Mélanges d'histoire sociale*, 105
Melis, Federigo, 96
Merleau-Ponty, Maurice, 204
Metals, precious, 41, 45, 95, 99, 102, 165–66
Métraux, Alfred, 181
Mexico, 102, 128
Meyerson, Ignace, 89
Michelangelo, 21
Michelet, Jules: Barthes on, 59; Febvre and, 20, 22; Roupnel and, 7; on history, 66; influence of, 186; and *longue durée*, 29; nature of his work, 8, 73, 150
Milan, 13
Minas Gerais, 212
Minas Velhas, 165–75
Mining, 102, 165–66
Mitteis, Heinrich, 121
Models: application by Brunner, 122–25; application by Sauvy, 141–49; application by Toynbee, 194–95; as historical concept, 40–41, 71–72. *See also* Strategy
Modigliani, Amedeo, 204
Mombert, Paul, 148
Mongols, 126
Montaigne, 14
Moore, Geoffrey, 101
Morgan, J. P., 41
Morgenstern, Oskar, 42
Moscow, 127, 211–12
Moslem world. *See* Islam
Mule trains. *See* Caravans, mule

Napoleon, 189, 195
Near East, 14
Nef, John U., 206
New Guinea, 215
New Spain, 94–95, 99, 102. *See also* America, Latin
Newton, Sir Isaac, 32
Niceforo, Alfredo, 206
Nicolle, Charles, 117n
Nietzsche, Friedrich, 84, 187, 195, 201–2
Nile River, 14
Novgorod, 126

Olives, 110
Otte, Enrique, 96

Pacific Ocean, 14
Palermo, 113
Panama, 95
Parent-Duchâtelet, A. J. B., 156
Pareto, Vilfredo, 195
Paris, 150–59
Pascal, Blaise, 42
Pavia, Battle of, 67
Perroux, François, 29, 58, 96, 119n
Peru, 94, 99
Péten, 118n
Peter the Great, 127–28, 180
Philip II, 4, 21, 100
Philippines, 96, 99
Philosophy, 62, 77
Phylloxera, 109
Picasso, Pablo, 204
Piganiol, André, 20, 66, 195
Piracy, 99
Pirenne, Henri, 36, 59, 73, 87, 183
Plato, 36, 121
Poincaré, Raymond, 11
Poland, 211
Population. *See* Demography
*Population* (journal), 154
Portugal, 14, 165, 175, 204
Potosi, 128
Potsdam Agreement, 39
Prices, 13–14, 101–2, 153
Productivity, 142–44
*Protocolos. See Archivo de Protocolos*
Proudhon, 6, 20
Prussia, 139
Psychology, 36, 56
Puerto Rico, 94

Quesnay, François, 147
Quételet, L. Adolphe J., 147

Rabelais, François, 20, 32
Ragusa, 14–15
Rambard, Alfred, 182
Ranke, Leopold von, 4, 8–9, 10–11, 29
Ratisbon, 204
Ratzel, Friedrich, 201
Recife, 128
Reformation, 16, 204–5
Rémond, M. A., 87
Renaissance, 32, 185–86

Renaudet, Augustin, 20–21
Renouvin, Pierre, 206
Revolution, French, 6, 74, 100, 124, 188–89, 210
*Revue de l'enseignement supérieure*, 62
*Revue de synthèse historique*, 34, 68
*Revue économique*, 83
Rhine, 203–4
Rieger, Marianne, 148
Rimbaud, Arthur, 4
Rio de Janeiro, 139, 212
Rio de la Plata, 100, 127
Ritter, Gerhard, 121, 127
Rocroi, Battle of, 67
Romano, Ruggiero, 99
Rome, 203–5
Rome Historical Congress (1955), 30, 70
Röpke, Wilhelm, 134
Rosenblatt, Alfredo, 148
Rostow, Walt, 58
Roumeguère, Dr., 72
Roupnel, Gaston, 47, 77, 117n; *Histoire et Destin*, 7
Ruiz, Simón, 96
Rumania, 211
Rümelin, Gustav, 134
Russia: and Arctic, 117n; in area studies, 26, 61; bourgeoisie in, 120; 1917 Revolution, 210; social development of, 126–28

Sahara Desert, 216
Saic. *See* Ships and shipping
Saint-Hilaire, Geoffroy, 109
Saint-Simon, 6
Sakhiet-Sidi-Youssef, Battle of, 39
San Salvador, 204
Santa Leopoldina, 139
Santiago, 133
Santo Domingo, 94
Santos, 173
São Francisco River, 169
São Paolo, 169, 173
São Paolo State, 173
Sapori, Armando, 125–26
Sartiaux, Félix, 216
Sartre, Jean-Paul, 28, 50, 204
Sauvy, Alfred, 141–49, 154, 160; *Richesse et population*, 141; *Théorie générale de la population*, 141
Saxony, Lower, 138
Sayous, André E., 89, 95

Schmoller, Gustav, 134
Schumpeter, Joseph Alois, 60
Science, 7. *See also* Sciences, human; Sociology
Sciences, human: and demography, 132–60; and history, 205–7. *See also* Economics; Geography; History; Sociology
Segovia, 101
Seignobos, Charles, 34, 57, 64, 199–200, 210. *See also* Langlois, Charles-Victor
Serial history. *See* History
Serra do Ouro, 167
Seville, 13–14, 91–103
Ships and shipping, 14–15, 100, 189. *See also* Technology
Siberia, 117n
Silver. *See* Metals, precious
Simancas, 96–97
Simiand, François: and conjunctures, 75–76; and *l'histoire événementielle*, 3–4, 27, 67, 71; and human sciences, 68, 73, 137; nature of his work, 17–18, 64–65, 137
Sincora, 172
Sion, Jules, 68
Social mathematics. *See* Mathematics
Social Sciences. *See* Sociology
Sociology: as a discipline, 56; and discontinuity, 89, 192; and history, 4–5, 7–8, 17, 25–52, 57, 64–80, 206; theories of, 147; urban, 126
Sombart, Werner, 76, 89, 118n, 121, 126, 198
Sorokin, Pitrim Aleksandrovich, 203, 206
Sorre, Maximilien, 154; *Les Bases biologiques de la géographie humaine*, 105–16, 147
South America. *See* America, Latin
Spain: and Arab conquest, 197; Bataillon on, 21; and Brunner's theories, 126; Catholicism in, 175; and concept of civilization, 182; and demographic changes, 146; education in, 60; influence on Brazil, 204; and Reformation, 205; and Weber, 186
Spanish Empire, 97
Spencer, Herbert, 201
Spengler, Oswald: and concept of civilization, 182, 186–89, 195–97; nature of his work, 122, 201, 215–16; *Decline of the West*, 186
Spix, Joh. Bapt. von, 168
Spooner, Frank, 41, 45

Sprenkel, Van den, 148
Sputniks, 39
Staël, Madame de, 204
Statistics, 206
Stendhal, 20
Strategy, as historical concept, 41
Structural anthropology. *See* Anthropology
Structural history. *See* History
Structure: and concept of civilization, 208–9; as historical concept, 31, 38, 71–72
Sue, Eugène, 156
Sugar, 95
Sweden, 180
Synchrony, 38–39, 48, 76, 78

Tartane. *See* Ships and shipping
Taubaté, 173
Technology, 14–15, 211–12, 216
Thibaudet, Albert, 9
Thirty Years' War, 99, 135
Thresholds, as historical concept, 133–41
Thünen, Johann Heinrich von, 134
Tintoretto, 50
Titian, 21
Tobacco, 95
Toledo, 101
Tönnies, Ferdinand, 182
Towns, 124, 126. *See also individual towns*
Toynbee, Arnold: Bagby and, 199; and concept of civilization, 185, 189–97, 206; and demography, 206; and "diffusion," 203; nature of his work, 201, 208, 215–16; quoted, 212; *A Study of History*, 190
Treitschke, Heinrich von, 10
Tupi-Guarani, 181
Turin, Yvonne, *The School and Education in Spain, 1874–1902*, 60
Tuscany, 13
Tylor, Edward Burnett, 183

Ubatuba, 173
United States of America: and area studies, 26, 61; and concept of civilization, 190, 192; cultivation of, 127; diseases in, 113; population density in, 138–39
Universities: Basel, 6; Columbia, 62; Harvard, 60, 62; Lyons, 60; Nuremberg, 59; Santiago, 134; Seattle, 62; Sorbonne, 21
Usher, A. P., 148–49
Usumacinta, 118n

Valencia, 102
Valéry, Paul, 50, 204, 209
Van Gogh, Vincent, 204
Vavilov, Nikolai Ivanovich, 109
Venice, 13–16, 88, 101
Vera Cruz, 96–97
Vico, Giovanni Battista, 201
Victoria (Brazil), 139
Vidal de la Blache, Paul-Marie, 51–52; *Principes de la géographie humaine*, 116, 147; *Tableau de la géographie de la France*, 17
Vienna, 120, 123
Vienne-en-Dauphiné, 37
*Vierteljahrschrift für Sozial-und Wirtschaftgeschichte*, 120
Vila Nova, 166–67, 174
Villena, Guillermo Lohmann, 95–96
Vines, 110. *See also* Phylloxera
Voltaire: *Essai sur les moeurs*, 177; *Le Siècle de Louis XIV*, 181
Volta Redonda, 212
Von Neumann, John, 42

Wagemann, Ernst, 133–42, 147, 159; *Population in the Destiny of Peoples*, 133; *The World Economy*, 133; *Die Zahl als Detektiv*, 133
Wagner, Richard, 189
Wallon, Henri, 68
Waxweiller, Émile Pierre, 201
Weber, Alfred, 182, 193, 197–98, 216; *Kulturgeschichte als Kultursoziologie*, 186, 197
Weber, Max: and brother Alfred, 197; Brunner and, 121; and demographic changes, 135; on Europe, 199; Marrou and, 66; urban sociology of, 126–27, 131n
Weill, André, 44
West Indies, British, 139
Wheat, 110
Wilhelm I (of Germany), 11
Witthauer, Kurt, 147
Wright, Harold, 139

Yalta, Treaty of, 39

Zola, Émile, 156